Torn halves

for my mother

Torn halves.............................

Political conflict in literary and cultural theory

....

Robert J. C. Young

MANCHESTER UNIVERSITY PRESS

Manchester and New York

distributed exclusively in the USA and Canada by St. Martin's Press

Copyright © Robert J. C. Young 1996

Published by Manchester University Press
Oxford Road, Manchester M13 9NR, UK
and Room 400, 175 Fifth Avenue, New York, NY 10010, USA

Distributed exclusively in the USA and Canada
by St. Martin's Press, Inc., 175 Fifth Avenue, New York,
NY 10010, USA

British Library Cataloguing-in-Publication Data
A catalogue record is available from the British Library

Library of Congress Cataloging-in-Publication Data
Young, Robert, 1950–
    Torn halves : political conflict in literary and cultural theory /
Robert J. C. Young.
        p.   cm.
    Includes bibliographical references (pp. 223–36).
    ISBN 0–7190–4776–5 (hard : alk. paper). — ISBN 0–7190–4777–3
(pbk. : alk. paper)
    1. Culture—Philosophy. 2. Politics and culture. 3. Criticism.
4. Philosophy, Modern—20th century. I. Title.
HM101.Y68   1996
306′.01—dc20   95–30849

ISBN   0 7190 4776 5 *hardback*
         0 7190 4777 3 *paperback*

First published 1996

99 98 97 96   10 9 8 7 6 5 4 3 2 1

Printed in Great Britain
by Bell & Bain Ltd, Glasgow

Contents..............................

Acknowledgements....................

All of the essays in this book have been written in dialogue with others. I am very grateful to all those who have discussed with me many of the issues developed here: in particular, I would like to thank Isobel Armstrong, Derek Attridge, Gargi Bhattacharrya, Rachel Bowlby, Jonathan Dollimore, Terry Eagleton, Maud Ellmann, Robin Fiddian, Daniela Havenstein, Ken Hirschkop, Christina Howells, Kadiatu Kanneh, John Knight, Rodney Livingstone, Laura Marcus, David Norbrook, Richard Rand, Jacqueline Rose, Nicholas Royle, Jonathan Sawday, Allon White (for whom there is another note elsewhere), and Clair Wills. I want too to express my gratitude to those students who have worked through with me in seminars many of the ideas developed in this book. Antony Easthope read the manuscript with great care and made some very useful suggestions; I am grateful to him for his scrupulous criticisms. Anita Roy has been an exemplary editor, for which much thanks. Some of these essays were written in the context of work on *The Oxford Literary Review*: I thank Geoffrey Bennington for his stimulating collaboration during the course of our long labour – now ended – on the *OLR*. Homi Bhabha as always has been a challenging and rewarding reader, and I thank him warmly once more. Susan Matthews and Matthew Meadows have given constant sustenance. My lasting gratitude to Badral, Maryam, and Yasmine, for teaching me what is worthwhile. Finally, this book is dedicated to my mother, Mary Young, a son's small gift towards love's irredeemable debt.

Earlier versions of some of these essays have appeared as follows: 'Back to Bakhtin', *Cultural Critique* 2 (1985–86), 71–92; 'Psychoanalysis and Political Literary Theories', in *Thresholds: Psychoanalysis and Cultural Theory*, ed. James Donald London, Macmillan, 1991, 139–57; 'The Politics of "The Politics of Literary Theory"', *Oxford Literary Review* 10 (1988), 131–57; 'The Idea of a Chrestomathic University', in *Logomachia: The Conflict of the Faculties*, ed. Richard A. Rand Lincoln, Nebraska University Press, 1992, 97–126.

Frontiers....................................

Theories of conflict

....

Introduction............................

Capitalism and theory

What is the relation of politics to theory? Theories make political claims, theorists make political critiques, and academics use theory in the pursuit of institutional ends: theory is not only about politics but itself forms a political practice. The contemporary pressure for theory to deliver a politics cannot be dismissed as mere fashion, easy moralizing or academic casuistry; it is also a product of the reformulation by theory of the very concept of the political. Instead of traditional political oppositions, there are now more difficult sets of related but often conflictual positions, a shift which forms part of a wider interrogation of the role of knowledge and power in the history of the West. This change has also involved the loss of Marxism's dominance of the realm of political and cultural theory, with the assertion against class politics of questions of minorities, gender and ethnicity, and the interrogation of the conditions of the production, operation, and transmission of academic knowledge in the institution and the State.

The essays in this book are concerned with the character of the conflict within that culture of theory. In retrospect, what was distinctive about the eruption of 'theory' within the humanities in recent years was not just that different theories developed through conflictual and productive engagements with others, but that the focus of antagonism between them was consistently the theory of conflict itself. This preoccupation can be seen to materialize in a repetition effect that is charted through the debates examined in this book. While the content of particular controversies ranges across the spectrum of recent preoccupations in literary and cultural theory, the recurrent dialectical form of such theoretical conflicts unfolds as a performative repetition of what is finally shown to be the constitutive structure of the academic institution itself. But what determines the institution?

In these essays, written between 1985 and 1993, I analyse the operations of conflictual theory in a number of areas: in relation to cultural theory, to historicism, to psychoanalysis, to racism, to the history and system of the academic institution. In each instance, a polarity emerges between the perspectives of inside and outside, content and frame, theory and the realities of society or history. More often than not the debates involve the juxtaposition of incommensurable arguments from two or more sides, their opposition constituting the founding division by which the field has been both developed and contested. At the centre of such conflicts has been the engagement of Marxism with a range of contemporary theoretical adversaries. While the confrontation between Marxism and rival theories lies at the heart of the debates discussed here, it is argued that this does not just consist of competing, mutually exclusive positions, but rather that their antagonism repeats the ambivalence of an incompatible dialectic that operates today within the forces that determine the material culture that frames them.

Far from ever collapsing from contradiction, it becomes increasingly clear that capitalism works most effectively through its contradictions. This insight can already be found in Adam Smith's gnomic invocation of 'the hidden hand'. Today it is often more obvious: open up 'emerging markets' (the banks' and brokers' term for much of the former Third World) for investment, extol the virtues of the introduction of free-market economies throughout the world. But as soon as an economy or a currency threatens to collapse, forget *laissez-faire* and arrange for intervention: call in the IMF and World Bank to prop it up with loans, the conditions for which allow the West to dictate its own terms for political freedoms or repression, according to investors' requirements. The free market only works properly by being carefully controlled. The same contradictory structure works at the interface of ideology and economics: formerly it was most glaringly evident in the irreconcilable moralities of the home and the market-place. Today it is equally visible in the way in which the demand for human rights, free speech and democratic institutions is directed at totalitarian governments as a matter of humanistic Western virtue, the minimum values necessary for a civilized society; yet, the introduction of human rights, political choice, and freedom also functions as the stealthy vanguard, the necessary requisite at the level of individual freedom, to produce the identificatory needs of consumer capitalism, destroying social forms of identity and creating a demand that enables outside politico-economic control through the introduction of a free-market economy, the opening up of new markets to corporate Western capitalism, the importation of Western consumer goods, and the parallel exploitation of new sources of cheap labour.

The demonstration of the successful functioning of this form of logic in the philosophical and cultural realm formed the basis of 'deconstruction'; its main adversary was a Marxism which, for the most part, held on to a rationalist logic of contradiction, and of its own role in such a structure. Even Ernesto Laclau and Chantal Mouffe base their work on this assumption: 'Now, if the tendency towards division is inscribed in the very structure of modern capitalism, what is the source of the opposite moment, the tendency towards unification?'[1] A succession of answers: the party, socialism as a party programme, or for Laclau and Mouffe, a new logic of hegemony, none of which is prepared to consider that such a unifying tendency could be just as effectively inscribed in the structure of modern capitalism as that which drives towards division. In fact, Marx and Engels had already suggested this possibility in *The Communist Manifesto*. They begin by stressing the inherent instability of a revolutionary capitalism:

> The bourgeoisie cannot exist without constantly revolutionising the instruments of production, and thereby the relations of production, and with them the whole relations of society.... Constant revolutionising of production, uninterrupted disturbance of all social conditions, everlasting uncertainty and agitation distinguish the bourgeois epoch from all earlier ones. All fixed, fast-frozen relations, with their train of ancient and venerable prejudices and opinions, are swept away, all new-formed ones become antiquated before they can ossify.

But this argument is immediately followed by a paragraph that stresses capitalism's simultaneous mechanism of totalization – political and economic imperialism: 'The need of a constantly expanding market for its products chases the bourgeoisie over the whole surface of the globe. It must nestle everywhere, settle everywhere, establish connexions everywhere.'[2] Among later Marxist writers, only Theodor Adorno and Walter Benjamin could be said to have fully followed through the dialectical implications of this powerful image of an untotalizable totality. In response to deconstruction's charting of the long-term survival and strength of such contradictory logics, some commentators accused it of merely presenting a neo-Nietzschean model of indeterminate conflict against a Marxist dialectic – itself, as Marx and Engels' comments indicate, a profoundly undialectical objection. At the same time, it has to be conceded that it was only after much prodding of this kind from the Left that it became clearer that deconstruction was articulating in an immanent way the secret doubled logic of capitalism itself. The history of the assimilation of deconstruction in the academy has involved the slow transformation of that immanent analysis into the form of a politico-critical instrument.[3]

Deconstruction did not initially appear to comprise a new kind of political or cultural critique. Early in the 1980s, Jonathan Dollimore succinctly put the issues as they then appeared:

> Currently, the important arguments are not between theory and what it has superseded but within theory itself – most importantly, perhaps, between materialism and deconstruction. They are arguments which keep coming back to one very important question: how far has the theorizing of literature and the humanities succeeded in what was, after all, one of its principal objectives, namely to politicize them?
>
> To attend the 1981 Southampton Conference 'Theory and Text', and that at Essex in 1982, 'Theory Ten Years On', was to realize that the present theoretical 'moment' is characterized by a real dilemma, and one which may yet be resolved only by a parting of ways.
>
> In virtue of their own remorseless logic, their own irresistible trajectory, certain forms of theory have been problematizing a range of concepts which, in terms of present political practice, some socialists reckon to be indispensable.[4]

But what then occurred was unanticipated, unexpected, and inconceivable: not just a transformation of the status of 'the political', but the abandonment of socialism itself. The collapse of the absolute dominance of Marxism among radical intellectuals in the early 1980s was no more imaginable at that time than the break-up of the Soviet Union. If some of the essays in this book took part in that challenge to the protocols of certain Marxist conceptualizations, they participated in a movement that became too successful. Oppression, exploitation, and poverty now strike without risk of systematic challenge.

The point of the deconstructive critique of Marxism, too often hastily assumed to be simply anti-Marxist, was not to destroy it but to expand its modalities, to refine its edge. What deconstruction proposed was a challenge to accepted ways of formulating certain conceptual problems in contemporary politics, and in knowledge. This explains on the one hand its lack of immediate and obvious political engagement, of which many have been so critical, and on the other hand the frequent feeling that somehow Marxism was its main object of attack. Deconstruction was most fully engaged in a conflict with the allegedly closed form of the Marxist dialectic, into which it sought to insert an opening, a dialogical interruption that would allow the dialectic to carry certain irreconcilable elements along with it. In that sense Marxism, particularly the legacy of the

Marxism of Louis Althusser, was indeed deconstruction's contemporary intellectual adversary, against which it began to assert a rival oppositional voice in Western cultural discourse.[5] This is not to say, however, that it was its political opponent; contrary to the assumption of some early commentators, deconstruction was not hostile to Marxism as such. Within the context of a powerful, but in many ways still Stalinist French Communist Party, it was hostile to certain rigidified Marxist dogmatisms. At the same time, as others have recognized, a profound affinity exists between deconstruction and Marxism: the wrestling between them tells the story of their complex engagement with each other.[6] Deconstruction needs Marxism, needs to work from it and through it, in order to produce its own forms of articulation and disturbance.[7] This has become clearer since the evanescence of Marxism as the dominant contemporary intellectual force in Europe, the result of which has been that deconstruction has also lost much of its effectivity, and has found itself conceptually and politically orphaned. The paradox that deconstruction has yet to confront is that if closed systems inhibit change, it is also the place of the aporetic within their impossible structures that provides the best hinge for effective political transformation.

Today, at a theoretical as well as a political level, many assume that Marxism has entered upon an inexorable and irreversible decline. What, though, of its once commanding dialectic of opposed entities in contradiction to each other, with no recourse but to work themselves through into a distinct, fused third term – the classical model of revolution (and of organic totalization)? This has been revised into an apparently less politically powerful paradigm: a dialectic of neo-Kantian antimonies in which contradictions may be mutually modifying but live on in an economy in which they neither merge nor become wholly distinct, a form of contestatory hybridization which repeats its own contemporary cultural and social situation. The messy mixes of poststructuralism and postmodernism, which rehearse the cultural condition of late capitalist society in the late twentieth century, are indeed the symptomatic theories of their era, but depend on the dialectical Hegelian–Marxist model which it is often assumed that they have replaced, playing themselves out in an apparently contradictory, antithetical economy of totalization and globalization balanced against decentralization and difference.

Ambivalent, contestatory doubling becomes apparent in this book as the distinctive form of many of the key conceptual apparatuses that have been developed in twentieth-century theory:

dialogization, differance, differend, the oscillations of centripetal and centrifugal forces, of diaspora and centralization, of displacement and condensation, of identity and difference, of immanence and transcendence, of monoglossia and heteroglossia, of power and resistance, of relativism and universalism, of subversion and containment, and of totalization and detotalization. Such reversible power relations cannot be analysed according to their individual terms: the discontinuous dialectic between them makes up the incommensurable dynamic, both creative and destructive, positive and negative at once. Gilles Deleuze and Félix Guattari's concept of flow represents one attempt to describe what happens within such oscillations, a forceful antithesis working in between this contradictory movement which, according to them, constitutes the effective drive of capitalism itself. And we have to concede that it's not for nothing that we speak of the *economy* of capitalism: its duplicitous extravagances not only play themselves out in the stock markets, finance houses, and treasuries of the world, but also determine the conceptual and theoretical formulations of its academies. Contemporary theory, be it dialogism, New Historicism, postmodernism, poststructuralism, postcolonialism, or psychoanalysis, repeats this structure and, in describing it, re-enacts and reinforces it.

Increasing cultural hybridity is evidently the product of the disruptions and dislocations that are the effects of the economic system, even while the agents of that system always seek to increase its control and the extent of its globalization. In this situation it can appear as if the productive political and theoretical move would be to oppose totalization with anti-totalization, necessity with freedom, as the range of 'post' theories are sometimes taken to imply. However, the specific intervention of deconstruction as a theory was to demonstrate that these two manoeuvres, although often operating at different levels, are nevertheless mutually determined, even if their imbalance in power can involve local and particular forms of subversion and resistance. Though operating against each other, these incompatible dialectics together make up a larger dialectical economy that manages to work effectively despite its contradictoriness and apparent theoretical impossibility. What becomes clear from the contemporary political and cultural situation is that a radical logic of incompatibility between centrifugal and centripetal forces, simultaneously forcing cultures and peoples together as it pulls others apart, operates as the cultural and economic dynamic of late capitalist society.[8] The logic of unity and diversity, fusion and separation, the imbrication of different cultures in which elements become irretrievably grafted on to one another, mixed even while remaining distinct, is also inscribed in the relations between societies of the North and the South. Capitalism's extraordinary adaptability and ability to metamorphosize itself into different forms, its inherent instability and constant mode of revolutionary change, that is, its skill – the central dynamic of the system – in deferring indefinitely that lonely last instance when its contradictions would produce its own self-destruction, can be understood in terms of the flexibility of its antithetical forces that certainly exist in contradiction to each other but which remorselessly reiterate and play out infinitely adaptable dialectics of simultaneity and disjunction, of centralization and dispersion, aggregation and disaggregation, of deterritorialization and reterritorialization. But if history repeats itself then it must also re-enact the convulsive protest of socialized voices coalescing antagonistically against diaspora, deprivation, and despair.

Notes

1 Laclau and Mouffe, *Hegemony and Socialist Strategy*, 32.

2 Marx and Engels, *Manifesto of the Communist Party*, 45–6.

3 For an account of the politicization of deconstruction in Britain (which includes a critique of my own work, characterized as retaining at least 'a commitment to politics'), see Easthope, *British Post-Structuralism Since 1968*, 161–90.

4 Dollimore, 'Politics Teaching Literature', 108.

5 For a detailed discussion of the controversial question of history in Althusser's work, see my 'The Scientific Critique of Historicism', in *White Mythologies*, 48–68.

6 On Marxism and deconstruction, see 'Séminaire "Politique"', in Lacoue-Labarthe and Nancy, *Les Fins de l'homme*, 487–529; Derrida, 'Politics and Friendship', and *Specters of Marx*. Other commentators include Bennington, *Legislations*; Mohanty, 'Marx After Derrida'; Ryan, *Marxism and Deconstruction*; Spivak, 'Scattered Speculations on the Question of Value', *In Other Worlds*, 154–75, and 'Limits and Openings of Marx in Derrida', *Outside in the Teaching Machine*, 97–119.

7 Derrida, 'Politics and Friendship', 221.

8 Cf. Hall, 'The Local and the Global'.

1

The dialectics of cultural criticism

Literary theory: exceeding the boundaries

> Imagination, a licentious and vagrant faculty, unsus-
> ceptible of limitations, and impatient of restraint, has
> always endeavoured to ... perplex the confines of dis-
> tinction and burst the enclosures of regularity.
>
> Dr Johnson

> I suggest that real reading, when it occurs ... is out-
> side the institution, allergic to institutionalization, pri-
> vate, solitary.
>
> J. Hillis Miller

Literature: a licentious and vagrant category, unsusceptible of limitations, and impatient of restraint: a melange of poetry, novels, plays,
sermons, political tracts, diaries, letters, books of philosophy and
science once thought to be true but now read as fiction. It is hard
to defend literature as a stable category: its sameness is made up
entirely of difference. What's apparently wrong with it, however, is
also what's right with it: literature is flagrantly hybrid. It can be
crossed with anything: the *Orlando* effect.

Inevitably, therefore, for literary criticism, which seeks to secure an object on which to build a discipline, the difficulty with
literature always comes in defining its boundaries. Perhaps that
was what the fuss about 'imagination' was always about. Literature
is always taking the reader beyond itself: discussion of books about
the world quickly turns into deliberations about the world which
they represent. Critics perpetually find themselves looking through
and beyond their window on to the world. It does not help much to
look closely at the text instead: language too tends to exceed its
limits at every level, whether of reference, representation, connota-
tion, metaphor, symbolization. The haemorrhage is habitually stemmed with notions such as text and context, interacting realms that
are also apparently discrete. Yet each seeps so easily into the

margins of the other that literary criticism seems perennially uncertain about the borders that it is supposed to defend. The long tradition in which the task of the critic was to divide authors into 'major' and 'minor' literature, as if they were identically named pupils at an English public school, has given place to an uncertainty derived from a recognition of the ways in which literature is relentlessly entangled with other discourses. It is no longer possible to define or prescribe its confines. Hence the attraction of the term 'culture', which seems to have no boundaries, encompassing the context of all literary production, the social world that goes on around it, while at the same time including literature. But if culture is 'insatiable', as Adorno suggests, it is also a boundary concept, or rather a concept about barriers, boundaries, frontiers, and limits.[1] My culture, my literature, my race, my nation. Here theory's work in relation to culture operates as a kind of enforced nomadism, crossing frontiers, borders, raiding disciplines, plagiarizing, kidnapping, transgressing. Its illicit operations are carried out across front lines, often deep in the exclusive territory of others. This radical activism would be entirely reassuring if such dislocations did not also mimic the transgressive cultural formations and operations of capitalism itself.

The relation of literature to culture goes much deeper than any recent conversion of the first into the second. If criticism's fundamental task is to police the limits of literature, the history of criticism also demonstrates a constant desire on its part to overflow its own measure, to stray beyond the limits of the literary into the frontier territories of cultural criticism. In that sense it is also a hybrid, ambivalent institution, enacting an institutional anxiety which hinges on the relation of academic knowledge to the outside world, a socialized echo of the philosophical complexities of subject–object relations. Misgiving about the institution's own knowledge in relation to that of the world of everyday life is as old as the institution itself. An uneasiness about the relation of inside to outside is apparent, for example, in the whole history of thinking about institutions of higher education and their function from the very beginning.

In recent years there has been an insistent emphasis upon the relation of literature to the culture of which it forms a part. If New Historicism, Bakhtinian criticism, or Cultural Materialism, for example, all invoked or defined themselves via 'culture' – very often as some form of the outside that was considered to transcend the formalism ascribed to the inside – this suggests that the contemporary movement from Literature to Cultural Studies was not something that was going on outside the academy, but rather amounted to the academy turning itself inside out. The definition of its subject, its proper object of attention, simply shifted from its interior to its exterior, from the private to the public, from the immanent to the transcendent. New literary theories consistently alternated around the same division: seeking to cross the boundary to the social (hence Mikhail Bakhtin's popularity), by using history (New Historicism) or culture (Cultural Materialism) or the history and culture of colonialism, or sexuality (which necessarily, according to this model, invoked the notion of 'transgression', the crossing of the law as the supremely human and therefore political act) – or, in the remarkable, if rare case of its inverse, attempting to refuse knowledge of the outside, or the racialized other (Paul de Man). The seemingly endless proliferation and succession of new theoretical positions was not just a question of fashion and the increasing commodification of academic production, but also the mark of a repetition compulsion, the constant preoccupation of theory confined to a particular discursive dynamic from which it sought to break out to become something beyond itself, to achieve its own negation.

The culture of institutions

'Culture' has now deviated decisively from a category of art to the category of the social, from the academy's own activities to its other, the outside world. In many ways, it may be too simplistic to describe the relation of the academic institution to society in such schematic inside–outside terms, for almost every such institution constitutes a complex economy of procedures that, far from being autonomous, interact at most levels with other social and economic processes. But at the same time, the operation of the institutional establishment as a determinate, separable entity has continued to dominate its conceptual thinking and its production of knowledge. This situation is reinforced by the long tradition in which the intellectual has regarded herself or himself as separated from society in general, whether in a state of alienation from society or as its avant-garde. Indeed it is arguable that the popular image of the institution as a monolithic, isolated totality is itself simply a version of the academic subject writ large, itself a form of the typical Romantic reversal of knowledge from the social world of the public sphere into a secret, interior higher life within an individual consciousness. At this level, the pressure for the inside to turn itself into the outside, like an empty trouser pocket, betrays a fantasy of escape which, as in Shelley's *Alastor*, has nowhere to go but itself.

This inside–outside paradigm is not merely one among many, but is rather a structure that has dominated the intellectual history of the institution as such. The customary opposition which Jacques Derrida has highlighted between the desirable presence of speech and the dead letter of writing itself mirrors the division between the world and the university, or, in F. R. Leavis's extraordinary inversion, between the technologico-Benthamite mechanical world outside, and the 'life' preserved within the beleaguered, chalk-dusted walls of university English departments. In a similar way, the whole philosophical question of the same and the other which has dominated European philosophy for the past two centuries amounts to a long meditation upon the relation between the subject and the object of knowledge, the institution's inside and its outside, the private and the public sphere. Most recent theory has oscillated according to this dichotomy of self-reflexivity and critical distance: either theory has been caught within the prison house of language, apparently celebrating the limits of its self-reflexive status, and finessing Kant by arguing that it cannot be certain about the status of even its own knowledge of itself, or it has urged the necessity of a breaking through the mirror of self-reflexivity to the outside, to the real, the material, to history.

Self-reflexivity must be changed for critical distance, its apparent inverse. The critique of self-reflexivity has always been accompanied by an urge to the exterior, to history, culture. Against this empirical impulse, poststructuralists scorned the assumption that language was a transparent medium, that literature provided a window on to the world, while espousing the Kantian paradigms that warned of the breakdown of representation, of the inability to cross from the structures of language to knowledge of the world. The only sphere deemed knowable became the world as text, the structures of representations and the systems of signs through which uncertain meaning was created. Humanity was condemned to living (on) in this world of simulacra, where it saw not the world but the hyperreal world of created images of the world. There was no 'outside' to this text. No outside: nothing produced so strong a reaction in the whole business of poststructuralism as the claim that there was no outside to a text. All reference, empirical reality, meaning itself, it was assumed, was denied. There was, apparently, only an inside, with the desired outside threatening to vanish altogether out of reach, thus dramatically highlighting the anxiety about the relation of academic knowledge to society at large.

Cultural theory's tendency to alternate between these inside–

outside polarities opens up the possibility that culture is the institution's own name for this anxiety, an oscillating antagonism operating within itself, formulated as the split between aesthetics or high culture (the inside) and mass or popular culture (outside). In this connection psychoanalysis reveals itself as a theory of the anxieties not of the patient but of the analyst, theorizing the incompatibility of inside and outside and, therefore, the troubled relation of the institution's link to the world outside. The polar division on which cultural theory is based and on whose tension it thrives, thus reproduces simultaneously both theory's relation to its object of analysis and the institution's own inside–outside structure.

What has characterized modern theory therefore is the way in which all theories themselves have shared an anxiety about this exterior, and have sought to move beyond the barrier of representation, beyond the institution itself, to the remote and exotic other. Or, in a twist of the Cartesian paradigm, this is reversed: if we cannot ever know the other, then we turn back to the self – hence the increasing tendency of academics to base their politics on, and to work from, their own gendered and minoritarian identities, which provide a means through which the individual can establish access to the social world outside. The intimate revelations of the inquiring self stand in as a typical example of the wider social structure. The dichotomy of the self and the other, the preoccupation with an otherness that remains other, the attempt to find a way of allowing the other to speak in its absolute alterity, or the self to speak in its unutterable sameness, are not only, as in Emmanuel Lévinas, an ethical issue, nor even, as in anthropology, a paradox of the impossible knowledge on which a discipline is founded, but are also part of a deep misgiving about the limits and boundaries of institutionalized knowledge as such. The formulation of knowledge in general into the various, carefully demarcated disciplines of academic knowledge is a matter of remarkably recent history. The institution remains haunted by the spectre of what, in order to achieve that conversion, it had to eliminate or demonize. The tendency of institutions has always been either to incorporate and assimilate the other or to exclude it, repeating the very structures through which knowledge is created. This history repeats to haunt the conscience of those working in institutions today, who find themselves enforcing the same formation even as they argue against it.

A distinctive feature of the contemporary intellectual milieu in humanities departments can be found in the dissatisfaction with the idea of the university as the preserver and guardian of high culture, the medieval, pre-print image of the university that was resuscitated so effectively by Matthew Arnold. The university now seeks to renounce its own culture for another culture beyond itself, attempting to relate its erudition to the world outside which is reckoned to possess a knowledge of greater validity than the institution's own. But does it ever manage to partake of that other culture or does it rather produce its own representation of it? Does it succeed in participating in it or does it rather create an oppositional virtual reality within the institution? Can those in the institution achieve a genuinely alternative position, or do they tend to act out the antithetical impulse which already makes up the institutional account of culture? Can those inside renounce themselves for the outside?

Those theories which attempt to break into the real world of the social do not generally acknowledge the institutional factors which determine and contain them. This is partly because those conditions themselves define the structures of knowledge within the institution and the desire of knowledge itself. Aside from the work of Pierre Bourdieu, there has been comparatively little reflection on the institutional context of the cultural institution across a range of different disciplines, or of the extent to which 'culture' itself constitutes an historically determined, discursive construction. The very concepts of culture, as they are used today, are all institutional creations even if they are no longer, as they were for Edmund Burke, Coleridge or Arnold, embodied in institutions. The contemporary preoccupation with culture not only involves something that goes on outside the institution but is also a phenomenon of the institution which defines it and creates it through its own culture of theory. Culture may constitute a name for that outside, but in a profoundly dialectical way the outside is constituted from the inside. 'Culture' is the product of the culture of theory within contemporary academic institutions.[2]

In *The Politics and Poetics of Transgression* (1986) Peter Stallybrass and Allon White offered a dynamic perspective on this inside–outside structure so characteristic of the academic institution.[3] They recast Bakhtin's theory of carnival into a powerful model of 'symbolic inversion': a form of displacement which operates through 'symbolic substitution from one domain to the other' (196). Stallybrass and White argued that a dualism of 'high' and 'low' structures a whole range of practices that have organized society since the rise of the bourgeoisie. While they themselves concentrated on high and low because of its association with differences of class, its polarization continually shifts in their analysis from determined class boundaries towards those of cultural difference, the polite and vulgar, the civilized and the savage, always towards the constitution of the inside by its exclusion of an outside. For Stallybrass and White, symbolic inversion comes to depend upon a pattern by which the 'high' attempts to exclude the 'low' in order to create and maintain itself, only to find that this makes it paradoxically dependent on this rejected other. Having shown the operation of this structure throughout the cultural history of bourgeois society (itself an example of 'low' and 'high': social history as opposed to political history), the authors end by considering the problem that their analysis applies equally well to their own book. They suggest that in the 'high' institution, the idealizing fascination of those on the Left with the vulgar forms of everyday life betrays nothing less than the workings of their own bourgeois identity:

> On the one hand, these sites have been singled out by some social historians in a nostalgic and privileged way as the ever-vanishing trace of 'real community'. But this precisely duplicates, at the level of academic discourse, the object of analysis. On the other hand, 'rigorous theory' has tended to look down upon 'mere content' as obvious, crude and vulgar, redeemable only through a process of abstraction and refinement. Here we find the opposite but equally characteristic gesture of 'the civilizing process'. In other words contemporary analysis has tended either to fetishize or repress the *contents* of these domains. In so doing, academic work clearly reveals its discursive mirroring of the subject-formation of the middle classes. (191–2)

On the one hand, a high cultural aesthetic or formalism eschews the vulgarity of the outside, a means of establishing bourgeois identity and of identifying the institution with its values in opposition to the vulgar world outside. On the other hand, those on the Left who challenge this, and regard the outside with fascination and nostalgia and seek to turn it into their object of study are, according to Stallybrass and White, merely indulging in a fetishization of the excluded other – a form of hysterical eroticization. This double bind with which they leave the radical institutional critic suggests that there is no easy turn from one domain to the other – whether the gesture be one of exclusion or incorporation.

Self-reflexivity and critical distance

As long as criticism operates according to this polarity, then the possibility remains that what the academic institution sees in 'culture' as its other is nothing less than a mirror of itself. Must culture always be an institutional product even if – especially if – it is represented as in fact existing outside it? Such an argument would imply that there is no more an actual object corresponding to culture than, as Edward Said argues, a real Orient that corresponds to the projections of Orientalism. Orientalism is a discursive construction of the West that has no necessary relation to the actual although if Westerners want to say anything about that actuality then they still have no option but to use Orientalist discourse. Nowhere is this kind of institutional construction of a new object for analysis more apparent than in the current postmodernism debate, a particularly obvious production of the culture of institutions. The theoretical shift of recent years from a preoccupation with poststructuralism to one with postmodernism, itself constitutes another example of the pressure towards culture which has produced its own symptomatic dilemma. The construction of a discourse about postmodernism mimics the discursive construction of all knowledges: the only difference being that postmodernism is a theoretical practice and cultural discourse without an object as such, refusing to reveal whether it is describing a discernible historical event, or an intellectual condition which its own discourse is simultaneously bringing into being. This may well be because, as Jean Baudrillard argues, postmodern theory has in effect reversed the order of things so that its discourse analyses not the object world but signs and representations with no necessary referent in the object world, which have therefore become the hyperreal, insurmountable limit of postmodern analysis.[4] The sign has become the referent, the inside has become the outside, a further twist of the knife in the seemingly uncontrollable and unavoidable oscillation between inside and outside of modern theory. Whereas formerly those in the institution could paradoxically claim to see the outside from a privileged point of exteriority more or less unavailable to those who really were outside, the situation has now been reversed. If today's culture is marked by an institutional anxiety about the institution's outside, its effect is to position the latter in the place of knowledge. The history of the institution is made up of these two transcendent impulses: the speculative moment in which the institution itself forms the point of exteriority through which it can comprehend and account for the world, and the empiricist counter-movement in which the institution's removal from the world is reversed so that it is posited as an inside which neglects the outside world, which now becomes the point of exteriority.

   This dialectic also impinges directly on the question of legitimation, a term today often associated with Jean-François Lyotard's
The Postmodern Condition of 1979: who, and by what criteria, has
the authority to judge the knowledge of the university, and by what
criteria can it be judged? The question centres on the prospect of
the legitimation of the university's knowledge in terms other than
its own. Ultimately, government has exercised political control over
every other institution, but the university has traditionally resisted
this on the grounds that politics is incommensurable with true,
objective knowledge. Its objectivity is jealously guarded, though
hard to demonstrate historically. At the same time, some of its own
practitioners are happy to bring political arguments to bear whose
authority is derived from the outside, and this has been a major
mechanism of institutional change. This problem of legitimating the
university's knowledge correlates with an inside–outside dichotomy
that recurs at the heart of its own account of knowledge as such.
   Lyotard's book is best known for its argument that postmodernism involves the substitutions of *petits récits*, singularities, for
the grand narratives of the Enlightenment, particularly that of Marxism (though not apparently that of postmodernism itself). The
postmodern condition, Lyotard argues, is one in which it has become impossible for any theory to legitimate itself in the way in
which Marxism, in particular, once claimed to be a science.[5] The
demise of Althusserian theory in this respect marks the historic last
attempt of Marxism to accede to a scientific moment, and thus a
uniquely privileged status. With the end of Althusserianism, the
major theoretical problem for Marxism in the cultural sphere became the maintenance of critical distance and the grounds for the
claim to objectivity. Inevitably this merged into the larger related
question of the breakdown of representation, the common-sense
division between the sign and its referent, which led to the problematics explored in Deleuze's simulacra, or Baudrillard's escape
from the reflexivity of simulacra through a principle of reversibility. Baudrillard's methodological technique of reversal constituted
a cunning way to allow him a form of ideology critique without
having to use the metaphor of (critical) distance. Avoiding the spatial
method of the appearance–essence model, Baudrillard achieved a
certain difference through seduction: by leading astray, inverting
or reversing any form of thought. However, this left it entirely
ungrounded, and without political principle or direction.
   Baudrillard's move was made in response to the technical
but significant political difficulty characteristic of the culture of

postmodernism, and it is in relation to this problem of the loss of critical distance and the threat of self-reflexivity that the theoretical attractions of cultural studies and cultural theory in humanities departments become apparent. If 'culture' stands in for 'the social', the investigation of culture acts as a substitute for the former analysis of ideology and its reassuring dichotomy – when consciousness of the world could be divided into the true and the false, and all was well with the world. The current shift towards cultural theory marks not so much a disciplinary change as a shift in the theorization of ideology: culture is another way of talking about ideology, the so-called lived relationship of men to their world, without having to invoke the disgraced category of consciousness or to contemplate any dangerous association of Marxism with psychoanalysis. A major attraction of culture is that it seems to avoid the whole problem of distance, of the relation of ideology to science (knowledge). However, as Claude Lévi-Strauss has shown, culture is equally beset by the problem of how the anthropologist, or critic, steps outside.[6] Transposed into the terms of Jürgen Habermas, the issue becomes the competing claims of universalist and relativist theories.

This urge to exteriority also fashioned the attraction of the New Historicist identification of an analogical model between textual representation and forms of symbolic practices 'outside'. In one move, the critic could glide effortlessly on the wings of homology to the exterior world, untroubled by the epistemological difficulties so painfully explored in the past fifty years. A comparable solution was to substitute the distance of time rather than space. This move reproduced the paradoxical situation of all historiography which repeats in a different form the inside/outside structure of cultural criticism. Just as the critic has to be both inside and outside the culture at the same time, so historians seek to be inside the past time that he or she is outside, and outside the present time which he or she is inside. Historiography, therefore, can only proceed through a dialectic of impossibilities – which is not to say that it is impossible, only that the historian, like the cultural critic, has to be the same and different at once. In the same way, if history involves an analysis of a culture of the past, it can also be a way of using the past to provide a critical perspective upon the present. The return to history, therefore, characteristic of New Historicism and Cultural Materialism, could be seen as having made a constructive response to the dilemma produced by the spatial model of theoretical analysis, even if its version of the inside–outside dialectic did not manage to demarcate clear-cut boundaries between the two.

The question of critical distance articulated the theoretical consequence of the polarity between the institution's inside and its outside, the sustained resistance to the alleged threat of formalism (from whom, though?) and the collapse into self-reflexivity. This was the reason for the importance of Fredric Jameson's early understanding of the problem and his sustained theoretical resistance to the implications of its consequences. It also provides the context for understanding the significance of his sudden abandonment in *Postmodernism* of the claims to critical distance, asserted so forcefully in *The Political Unconscious*. For Jameson postmodernism means, above all, the loss of critical distance, based on 'a certain minimal aesthetic distance', and the acceptance of the very world of representation and self-reflexivity that had hitherto been so forcefully resisted.[7] It thus heralds the end of the doubled system according to which thought could be split in two, and science (knowledge) be set against ideology, and the world understood in its proper meaning: in other words, postmodernism means the end of the possibility of critique as such. The point outside the dominant culture for so long adopted by the Marxist critic as the basis for a critical perspective is thus no longer available. Postmodernism has apparently broken down the inside–outside dichotomy on which institutional knowledge is based. This is the epistemological basis of the apparently entirely ethical pursuit of the other and forms of alterity so characteristic of postmodernist work. When science could set its knowledge against ideology, there was a noticeable lack of interest in the otherness of the other. Now that we are inextricably within the culture of postmodernism, the alterity of the other becomes the last trace of a ghostly knowledge.

What was particularly telling in this context was Jameson's celebrated use of the Bonaventure Hotel as a metaphor of the postmodern condition of an irresolvable oscillation between totalization and fragmentation.[8] The Bonaventure Hotel, a postmodern building well-known to academics as the place where the Los Angeles meeting of the Modern Language Association was held, was cited by Jameson as an illustration of the extent to which the individual is deprived of all coordinates in the postmodern world, literally finding it impossible to find her or his way around or out of the building in which the inside and outside have apparently become indistinguishable. The experience of the hotel breaks down the division between the two in an image of the critic's inability to distinguish science from ideology; and yet at the same time it also reinforces the division of outside from inside, for the postmodern academic remains in fact trapped inside. Nothing could be a more graphic illustration of the fact that what is at stake here is an institutional anxiety, in which the academics in the hotel are cut off from the surrounding city, and, to the extent that the hotel's exterior mirrored surface reflects only the city that it faces, have indeed themselves become invisible. The institution no longer works as the speculative moment for culture, but rather the reverse whereby the institution can only reflect the totality of culture outside.

The tables have been turned. It is no longer the intellectual who has established a critical distance from the society around her or him, but society which encompasses the intellectual. Society no longer depends on the institution to guard and preserve the treasures of its culture, but instead uses the institution as a form of self-reflection. The cultural critic appears to be remorselessly trapped inside, trying to get out.

Cultural criticism and society: Adorno's torn halves

The dilemmas of this inside–outside dichotomy have found themselves endlessly perpetuated while critics have continued to validate one against the other. But in a typically postmodern inversion, by which before comes after, Adorno had already offered a particularly acute and productive analysis of the problems involved. Writing to Walter Benjamin from London in 1936 (the year in which he was writing under the pseudonym Hektor Rottweiler), Adorno made what was to become his most famous statement about the relation of high art to popular culture.[9] Discussing Benjamin's essay 'The Work of Art in the Age of Mechanical Reproduction', Adorno criticizes his friend's tendency to lament the loss of the aura of high (or autonomous) art even as he celebrates the introduction of populist mechanical arts such as the cinema. Adorno argues that it is a mistake to see the one as a substitute for, or alternative to, the other, for they are both marked by a common dialectic: 'Both bear the stigmata of capitalism, both contain elements of change. . . . Both are torn halves of an integral freedom, to which however they do not add up. It would be romantic to sacrifice one to the other'.[10] The essential point about culture under capitalism, according to Adorno, can be found in its dialectical structure of perpetual antagonism in which the different kinds of art never add up to a totality, truth or freedom. This schismatic formation of irreconcilable torn halves (*auseinandergerissenen Hälften*) has resulted from the institution of the division of labour, whose effect has been to produce a culture perpetually set against itself, its products simultaneously producing both ideology and truth. For Adorno, the critic can only hold on to this understanding by maintaining the two sides of the impossible dialectic simultaneously together, not by affirming the one against the other. The conflictual structure of culture is the product of the divisions instituted by capitalism, and bears the stigmata (*Wundmale*) of its agony; but the repetition of those scars is also a sign of divine favour, whereby the irreconcilable antagonisms of capitalism provide the fissure that facilitates a critical perspective upon society.[11] The split between consciousness and social life-processes which Marx saw as a deleterious effect of capitalism also paradoxically empowers a singularly positive form of political critique, even if it is predicated on the eventual obliteration of the conditions which make it possible. So the reduction of the labourer to 'mere spectatorship, to mere *contemplation* of his own estranged activity and that of his fellows', for example, which is considered to be such a negative reifying effect of capitalism, is repeated in a more positive form in the critical distance which for the contemplative critic provides the basis for her or his analysis of capitalist society.[12] Thus alienation can be transformed into a determinate irreconcilability that provides the dissonant basis for critique.

The complicity of the cultural critic

Adorno argues that we must carefully distinguish dialectical from conventional cultural criticism. His most substantial analysis of the differences between the two is to be found in the short but complex essay, 'Cultural Criticism and Society'.[13] Here Adorno unravels the difficult paradoxes of cultural criticism, beginning with the fact that cultural criticism in itself involves a 'flagrant contradiction': 'The cultural critic is not happy with civilization, to which alone he owes his discontent. He speaks as if he represented either unadulterated nature or a higher historical stage. Yet he is necessarily of the same essence as that to which he fancies himself superior' (19). The whole of Adorno's argument depends on, and develops, the implications of this situation in which the critic claims difference, but must necessarily also be the same as that from which he or she differs.

The cultural critic is a part of that which he or she speaks against: the very project of cultural criticism involves an impossible contradiction in which the critic places herself or himself simultaneously inside and outside the culture. Here we find the basis for the interminable dialectic between inside and outside so characteristic of critical thinking. In general, individuals are inclined to endorse one side or the other, and much of Adorno's essay is addressed to the tendency of cultural criticism to hypostatize alternative positions rather than to address the paradoxical situation which produces them. The result is that the options remain entirely within the culture's own terms, and thus either repeat it uncritically (Adorno describes this as 'total immanence', 26), or take up a transcendent position outside it and dismiss it in its entirety, with the critic implicitly claiming that he or she possesses the true knowledge (or the true culture) which the culture itself lacks. We can compare the tendency of criticism to seek to move from the formalist inside to a culture outside, with the dialectic that Adorno here describes.

The dialectic of immanent and transcendent criticism

The answer to the quandary of the choice between them, according to Adorno, is not to choose between the two at all but to practise both at the same time dialectically:

> Criticism retains its mobility in regard to culture by recognizing the latter's position within the whole. Without such freedom, without consciousness transcending the immanence of culture, immanent criticism itself would be inconceivable: the spontaneous movement of the object can only be followed by someone who is not entirely engulfed by it. (29)

The most important section of Adorno's essay is to be found in the development of this distinction between transcendent and immanent critique. Asserting that 'the traditional transcendent critique of ideology is obsolete' (33), he argues that it must now be historicized, for it was conceived against a dominant idealism, a bourgeois subjectivism and concomitant fetishization of culture, which no longer exists. In a situation where ideology has become the practice of everyday life, the standard alternatives of cultural criticism, 'either calling culture as a whole into question from outside under the general notion of ideology, or confronting it with the norms which it itself has crystallized', are no longer acceptable.

Whereas the immanent method 'presupposes the questionable whole', the transcendent method, has inevitably seemed the more radical alternative, because it 'aims at totality'. Marxism has traditionally positioned itself *vis-à-vis* its object of analysis by establishing a critical distance, in the form of what Adorno calls 'transcendent critique'. It is necessary to get outside culture in order to criticize it objectively, according to terms other than its own. The transcendent critic therefore assumes an 'Archimedean position above culture and the blindness of society, from which consciousness can bring the totality, no matter how massive, into flux' (31). But such a position has to take out culture *en bloc*, and this produces a theoretical and a moral dilemma. In the first place it means that there is no point left on which the Archimedean lever can be placed. 'The choice of a standpoint outside the sway of existence is as fictitious as only the construction of abstract utopias can be' (31). At the same time, for Adorno, the necessity to get outside involves the danger that such external critique will tend to totalize the object and therefore necessarily involve complete rejection of it. 'In wishing to wipe away the whole as if with a sponge', Adorno comments, such critics 'develop an affinity to barbarism' (32). A good example of this throwing of the baby out with the bathwater would be his own analysis of the culture industry. Such fundamental critique may be all very well for certain forms of political analysis, but in the case of cultural analysis, the demonstration of the complicity of culture with a dominant ideology only allows its rejection: in a form of paranoia, the whole world is divided into black and white, and prepared for a new form of domination. In this example we encounter a problem which resurfaces with Adorno's later tendency increasingly to validate high art against all forms of popular culture. The issue here is that his criterion of culture is itself set up in a dialectic with barbarism, and thus reproduces most faithfully the dialectic upon which the Western notion of culture is formed. A further complicit moment of Adorno's own over-immanence within his own culture can be detected in his unguarded comment that 'Cultural criticism must become social physiognomy' (30), which invokes the racialized language of nineteenth-century accounts of culture and which finds its echo in his hostility towards jazz. He fails to see that this dialectic of culture and barbarism operates as another set of torn halves, another tension within the concept of culture itself.

Against the blanket rejection of culture which tends to be the outcome of the transcendent position, Adorno opposes the 'immanent procedure' which he regards as 'the more essentially dialectical':

> It takes seriously the principle that it is not ideology in itself which is untrue but rather its pretension to correspond to reality. Immanent criticism of intellectual and artistic phenomena seeks to grasp through

the analysis of their form and meaning, the contradiction between their objective idea and that pretension. It names what the consistency or inconsistency of the work itself expresses of the structure of the existent. Such criticism does not stop at a general recognition of the servitude of the objective mind, but seeks rather to transform this knowledge into a heightened perception of the thing itself. (32)

This form of criticism produces insight into the negativity of culture from within culture. It thus avoids the other major problem of transcendent critique, namely the question of how does such a critic achieve the position of distance from his or her own culture and history? We are, necessarily, a part of the culture which we wish to criticize. We cannot wash away the traces of our own history. From this point of view, immanent critique has the advantage that it looks not at the totality of a culture, but at a fragment of it, which, Adorno claims, will have a micrological relation to the totality. Art is privileged in that a detailed analysis can demonstrate the operation of the antagonisms which constitute society as a whole. Immanent criticism reveals how the individual work of art repeats, rather than resolves, the antimonies of its culture; this open-endedness forces a negative cognitive relation to its own cultural milieu. Where it finds inadequacies, it does not merely ascribe them to the failure of the individual artist, but seeks to understand how they are derived instead from the irreconcilability of the object's own cultural moment:

> It pursues the logic of its aporias, the insolubility of the task itself. In such antimonies criticism perceives those of society. A successful work, according to immanent criticism, is not one which resolves objective contradictions in a spurious harmony, but one which expresses the idea of harmony negatively by embodying the contradictions, pure and uncompromised, in its innermost structure. Confronted with this kind of work, the verdict 'mere ideology' loses its meaning. (32)

Here there seem to be two possibilities for criticism: one in which the work of art is seen as incorporating and therefore potentially revealing the antagonistic structures of society, the other in which its drive towards harmony itself highlights the difference between the ideal and existent reality.

In Adorno's account of immanent criticism it becomes evident that the autonomous work of art in effect repeats the autonomous mind of the critic. In the later *Aesthetic Theory*, the critical role would be fully assumed by the work of art.[14] Here it is through a parallel autonomy that both achieve a sort of internalized externality to culture, encrypted within its unconscious like a double agent.

Inevitably, however, immanent critique will always suffer from its own immanence, that is, the fact that the critic will be caught up within his or her own culture and be an unavoidable accomplice in its ideological structuring of reality. Immanent criticism remains under the spell of the object which it analyses, and cannot itself resolve the contradictions which it finds. It can therefore only reflect the conditions of existence, without altering them, and will always threaten to revert to idealism. At this point immanent criticism needs the perspective of transcendent criticism, but the opposite will always also hold true:

> the abstract categorizing and, as it were, administrative thinking of the former corresponds in the latter to the fetishism of an object blind to its genesis, which has become the prerogative of the expert. But if stubbornly immanent contemplation threatens to revert to idealism, to the illusion of the self-sufficient mind in command of both itself and of reality, transcendent contemplation threatens to forget the effort of conceptualization required and content itself instead with the prescribed label, the petrified invective, most often 'petty bourgeois', the ukase dispatched from above. (33)

The practitioner of a dialectical cultural criticism must guard equally against this tendency as against enthralment in the cultural object.

The deficiencies readily apparent in both methods led Adorno to propose that the practice of criticism must sustain an antimony between them, a critical dissonant doubling which parallels the fissure within the individual work of art or in culture itself. He argues that cultural criticism must operate through an incompatible logic of transcendent and immanent critique, even if that removes the finality associated with either and substitutes unresolved contradiction. Dialectical criticism must sustain a duality, which means a continuous mobility between contesting positions:

> It must relate the knowledge of society as a totality and of the mind's involvement in it to the claim inherent in the specific content of the object that it be apprehended as such. Dialectics cannot, therefore, permit any insistence on logical neatness to encroach on its right to go from one *genus* to another, to shed light on an object in itself hermetic by casting a glance at society, to present society with the bill which the object does not redeem. (33)

Criticism thus makes connections which the object avoids, and demands that society honours the unpaid bills which culture leaves behind. At the same time, in the constant self-criticism of critical procedures, the very dialectic between knowledge which comes from without and from within must itself become suspect, for it is itself a symptom of the reification which dialectics must accuse. The conflict between the two repeats the antagonistic structure that is the product of capitalist society. In that sense, dialectical criticism could be said to always be co-opted, merely repeating rather than challenging the structures of capitalism. But the cultural critic has one resourceful turn left: in mimicking it, he or she can reverse this dialectic against itself, 'give it a turn towards nonidentity', so that it becomes a hinge that is both negative and positive at once: 'The dialectical critique of culture must both participate in culture and not participate. Only then does he do justice to his object and to himself'.[15] If culture consists of torn halves that do not add up, then so too must the practice of cultural criticism be one of sameness and difference. As Tzvetan Todorov puts it, 'being outside is an advantage only if one is at the same time completely inside'.[16] For the cultural critic, as opposed to the anthropologist, it is imperative to maintain a critical edge while performing this impossible feat of a negative dialectics: the torn halves should be left in tatters, expressly because they are the immanent conditions of an untotalizable capitalism. At the same time they must be put together, mended in an enabling transcendent gesture to the utopic future towards whose ideal criticism must be directed.

Contrary to this difficult, paradoxical injunction, which Jameson describes as 'how to do something which is impossible, yet indispensable, and in any case inevitable', Adorno himself in his own practice increasingly emphasized immanence over transcendence.[17] The reason for this lay in what he regarded as the ever-increasing forces of totalization and reification of the culture industry which had begun to threaten civilization itself. Adorno therefore tended to reject popular culture *in toto*, his transcendent position being achieved primarily from the 'high' cultural position of the autonomous work of art. Thus high and low, the apparently torn halves of culture, themselves became the antimonies which provided the perspectives from which his cultural critique was conducted. As Adorno anticipated in his critique of Benjamin, today's emphasis on popular culture against high culture could be said to reverse these terms, but without altering them. In making this move into cultural pessimism, adopting one half against the other, Adorno repressed his own greatest insight, namely that the two concepts of culture, high and low, intellectual and aesthetic achievements versus everyday social practices, themselves offer a dialectic through which critique of that culture can be achieved. The critique is lost if one half of that dialectical encounter is simply validated against the other. Although each seems to offer a transcendent position of sorts, neither can escape qualification by the other. For the Adorno of the essay, a dialectical critique of culture has to be constructed through the perennially uneasy synthesis of immanent and transcendent critique.

A dialectical cultural criticism of this kind offers a much more powerful method than the reification which accompanied Adorno's own increasing pessimism, and which inevitably made it impossible to sustain the balance between antimonies in his own work. The challenge of reading the earlier Adorno is that he develops the operation of this technique to a refined degree in his own style, so that he is constantly oscillating between antithetical, contrary positions. The power of his account of culture derives from its being both positive and negative at the same time. Take the question of the way in which culture is described as originating from the divorce between mental and manual labour. Inevitably Adorno presents this both as a good and a bad thing – bad because it forms the basis of exploitation and alienation, but good because it produces culture as such, which cannot be all bad. Similarly, the cultural critic remains in the impossible but necessary position of fighting against the very conditions which make her or his own critique possible. Whilst positing the prospect of an ideal social harmony, he or she must not fall into the trap of endorsing the resolutions offered by the ideology of culture. Whilst attacking the contradictory situation of the torn halves, the critic must also emphasize them. Totalization and anti-totalization, inside and outside, must not be set against each other but sustained simultaneously in their incompatibility.

Just as it is not the choice between different forms of culture, high or low, in themselves but their estranged division that represents the critical potential for cultural criticism, so too it is not totalization or detotalization in itself that holds radical potential but the opening of an incompatible division between the two. It is in the split itself, the hinge between these two dissonant movements that the cultural critic needs to be located. Cultural criticism would consist of the critical practice of this dissonant incompatible dualism. Its first move would be to recognize that the close imbrication of culture and cultural criticism means that the open-ended dialectical conflicts that Adorno found operating in the work of art as in society can also be detected in contemporary theory and in many forms of critique. His own strategy was to transpose this into an enabling form of dialectical criticism which articulated immanent and transcendent critiques in a 'negative dialectics' articulated, according to Adorno, most effectively through the contemporary realm of the aesthetic. Though the dialectic is rarely to be found already enunciated self-consciously as a form of negative cognition, it can be shown to be at work in the inclusion of the nonconceptual within the conceptual, remorselessly repeating the antagonisms that construct and decompose the culture of everyday life. The scission within culture, between cultural forms, produces not a transcendent point for the critic but a differential reversible fulcrum from which critique can be constructed.

Adorno and the loss of critical distance

The question that follows is whether Adorno's analysis also applies to the particular situation characteristic of postmodernism. Clearly, the loss of critical distance which Jameson laments can be identified as the failure of what Adorno calls transcendent critique. To claim that this implies the end of critique as such, in the first instance seems to neglect the possibilities offered by immanent critique. However, since according to Adorno, transcendent and immanent critique operate dialectically, then the loss of one would always involve the loss of the other.

Adorno's argument suggests that if critical distance was founded on a clean break between science and ideology, then the whole idea operated on a premise which identified with a single polarity of the critical antimonies of culture. Far from being such a position of absolutism therefore, as proponents of the science/ideology distinction assumed, it was always inevitably subject to the qualifications and limitations which Adorno so shrewdly analyses. The recognition of these need not therefore mean a descent into the totalization of a dominant culture, or even the unanchored relativisms associated with postmodernism. The transcendent position was always achieved, as Adorno points out, through a 'delusion of being absolute'. What has happened in the postmodern situation is simply that this insight into its necessary error has been generally acknowledged. At the same time, however, transcendence has been displaced into the 'absolute reification' which Adorno was to claim for the culture industry, and which is now being invoked to describe the one-dimensional dominance of postmodern culture. But as Adorno himself shows, even this need not mean that critique has to be abandoned altogether. It rather suggests the need to utilize the more complex antimonies that deploy in a productive way the

paradoxical, impossible position of the cultural critic in society.
The story of theory over the past two decades has consisted of a
slow coming to terms with the requirements and demands of that
difficult aporetic place.

(1993)

Notes

1 Adorno, *Prisms*, 19.

2 Cf. Bürger, *Theory of the Avant-Garde*; Giddens, *The Consequences of Modernity* and *Modernity and Self-Identity*; Shiach, *Discourse on Popular Culture*.

3 Stallybrass and White, *The Politics and Poetics of Transgression*. Further
references will be cited in the text.

4 Baudrillard, *Seduction*. Cf. Laclau and Mouffe, *Hegemony and Socialist Strategy*, 107–10.

5 Cf. Habermas, *Legitimation Crisis*.

6 Lévi-Strauss, 'Race and History', in *Structural Anthropology*, vol. 2, 323–62.

7 Jameson, *Postmodernism*, 48.

8 Cf. my discussion of Jameson in *White Mythologies*, especially 111, and 203
n. 48.

9 Buck-Morss, *The Origin of Negative Dialectics*, 307.

10 Adorno to Benjamin, 18 March 1936, in Bloch, *Aesthetics and Politics*, 123.

11 Cf. Marcuse, 'The Affirmative Character of Culture', in *Negations*, 88–133.

12 Arato, *The Essential Frankfurt School Reader*, 195.

13 Adorno, 'Cultural Criticism and Society', *Prisms*, 19–34. Further references
will be cited in the text. Despite the range of recent critical work on Adorno,
few commentators consider this essay; the most useful discussion for an
understanding of Adorno's comparable argument in the *Aesthetic Theory*
is Peter Osborne's 'Adorno and the Metaphysics of Modernism'; for other
discussions of related issues in Adorno's work, see Bernstein, 'Introduction' to Adorno, *The Culture Industry*; Benhabib, *Critique, Norm, and Utopia*;
Dews, *Logics of Disintegration*; Eagleton, *The Ideology of the Aesthetic*;
Jameson, *Late Marxism*; and Zuidervaart, *Adorno's Aesthetic Theory*.

14 Cf. in particular, the irreconcilable but necessary dialectic of mimesis and
rationality in Adorno's *Aesthetic Theory*.

15 Adorno, *Negative Dialectics*, 12; 'Cultural Criticism and Society', *Prisms*, 33.

16 Todorov, *Nous et les autres*, 104. Cf. Adorno, *Negative Dialectics*, 145; Lévi-
Strauss, *Introduction to the Work of Marcel Mauss*, 30–1.

17 Jameson, *Postmodernism*, 205; cf. 185. Adorno's move is signalled already in
the discussion in the last page of 'Cultural Criticism and Society'.

Borders......................................

The culture of theory

....

2

Back to Bakhtin

In memory of Allon White[1]

In Britain in the 1970s there were two dominant positions in Marxist theory, symbolized by two names, E. P. Thompson and Louis Althusser, and by two rival annual gatherings, the Oxford History Workshop and the Essex Sociology of Literature Conference.[2] In intellectual terms they could be characterized as the Marxist humanism developed by the New Left after the 1956 Twentieth Party Congress in the USSR, and the anti-humanist structural Marxism of the late 1960s and 1970s which came to dominate Marxist literary theory of the time. The arguments between the two camps, finally devolving into the question of the poverty or necessity of theory, ceased only with the autocritical self-destruction of Althusserianism by the British Althusserians.[3] Althusser's assimilation even of 'practice' into theory, his absolute disdain for any empiricism, had meant that Marxist knowledge was effectively severed from the world outside. The crisis became acute after Barry Hindess and Paul Hirst's critique of Althusser and their dismissal of history as such – hitherto for most Marxists the final touchstone of reality – when it became common practice for ex-Althusserian Marxists to announce that 'there is no epistemology'. In an extraordinary development, Marxism either had or seemed about to turn itself into an idealism. At this point, Derrida's *Of Grammatology* appeared in English, with its powerfully argued charge that Marxism was a form of metaphysics. So Marxist theory found itself under an added pressure, this time stemming from the destabilizing claims of poststructuralism.

The anxiety over the prospects for Marxism in the literary sphere was signalled most graphically by *Re-Reading English* (1982), a work which attempted to capitalize on the 'crisis in English Studies' occasioned by structuralism and poststructuralism in order to dismiss both traditional Leavisite and poststructuralist criticism in favour of a return to 'History', and the 'concrete'.[4] Since Georg Lukács, these nouns have always been invoked to designate the desired object of Marxist knowledge, that elusive materiality outside the institution. Some contributors, however, accepted that history in its concrete form was hardly available as a straightforward option when even Marxism itself, in its Althusserian version, had apparently abandoned history as its given category of certitude.[5] In this beleaguered situation the work of Bakhtin seemed increasingly to offer the possibility of deliverance. So John Hoyles argued that:

> Perhaps one *way out of this impasse* lies in a reworking of sociological poetics following the example of the Bakhtin school; for it was this school . . . who [*sic*] in the twenties provided the first serious Marxist critique of the Russian formalists and paved the way for a theory and practice of textual politics whereby literary criticism would avoid the twin reductionisms of formalist poetics and vulgar Marxist sociology.[6]

Here the first suggestions emerge of the shift that was increasingly to characterize Marxist criticism of the 1980s, as it abandoned the apparently forlorn category of 'History' in favour of 'the social' – Habermas would be a case in point. In making his proposal for Bakhtin, Hoyles was following an initial suggestion from Raymond Williams in 1977, developed by Tony Bennett in 1979, endorsed in 1981 and 1982 by Terry Eagleton, further supported by David Forgacs in 1982, Graham Pechey in 1983, and Allon White in 1984.[7] These often programmatic declarations created a general consensus that the way forward was back to Bakhtin.

The attraction, as Graham Pechey put it bluntly, was that 'Bakhtinism catches Formalism on its way to Structuralism, diverting it in a Marxist direction'.[8] Bakhtin was heralded as offering a 'way out' of the impasse that had threatened to cut Marxist knowledge off from the social. Bakhtin's attraction was that he seemed to offer the possibility for Marxism to return to the old certainties of the everyday world outside. Although the work of Bakhtin and his collaborators Valentin Voloshinov and Pavel Medvedev – whom I will continue to distinguish by the books signed with their names – began to be translated in the late 1960s, it is striking that it had little impact on Marxist criticism until the 1980s. Jameson's *The Prison-House of Language: A Critical Account of Structuralism and Russian Formalism* (1972), for instance, makes no mention at all of the Bakhtin Circle.[9] In the USA the resurgence of interest in Bakhtin coincided with the 1981 translation, *The Dialogic Imagination* (available in French since 1978), but in Britain it was rather the carnivalesque *Rabelais and His World*, which had been translated thirteen years earlier, which became the central text. Thus in 1979 Tony Bennett announced that 'Bakhtin's study of Rabelais would seem fully to exemplify what a Marxist – that is, a historical and materialist – approach to the study of literary texts should look like'.[10]

What was disturbing, however, was that at the very moment when Marxist interest in Bakhtin began to quicken, everyone else's did as well. In June 1983, for instance, an article by David Lodge on 'Joyce and Bakhtin' appeared on the front page of the *James Joyce Broadsheet*. According to Lodge, Bakhtin's appeal stemmed from the way that he seemed 'to offer some kind of rapprochement between the analytical rigour of Formalism and a Marxist or humanist conception of literature as an institution serving the cause of human freedom'.[11] Lodge went on to apply a form of Bakhtin's typology of literary discourse to *Ulysses* and *Finnegans Wake* with little noticeable sense that he was producing an example of 'what a Marxist approach to the study of literary texts should look like,' or, it might be added, that James Joyce and Bakhtin had already been brought together by Julia Kristeva sixteen years earlier. Long articles on Bakhtin also appeared at about the same time from, among others, Wayne Booth, David Carroll, Paul de Man, and Dominick LaCapra, a newsletter was founded and an annual international conference on Bakhtin initiated. Literary journals soon produced a spate of special issues on Bakhtin.[12]

If Bakhtin seemed to offer a way out which would allow British Marxism to return to the real world, many others were also attracted by his egressive charms. The unprecedented extent of Bakhtin's appeal, comparable in recent critical history only to that of Derrida, led de Man to ask 'who, if anyone, would have reason to find it difficult or even impossible to enlist Bakhtin's version of dialogism among his methodological tools or skills?'[13] What was striking was that whereas de Man himself or Derrida produced passionate disciples and equally passionate opponents, it seemed that just about anyone could, and probably did, appropriate Bakhtin for just about anything. Conversely, it was extremely hard to find anyone actually writing against Bakhtin. Why and how could this be so?

Everyone was attracted to the fact that Bakhtin appeared to offer a reconciliation between poetics and hermeneutics, between questions of form and questions of interpretation in the context of their relation to society and history. But it was undoubtedly the advent of poststructuralism, particularly the spectre of Derrida, that accounted for Bakhtin's sudden appeal around 1980. This was complicated by the fact that the Derrideans themselves also liked

Bakhtin, finding support for their arguments by detecting a certain compatibility between deconstruction and dialogism. Samuel Weber, for example, remarked that

> 'Voloshinov' goes beyond the traditional notions of dialogue (as does 'Bakhtin,' in his notion of the 'polyphonic'), just as Derrida's practice of dissemination dislocates that of polysemy. In both, an irreducible alterity is shown at work in the very identification and identity that seek to efface its traces.[14]

Apart from the demonstration of the workings of heterogeneity within language, Bakhtin and Derrida apparently resembled each other in their insistence on the problems of closure in any system, the effects of iterability, and the boundlessness of context: 'The problem of boundaries between text and context. Each word (each sign) of the text exceeds its boundaries', Bakhtin declared in an essay written several years later than Derrida's '*il n'y a pas de hors texte*', and causing rather less offence.[15] The similarity was such that Terry Eagleton was even able to argue that 'Bakhtin recapitulates *avant la lettre* many of the leading motifs of contemporary deconstruction'.[16]

Bakhtin's relation to Derrida is itself in fact an example of a certain dialogic interaction: not direct in any way, but through their shared philosophical grounding in the nineteenth- and twentieth-century German phenomenological tradition, particularly the critiques of hermeneutics of Edmund Husserl (the *Logical Investigations* were translated into Russian in 1910) and Martin Heidegger (especially *Being and Time*, 1927). As Michael Holquist observes in an account of the formation of the 'Bakhtin Circle' from 1918 to 1920, 'the most frequent topic of discussion, the subject of most burning concern for the majority of the group – certainly for Bakhtin – was German philosophy. At this point Bakhtin thought of himself essentially as a philosopher and not as a literary scholar'.[17] This is the context cited by Voloshinov in *Marxism and the Philosophy of Language*:

> The trend-setting works of Husserl, the main representative of modern antipsychologism; the works of his followers, the *intentionalists* ('phenomenologists'); the sharply antipsychologistic turn taken by representatives of modern neo-Kantianism of the Marburg and Freiburg school; and the banishment of psychologism from all fields of knowledge and even from psychology itself! – all these things constituted an event of paramount philosophical and methodological importance in the first two decades of our century. (*MPL* 32)

Bakhtin's philosophical debts to Husserl and Heidegger, though often gesturally acknowledged, have still to be charted in detail; but

it is nevertheless clear that many of the apparently uncanny similarities between Bakhtin and Derrida can be fairly simply accounted
for by their close links to the same philosophical tradition of European phenomenology. The rather straightforward solution to this
intellectual mystery is that they had read the same books.

Despite, or perhaps rather because of, his affinity to Derrida,
it was the possibility of providing grounds for a critique of deconstruction that for many formed the basis of Bakhtin's appeal. If
structuralism and deconstruction seemed to have reduced the
material world and any knowledge of it into a hermetic realm of
language and sign systems, Bakhtin offered the possibility of moving out of the looking-glass back to the real world. For humanist
critics a key factor lay in the way in which Bakhtin's work emerged
as a critique of Russian Formalism and formalist work in general: he
thus appeared as a critic who had gone 'beyond' structuralism,
uncannily anticipating much poststructuralist thought but presenting it in a more traditional (if scarcely more readable) guise. He
talked reassuringly about characters, plots, the author, and consciousness, offering a humanist version of poststructuralism together
with a liberal politics centring on the idea of the word as guarantor
of human freedom. The humanist claim on Bakhtin is graphically
illustrated by the telling translation of a title which in Russian had
been the neutral *Questions of Literature and Aesthetics* (*Vosprosy
literatury i estetki*) into the resoundingly affirmative *The Dialogic
Imagination*.[18]

Some humanist critics, particularly in the United States, went
so far as to want to deny Bakhtin's Marxism altogether, in an exact
parallel to the case of Walter Benjamin. Bakhtin's sudden popularity came at the same time as the culmination of a movement to
assimilate the works of two members of his circle, Medvedev and
Voloshinov, to Bakhtin himself (Medvedev and Voloshinov having
died in 1938 and 1936 respectively, the former perhaps for the
privilege of publishing Bakhtin's work under his name).[19] The effect
of this monological drive to reduce multiple authorship to the works
of a single genius was always to reduce the importance of Marxism.
Voloshinov's translator, I. R. Titunik, for instance, claimed that 'the
sociological poetics of the Bakhtin group (minus Medvedev's eclec-
ticism; that is, minus Marxist pre-suppositions) and the formal
method . . . represented parallel overlapping, interdependent, and
ultimately completely reconcilable methods' (*MPL* 200). Take the
Marxist presuppositions out of Medvedev and Voloshinov – and
you get a perfectly acceptable Bakhtin.

The same dismissal of Bakhtin's Marxism can be found in Holquist's account of why Bakhtin entered into such polyphonic arrangements with his friends about authorship. According to Holquist it was merely a case of expedience: 'Bakhtin was notorious in Leningrad circles as a *cerkovnik*, a devout Orthodox Christian'. Bakhtin's Marxism was simply a disguise which can now be discarded: 'Marxist terms are . . . most often present in Bakhtin's books . . . as a kind of *convenient*, in the abstract, not necessarily inimical – but above all, *necessary* – flag under which to advance his own views: If the Christian word were to take on Soviet flesh it had to clothe itself in ideological disguise'.[20] Despite Holquist's later biography, conclusive evidence of this argument is still lacking; nevertheless it undoubtedly facilitated Bakhtin's American appeal.[21] A recent more plausible suggestion has been that the stories about Bakhtin's secret authorship were simply an expedient device to use the prestige of his name in order to get the books of Voloshinov and Medvedev republished.[22]

Streetwise with Bakhtin

For Marxists, meanwhile, Bakhtin's attractions were not altogether dissimilar: he provided an effective sociological critique of structuralism, as well as the materialist account of language so conspicuously missing in Marxist theory ever since Stalin's prescriptive intervention in the field.[23] Rather than offering an alternative to Derrida in the sense of an oppositional position, Bakhtin seemed to allow the assimilation of some of the more compelling aspects of his thought while placing them within a more acceptable sociohistorical framework. Derrida himself could then be more or less indifferently rejected altogether. In general, Bakhtin seemed to recapitulate many of the dominant motifs of poststructuralism while at the same time adding an historical basis to them.[24] According to Eagleton, Bakhtin united 'what we might now rhetorically call certain Derridean and Lacanian positions with a politics revolutionary enough to make much poststructuralism nervous' (79). Citing Bakhtin's notion of carnival as proof of this, he observed that here 'the Nietzschean playfulness of contemporary poststructuralism leaves the academy and dances in the streets'.[25] Nothing illustrates better the basis of Bakhtin's appeal than Eagleton's description here, where the theorist *'leaves the academy and dances in the streets'*. Bakhtin transports you from the inside to the outside, out of the academic institution into the pulsating life of the real world. So the invocation of history as an outside which poststructuralism lacked was developed alongside a corresponding inside/outside metaphor of theory and the people, the university and the real world outside it, the academy and the streets.

In this antithesis between the world of the academy and the life of the streets, it is noticeable that Bakhtin's own style remains remarkably erudite. He proposes in a conventional 'high' academic language, not noticeably comic, and full of authoritative jargon, a monological theory which paradoxically denies the possibility of a theory and celebrates laughter, subversion, parody, and 'low' genres. Or is there, as Hayden White suggests, a carnivalesque inversion of his own claims to authoritativeness taking place at the same time, illuminating 'the very grandiosity of his enterprise as a parody of the methods of scholarship and science alike'?[26] The length of Bakhtin's essays, their unreadability, their repetitive structure, their proliferating jargon, and ever bifurcating categories, are, as White points out, at odds with the thesis of their content, thus subverting any claim to authoritativeness. This would not be incompatible with some of the other curiosities known about Bakhtin:

> During some sixty years as a scholar, Bakhtin assumed many masks, spoke in many voices, published under a number of different names, parodied many methods. Is there any reason to believe that these essays [*The Dialogic Imagination*], published under the name of Bakhtin, represent the fixed position, the real centre of his thought, by which to measure the merely parodistic dimensions of his other works, both those recognized as having been written by him and those *thought* to be from his hand?[27]

Similarly, can we be so sure as Holquist that the *real* Bakhtin was the devout *cerkovnik* who wrote the religious magnum opus *The Architectonics of Responsibility* which, Holquist assures us, 'contains, in embryonic form, every major idea Bakhtin was to have for the rest of his long life'?[28] It is noticeable, at any rate, that, although Bakhtin's subject concerns dialogism in the novel, many of his critics, without showing any awareness of the transference that they are making, write as if such qualities are to be found in Bakhtin himself. Bakhtin begins to become the thing of which he speaks. His texts turn the outside in, just as much as the inside out. This makes it even harder to identify 'Bakhtin'.

Is there, in fact, a real Bakhtin that can be appropriated by a particular mode of criticism, or is it not rather that the ambivalence of Bakhtin's position seems to allow everyone to claim a particular version of him as their own? His ideas such as the contested nature of the sign, the determination of the utterance from without by social relations, the endless struggle for the word, and the reaccentuation of meanings in texts throughout history, evidently apply just as much to his own writings. Above all, Bakhtin's ambivalence results from the way in which he himself represents rather than resolves the conflictual struggles in society – so that by definition everyone can find somewhere in Bakhtin an image of themselves.

The 'directedness' of the sign

The indeterminacy of Bakhtin's texts is of course compounded by the authorship problem. But though the works of Voloshinov and Medvedev, published in the 1920s, have seemed to many to be more self-consciously Marxist both in word and spirit than Bakhtin's contemporary book on Dostoevsky or any of his later works, it does not necessarily follow that a straightforward separation can be made between them. For despite their differences, Bakhtin could also be said to have dramatically extended the implications of the work of his collaborators. Voloshinov's 1929 critique of Ferdinand de Saussure undoubtedly enabled a Marxist perspective – some fifty years later – on the kinds of privilege accorded to language by the Saussurian structuralism of the 1960s. But Voloshinov's own position also constituted the basis of an argument that was to be equally troubling to many of the fundamental assumptions of more orthodox dialectical theory.

Voloshinov's critique of Saussure is by now well-known, but it would still be helpful to reconsider some of its main components at this point. In general, Marxist criticism of Saussure has focused upon his initial separation of the analysis of language into synchronic and diachronic dimensions and disparaged his privileging of the first over the second, that is of structure over history.[29] Voloshinov, by contrast, did not object to Saussure on these grounds at all, which would perhaps be more surprising if it were not recalled that Saussure's *Course in General Linguistics* spends more time analysing the diachronic than the synchronic – it was in fact rather the structuralists, Lévi-Strauss in particular, who foregrounded space over linear time. Voloshinov himself took issue with a second separation, concerned not with the realm of history but the social, namely Saussure's division of language into the individual utterance (*parole*) as opposed to the overall system (*langue*). In concentrating on the latter, Saussure made the mistake, according to Voloshinov, of using a methodology developed for the analysis of dead, written languages which meant that the basis of his linguistics was flawed from the outset. For the utterance, says Voloshinov, can't be considered as an isolated phenomenon; there is no such thing as a merely individual expression because we do not (generally) speak into thin air – every utterance is not only spoken by someone but is also addressed to someone else. Even the academic silently writing at the typewriter, or today into a computer, performs an act of communication which must be regarded as 'a social phenomenon' (*MPL* 62). What is more, in so far as it forms a part of a process of communication, 'its organizing centre' Voloshinov argues, 'is not within but outside . . . in the social milieu surrounding the individual being' (*MPL* 93). This observation could be said to constitute the crucial move, enabling him both to avoid Saussure's implicit psychologism and to set up the whole basis of language as a kind of double-dealing, an idea that was later to be developed into dialogism: 'The *word is oriented toward an addressee*, toward *who* that addressee might be . . . *word is a two-sided act*. It is determined equally by *whose* word it is and for *whom* it is meant. As word it is precisely *the product of the reciprocal relationship between speaker and listener, addresser and addressee*. Each and every word expresses the "one" in relation to the "other"' (*MPL* 85–6). Orientation of the word toward the addressee means that the word is a kind of bridge thrown between the self and other, constituting a border zone between the two that belongs to neither. Voloshinov's word thus, crucially, breaks through from inside to outside, from the same to the other. In the same way, Bakhtin was to emphasize the 'directedness' ('*napravlennost*') of the word and of discourse, thus encompassing, as in Husserlian phenomenology, the intended orientation of the word towards an object as well as the speech-act.[30] Voloshinov himself emphasizes that such an orientation means that individual utterances are already determined by social relations. The sign, therefore, is invariably *motivated*: 'the immediate social situation and the broader social milieu wholly determine – and determine from within, so to speak – the structure of an utterance' (*MPL* 86). In this way, Voloshinov breaks down both the solipsism and psychologism of Saussure and opens up the study of language to its social dimension. Instead of becoming a world unto itself, as for the poststructuralists, for Voloshinov language dissolves the division between inner and outer spheres.

Literature and the psyche

This doubled structure of signification is reinvoked by Medvedev in his subtle account of the relation of literature to society in *The Formal Method* (1928). Here the connection between literature and the socio-economic base is described as one of direct mediation by other ideological forms, in a structure somewhat similar to Spinoza's distinction between efficient and final causes. Thus Medvedev simultaneously opposes the formalist separation of literature from so-called 'extrinsic' factors to Marxist assumptions that 'separate works, which have been snatched out of the unity of the ideological world, are in their isolation directly determined by economic factors' (*FM* 15) – a position which Bakhtin himself re-endorsed over forty years later (*SG* 140). This means that even the intertextual effect of literature upon literature can still be considered a sociological effect. Literature is thus determined from within and from without, except that the within is itself determined by the without, and vice versa. As Bakhtin put it in the 1929 Preface to *Problems of Dostoevsky's Poetics*: 'every literary work is internally, immanently sociological' (*DP* 276).

The same structure works for the relation of the psyche to the social: Graham Pechey notes that if Russian Formalism 'had only gone as far as to bracket out the authorial psyche as "cause" of the work, Bakhtin takes the more radical step of theorizing this "cause" as an effect of the same (discursive) order as the work itself'.[31] The distinction between the different realities of inner and outer realms is broken down by the sign which partakes of both: in *Freudianism*, Voloshinov describes them as the difference between 'inner' and 'outer' speech (*FMC* 21–4). Consciousness is not, therefore, analysable as an interior state of being as in conventional theories of psychology and ideology but can only be interpreted through, and as a part of, the semiotic system which is itself a social phenomenon. Thus the whole of social reality, signs, language, and the psyche are seamlessly stitched together.

Voloshinov's critique of Freudianism, which in general has always remained undervalued in comparison to the other works of the Bakhtin Circle, has the distinction of providing the earliest theory of a political unconscious in which the text of history produces revolutionary change, though Voloshinov senses no imperative to detect the traces of a vast, uninterrupted narrative of class struggle as Jameson does. The critique is particularly interesting in that for all his attack on the premises and categories of psychoanalysis,

Voloshinov does not dismiss the idea of the unconscious as such. Instead he suggests that, given the absence of a dividing line between the individual psyche and the formulated ideology of its social milieu, what Freud calls the conscious constitutes the official or dominant ideology, while what he calls the unconscious forms the unofficial or revolutionary ideology:

> Those areas of behavioural ideology that correspond to Freud's official, 'censored' conscious express the most steadfast and the governing factors of class consciousness. They lie close to the formulated, fully fledged ideology of the class in question, its law, its morality, its world outlook. . . . Other levels, corresponding to Freud's unconscious, lie at a great distance from the stable system of the ruling ideology. They bespeak the disintegration of the unity and integrity of the system, the vulnerability of the usual ideological motivations. (*FMC* 88–9)

Although not every motive in contradiction with official ideology will do so, any that is founded on the economic being of a whole group 'will develop within a small social milieu and will depart into the underground – not the psychological underground of repressed complexes, but the salutary political underground. That is exactly how a revolutionary ideology in all spheres of culture comes about' (*FMC* 90). On the one hand, Voloshinov admits that motives in contradiction with official ideology, in the social *déclassé* loner, 'little by little really do turn into a "foreign body" in the psyche' (*FMC* 89), thus in a certain sense validating the findings of psychoanalysis and providing a proleptic political interpretation of the cryptonomy of Nicolas Abraham and Maria Torok. On the other hand, Voloshinov also puts forward a theory of revolutionary change based on Freud's model in which contradictions and censored ideologies can 'ultimately burst asunder the system of the official ideology' (*FMC* 88). If this seems to anticipate Kristeva, Voloshinov also comes close to Wilhelm Reich when at one point he implies that psychoanalysis itself constitutes a revolutionary movement.[32]

The sign

Whereas Saussure stresses language's role as a system of social conventions, Voloshinov emphasizes the function of the sign above all as 'an ideological phenomenon, a product of social intercourse' (*FMC* 115). This might at first seem contradictory, in so far as ideology conventionally requires the category of consciousness. But Voloshinov redefines consciousness itself as the effect of the production of signs in social interaction, as 'a social-ideological fact', which means that it cannot be explained in terms of idealism or psychologism because it is always located between individuals: 'Signs can arise only on *interindividual territory*' (*MPL* 12). Thus ideology does not exist in an individual consciousness which can be opposed to the real, as inner to outer, because it both comments on and partakes of the real: 'Any ideological product is not only itself a part of reality (natural or social), just as is any physical body, any instrument of production, or any product for consumption, it also, in contradistinction to these other phenomena, reflects and refracts another reality outside itself' (*MPL* 9). Language therefore occupies a special place within the social sphere because it has a unique double role: it is both itself a part of reality but also simultaneously 'reflects and refracts another reality outside itself'. The basis for Bakhtin's main argument about the novel can be seen to be already available here. The sign does not merely reflect reality, but also 'refracts' it as an effect of the competing social interests in a society, in other words, as an effect of the class struggle:

> Class does not coincide with the sign community, i.e. with the community, which is the totality of users of the same set of signs for ideological communication. Thus various different classes will use one and the same language. As a result, differently oriented accents intersect in every ideological sign. Sign becomes an arena of the class struggle. (*MPL* 23)

This 'social multiaccentuality of the ideological sign' constitutes Voloshinov's most significant and influential theoretical contribution. It must be emphasized, however, that it is a concept incompatible with the category of consciousness, and therefore also with conventional accounts of ideology.

Since it never actually becomes the thing to which it refers, the sign can always remain contested, accented, stressed or evaluated according to the disposition of a particular system, language, or class. It is thanks to 'this intersecting of accents that a sign maintains its vitality and dynamism and the capacity for further development'. It is also just this aspect of the sign that allows it to become a force both for domination and for subversion:

> The very same thing that makes the ideological sign vital and mutable is also . . . that which makes it a refracting and distorting medium. The ruling class strives to impart a supraclass, eternal character to the ideological sign, to extinguish it or drive inward the struggle between social value judgements which occurs in it, to make the sign uniaccentual. (*MPL* 23)

This is the process that Bakhtin will describe as the drive to monology by the dominant class and its discourse. But Janus-like, the sign is two-faced: it has an 'inner dialogic quality' which means that it can become a kind of double-talk, its accent shifting ineluctably between truth and falsity, affirmation and disavowal. Although all language has the quality whereby 'any current curse word can become a word of praise, any current truth must inevitably sound to many other people as the greatest lie', this inner dialectical quality of the sign is normally restrained by the pressure of a dominant ideology which maintains a single established meaning. It is, according to Voloshinov, only at the time of social or revolutionary crisis that this antithetical aspect of the sign emerges. In the persuasive thesis of his book on Rabelais, Bakhtin was to add another privileged moment, that of carnival. At its simplest, Bakhtin's theory of 'dialogism' finds its basis here in the ambivalence of the sign, indeed of representation itself, whereby any sign can address or refer to anything outside itself without becoming or subsuming it – and thus potentially always stand open to reaccentuation or reinflection.[33] As Kristeva recognized, the contested nature of the sign also provokes as its corollaries the denial of univocal meaning, unfinalizable interpretation, the negation of originary presence in speech, the positioning of the subject in and by discourse, the breaking down of the identity of the subject, all inside–outside oppositions, the semantic identity of the sign, and 'the crumbling away of the representational system' as such (*RP* 114). Bakhtin takes the principle of dialogism very far, eventually developing it into a theory of the novel, society, and indeed of life itself.

'Inauthentic direct discourse'

The great attraction of Voloshinov's account of the struggle for the sign is that it brings the class struggle to the level of language and by implication also offers an immediacy to the politics of writing. Bakhtin's dialogism develops this basic idea of the multiaccentuality of the sign, but shows that when its logical implications are extended, an increasing complexity begins to make problems for the engaging politics which Voloshinov's prescription promises.

These difficulties begin in *Marxism and the Philosophy of Language* itself: if its thesis is summarized – as it often is – into 'the struggle for the sign', then all is well. But if there is a struggle for each sign, or word, so making it multiaccentuated, then discourse in general – the Russian *slovo* means both word and discourse –

becomes more problematic because your own language will always itself be marked by past struggles, very probably without your having any knowledge of it. This is particularly the case with reported speech: in Part III Voloshinov proposes a division of discourse into the typologies of 'direct speech' and 'reported speech'. He notes in the Russian language 'an extraordinary ease of interaction and interpenetration between reporting and reported speech' (*MPL* 127): it is not here a question of the use of indirect discourse as a formal literary style, but rather the way in which within ordinary direct speech there is, as Voloshinov puts it, 'anticipated and disseminated reported speech concealed in the authorial context and, as it were, breaking into real, direct utterances' (*MPL* 135). This means that even in ordinary speech 'almost every word . . . figures simultaneously in two intersecting contexts, two speech acts' (*MPL* 136). Voloshinov emphasizes the way in which this allows a continuous ironizing of speech – not only enabling the speaker to reinflect the reported speech he or she uses, but also allowing the reported speech to ironize the speaker unawares.

This argument for a 'double-oriented speech' problematizes the earlier argument for the struggle over the sign. Such a struggle assumes an intentionality on the part of the speaker that can be put into effect; double-oriented speech means, however, not simply that the other's signs can be shifted in meaning, recontextualized, but that your own signs were never your own in the first place. They are always already ironized and ready to shift into a different perspective from that which you intended, as an effect of the 'disseminated reported speech concealed' in your words. The subject is not in a position to control the alterity of discourse – the speech of the other will always be encrypted in your language. The subject thus becomes as much a tissue of conflicting forces as the sign itself. At this point the differences between Voloshinov's and Michel Foucault's theories of discourse become evident. The former's stress on the prevalence of reported speech within discourse must be incompatible with Foucault's notion of rival, and therefore distinct, stratifications of language and discourses of truth. For reported speech makes it impossible to maintain distinctions between discourses in the first place.

In the final section of the book Voloshinov broaches the question of 'quasi-direct discourse' (*uneigentliche direkte Rede*, improper or unreal direct discourse – or, to bring out its un-Heideggerian quality, inauthentic direct discourse). In a discussion of its definition as '*concealed* or *veiled* discourse', he observes that in a novel this means that the form of speech 'does not at all contain an "either/or" dilemma; its *specificum* is precisely a matter of *both* author *and* character speaking at the same time, a matter of a single linguistic construction within which the accents of two differently oriented voices are maintained' (*MPL* 144). So the proper has become improper: and at this arresting point Voloshinov anxiously tries to draw the line. He ends his book by denouncing the 'alarming instability and uncertainty of [the] ideological word', pleading for a return to 'the word that really means and takes responsibility for what it says' (*MPL* 159). But it is too late: his whole text argues otherwise, betraying the characteristic workings of the logic of alterity. It is this quality which Bakhtin, far from denouncing, celebrated as 'dialogism': not merely its simple form in which an utterance must be considered from the point of view of being spoken by someone and addressed to another, but in its radical implication that discourse cannot be proper or authentic, because it is double-voiced, a 'double-accented, double-styled *hybrid construction*' (*DI* 304). We have analysed elsewhere how dialogism in this guise of hybridity can be transformed into an interrogative, critical instrument. But can the same apply to dialogism itself?

Dialogism

Dialogism first appears as an important concept in the book on Dostoevsky where it is used to describe the particular discursive form of Dostoevsky's 'polyvalent' novel. Dostoevsky's world, says Bakhtin, is 'profoundly *pluralistic*' (*DP* 26): instead of the authorial position dominating the novel and the speeches of the characters, the speech and ideologies of the different characters compete without ever being concluded: 'In Dostoevsky's novels, the life experience of the characters and their discourse may be resolved as far as plot is concerned, but internally they remain incomplete and unresolved' (*DI* 349). This kind of novel, Bakhtin claims, developed from the same medieval comic genres to be described in his book on Rabelais: somewhere in the seventeenth century they lost their laughter – about the same time, interestingly enough, that Foucault argues that the Western world excluded folly and madness from normal life. According to Bakhtin, these comic genres developed through satire into the dialogic form used by Dostoevsky. Though from a conventional point of view Dostoevsky's novels appear 'a chaos, and the construction of his novels some sort of conglomerate of disparate materials and incompatible principles for shaping them' (*DP* 8), Bakhtin characterizes this as a new version of the carnivalesque, so that the novel takes on its anti-ideological and anti-totalizing functions. Accordingly Bakhtin praises the 'rigorous unfinalisability and dialogic openness of Dostoevsky's artistic world' in which the hero's consciousness of self 'lives by its unfinalisability, by its unclosedness, and its indeterminacy' (*DP* 272, 53). Later he would apply this to himself, commenting on 'a certain *internal* open-endedness of many of my ideas' (*SG* 155).

In *Dostoevsky's Poetics*, Bakhtin opposes the dialogic novel to the more usual monological form of which Tolstoy is given as the prime example. But already within this book, the ramifications of dialogism are extended quite dramatically. If dialogue began as a description of a feature of the utterance, it quickly becomes a principle of almost everything. Those things resistant to dialogism – which Bakhtin calls 'poetry' – retreat further and further from his gaze and indeed become less and less possible as dialogism spreads beyond language and subsumes ever greater areas of human activity. For the dialogic principle is everywhere and permeates everything: '*Life by its very nature is dialogic*' (*DP* 293, my emphasis). No material or historical explanation is offered for what Bakhtin describes: instead dialogism itself becomes a founding principle of language and meaning:

> Dialogic relationships exist among all elements of novelistic structure; that is, they are juxtaposed contrapuntally. And this is so because dialogic relationships are a much broader phenomena than mere rejoinders in a dialogue, laid out compositionally in the text; they are an almost universal phenomenon, permeating all human speech and all relationships and manifestations of human life – in general, everything that has meaning and significance. (*DP* 40)

Dialogism's ubiquity is such that, as Todorov points out, logically it becomes impossible to distinguish between monologic and dialogic discourse, since all discourse is by definition dialogic, that is, maintains inter-textual relations.[34] In the last analysis, dialogism breaks down all same/other oppositions even while it is itself predicated on them. Insisting on differences, dialogism simultaneously negates their very possibility, just as carnivalization not only involves a decentring of the official discursive norms (such as Bakhtin claims for Laurence Sterne – 'a parody of the logical and expressive structure of any ideological discourse as such'), but ultimately becomes, as in Rabelais – 'a parody of the very act of conceptualizing anything in language' (*DI* 308–9). All conceptual distinctions that Bakhtin proposes in his texts are inexorably propelled as if towards their own dissolution in the same way.

The function of dialogism is more than one of mere negation and dispersal however, for while, like the carnival, it denies and destroys it also simultaneously revives and renews. The movement of dialogism is moreover the means by which ideology is changed and generated rather than remaining given; it both portrays and enacts the struggle for meaning and dominance among different socio-political groups in society. This linguistic and ideological conflict over representation is unending and cannot achieve closure, utopic or otherwise: it is not a contradictory struggle in the usual sense of a dialectical materialism. Representations, ideologies, are generated and die: there is no possibility of any ultimate resolution into a realm of truth, because dialogism always enforces 'a radical scepticism toward any unmediated discourse and any straightforward seriousness, a scepticism bordering on rejection of the very possibility of having a straightforward discourse at all that would not be false' (*DI* 401). Of course by the same token a dialogized discourse cannot be true either. It will always be ironized. In this sense what we get in Bakhtin is a kind of negative knowledge reminiscent of Adorno's, implying the impossibility of all hermeneutics: truth and dialogism can only contradict each other. So, for Bakhtin, the novel can unmask, but it can never reveal truth: 'Truth is restored by reducing the lie to an absurdity, but truth itself does not seek words; she is afraid to entangle herself in the word, to soil herself in verbal pathos' (*DI* 309). Truth, then, is a word which can never mean itself, can never, paradoxically, as a word be made to mean anything but the shadow of its opposite. What we get is what Bakhtin calls a 'gay deception', an 'interillumination', a 'verbal and semantical decentring of the ideological world' comparable to Adorno's claim that what a negative cultural criticism can achieve is the 'defetishization' of ideology. However Bakhtin leaves the humourless Adorno behind in his Nietzschean celebration of what is variously translated as a 'gay' or a 'jolly' relativity (*DI* 401, 363, 367). For Bakhtin, as for Gogol, 'laughter is the only serious element'.[35] Laughter disrupts all closure and, like death, will always introduce alterity.

Carnival

In his best known example, Bakhtin found dialogism embodied in carnival. Here the dialectical quality of the sign, its two-facedness, becomes manifest in a social institution, the medieval carnival which comprised, he suggests, 'a second world and a second life outside officialdom' for medieval people. The laughter of carnival produced a moment of freedom:

> carnival celebrated temporary liberation from the prevailing truth and from the established order; it marked the suspension of all hierarchical rank, privileges, norms and prohibitions. Carnival was the true feast of time, the feast of becoming, change, and renewal. It was hostile to all that was immortalized and completed. (*RW* 10)

Carnival's significance was thus not so much that it constituted a form of resistance but rather that it gave the people a break; moreover it enabled the kind of transparent communication without let or hindrance between all subjects of society which Habermas looks forward to:

> a special type of communication impossible in everyday life. This led to the creation of special forms of marketplace speech and gesture, frank and free, permitting no distance between those who came into contact with each other and liberating from norms of etiquette and decency imposed at other times. (*RW* 10)

According to Bakhtin, in Rabelais we find the representation of this kind of carnivalesque expression, as well as the whole related tradition of folk humour embodied in the comic genres of medieval literature.

As we have seen, some literary critics have tended to emphasize carnival as the centre of Bakhtin's work.[36] It is not certain, however, that it can be detached from its place in Bakhtin's larger argument: by the time of its re-emergence in the form of the nineteenth-century novel, for example, carnival has simply become a name for a new manifestation of the ubiquitous dialogic principle. In its historical manifestation as a medieval and Renaissance institution, carnival is often offered as an example of a revolutionary dispersal of hegemonic feudal order, its uncontrollable laughter allegedly performing a political, anti-ideological role. But if carnival also allows a special kind of communication which momentarily restores a lost 'utopian realm of community, freedom, equality, and abundance' (*RW* 9), this means that these functions are in contradiction with each other – which means that carnival as a concept is itself dialogical. Carnival both produces and abolishes dialogism: it enforces a distance from the official culture, but permits no distance between its participants. It is both parodic, subversive of the official ideology but necessarily remaining within its terms, and an uncensored realm of free expression, implying an originary utopic realm rather than the competing points of view of heteroglossia. It is as if carnival works according to the contradictory descriptions of both the Freudian and the Jungian unconscious. Like the former, it requires repression in order to have any force; carnival necessarily declined with the rise of democratic forms of government. Any anti-ideological function is further complicated by the frequent objection that carnival was permitted, often organized, by the State authorities and thus could be said merely to constitute an instance of repressive tolerance, a structure perfectly illustrated in Adam Smith's suggestion in *The Wealth of Nations* that the State should arrange carnivals so as to mitigate the disabling effects of capitalism – an idea he doubtless got from the contemporary practice on the slave plantations in the Caribbean.[37]

Despite the widespread celebration of carnival for its invocation of the social realm, it is noticeable that for Bakhtin himself the carnival in which he takes any interest remains very much within the bounds of the literary. The 'dialogic resistance' which Bakhtin promises occurs at the level of language, particularly the novel (necessarily, therefore, within discourse) and not in the realm of a 'social history' that is somehow outside it. It involves antithetical institutional discourses: carnival's 'lively play with the "languages" of poets, scholars, monks' is described as 'consciously opposed' to authoritarian literary language: 'It was parodic, and aimed sharply and polemically against the official languages of its given time. It was heteroglossia that had been dialogized' (*DI* 273). Parody necessarily has to remain within the orbit of monological languages in order to dialogize them; the ordinary language of the people outside these discourses makes up a heteroglossia that has not been dialogized and therefore remains politically ineffective, simply disorganized, even if attractively anarchic:

> As distinct from the opaque mixing of languages in living utterances that are spoken in a historically evolving language . . . the novelistic hybrid is an *artistically organized system for bringing different languages in contact with one another*, a system having as its goal the illumination of one language by means of another. (*DI* 361)

The novel achieves its special status, and special perspective, by 'artistically organizing' the languages of heteroglossia. In itself heteroglossia is 'mindless', 'an opaque mechanistic mixture of languages' (*DI* 366); it is because of this that Bakhtin places so much emphasis on carnival. In his view carnival provides the only historical moment in which the heteroglossia of the world is dialogized. Dancing in the streets thus partakes of the utopic, nostalgic element in carnival; parody of the official discourses by contrast makes up the subversive, politically effective component. The implication of this is that while on the one hand social carnival is the realm of freedom from constraint, it is only when it is directed by being given form in the novel that it becomes politically effective. Carnival itself, as Eagleton has observed, is 'a spasmodic, officially licensed affair, without the rancour, discipline and organization, essential for an effective revolutionary politics. Any politics which predicates itself on the carnivalesque moment alone will be no more than a compliant, containable libertarianism'.[38]

Although this is probably over dismissive, it is clear that carnival is too ambivalent a concept to use as a general category of political subversion; even when dialogized, its politics is likely to be as open-ended as anything else in Bakhtin. Bakhtin's 'unfinalisability' is only subversive when open-endedness itself is subversive, as was of course the case during the Stalinism of his own day. The suppression of *Rabelais and His World* in 1946 (it was failed when submitted as a thesis) at least testifies to its potential political effectivity at a particular historical moment. Even if it was in fact prevented from making any intervention, someone in Soviet academia seems to have feared the disruptive force of carnival in Bakhtin. Dehistoricized and extracted as a concept, a quasi-metaphysical principle, or as a general axiom of revolutionary textual politics, carnival becomes less workable. This is the general conclusion of Stallybrass and White's *The Politics and Poetics of Transgression*, the most sustained example of the use of carnival for a transhistorical cultural study. The politics of carnival, they argue, cannot be essentialized but must depend on examination of the specific historical conjuncture at issue. For them, carnival's political and analytic force can only be preserved by considering it as merely 'one instance of a generalized economy of transgression and of the recoding of high/low relations across the whole social structure'.[39] Carnival therefore becomes a privileged example of the symbolic inversions in the characteristic binarisms of a class society. We have already discussed in the previous chapter the way in which Stallybrass and White end by showing how the dualism of high and low applies equally well to the nostalgia of academics for the rough world outside the institution. Perhaps this bleak analysis explains why in the same year that *The Politics and Poetics of Transgression* was published, Eagleton commented:

> The concept of carnival, looked at in another light, may be little more than the intellectual's guilty dues to the populace, the soul's blood money, to the body; what is truly unseemly, indecent even, is the apparent eagerness of deans, chaired professors and presidents of learned societies to tumble from their offices into the streets, monstrous papier mâché phalluses fixed in place.[40]

Bakhtin's carnival does not then, after all, enable you to leave the academy to dance in the streets. For the institutionalized critic, there is no easy passage from one domain to the other – if only because Bakhtin has broken down the distinction between the two. The academic fantasy of moving out on to the streets is itself disrupted by the carnivalization of academic disciplines.

Dialogism and dialectics

Bakhtin, therefore, offered a somewhat perilous 'way out' for Marxist criticism, although of course it all depends what kind of Marxism you're talking about. While an orthodox Marxist would consider Bakhtin's notion of the word as the guarantor of human freedom idealist, it has been considered perfectly compatible for followers of Habermas.[41] Let us say instead therefore that Bakhtin involves major difficulties for a number of significant classical Marxist concepts. The eagerness to claim Bakhtin as a major Marxist aesthetician meant that there was little sustained analysis of these problems.[42] Bakhtin's strength, Eagleton has argued, was that he put the motifs of deconstruction 'scandalously, in a firmly social context'.[43] But the notion of a social and historical framework begins to seem less secure when Bakhtin explores the ways in which context and framing destabilize rather than produce fixity of meanings in a sociohistorical framework. The theories of the sign and of dialogism of Voloshinov and Bakhtin themselves break down the possibility of this conventional inner/outer, psyche/social division. Bakhtin's emphasis on the prevalence of 'reported speech' in discourse makes the whole notion of placing anything 'firmly' in context much more problematic. The point is rather that the context can always be changed:

> The speech of another, once enclosed in a context, is – no matter how accurately transmitted – always subject to certain semantic changes. The context embracing another's word is responsible for its dialogizing background, whose influence can be very great. Given the appropriate methods for framing, one may bring about fundamental changes even in another's utterance accurately quoted. (*DI* 340)

Bakhtin argues that the transmission of speech provides a means for 'an interpretive frame, a tool for reconceptualization and reaccenting' (*DI* 339); it is only through the fluidity of context, which allows a constant decontextualizing and reframing, that the sign can be multiaccentuated rather than monological. This means that texts can never be anchored to a particular context, social or otherwise: 'There cannot be a unified (single) contextual meaning. Therefore, there can be neither a first nor a last meaning; it always exists among other meanings as a link in the chain of meaning. . . . In historical life, this chain continues indefinitely' (*SG* 146). The fixity of meaning produced by social context is therefore the very thing that Bakhtin's work disallows. In the same way, the refusal of teleology in favour of repetition goes directly against any conventional Marxist account of history. Indeed history itself loses all stability as it becomes dialogized: 'Even past meanings, that is, those born in the dialogue of past centuries, can never be stable (finalized, ended once and for all) – they will always change' (*SG* 170). History as a form of understanding cannot therefore be said to constitute either a ground or a context.

Above all, though, there is the difference between dialogism and dialectics. There have been attempts to assimilate the two. In *The Political Unconscious* (1981), Jameson readjusted Bakhtin's dialogism so that it could be employed as a description of straightforward class struggle within the overall framework of dialectical materialism. Because Bakhtin's work was, he claimed, restricted to the notion of carnival, it was 'necessary to add the qualification that the normal form of the dialogical is essentially an *antagonistic* one, and that the dialogue of class struggle is one in which two opposing discourses fight it out within the general unity of a shared code'.[44] Jameson then went on to argue that Bakhtin's dialogism was indistinguishable from orthodox Marxist dialectics – 'the basic formal requirement of dialectical analysis is maintained, and its elements are still restructured in terms of *contradiction*' (85). Such an argument that Bakhtin's ideas were restricted to carnival and therefore needed to be extended – into a traditional dialectics – signals a move of annexation and limitation. Bakhtin himself, in fact, frequently stressed that dialogism should not be confused with Hegelian or Marxist dialectics. Dialogism cannot be resolved; it has no teleology. It is unfinalizable and open-ended. It defines itself by its refusal of all forms of transcendence, all attempts to unify. Bakhtin always maintained a distrust of what he called 'Hegel's monological dialectic'.[45] So, for example, he criticized Boris Engelhardt's analysis of Dostoevsky precisely on the grounds that he attempted to turn the novelist's dialogism into a transcendent dialectics:

> Engelhardt . . . monologises Dostoevsky's world, reduces it to a philo-
> sophical monologue unfolding dialectically. The unified, dialectically
> evolving spirit, understood in Hegelian terms, can give rise to nothing
> but a philosophical monologue. (*DP* 26)

In Bakhtin's own terms, any individual elements that are contained will be set against each other unmerged, rather as in Dante's world where 'multi-leveledness is extended into eternity' (*DP* 27).

As early as 1966, Kristeva had argued that an 'other logic' permeates Bakhtin's work, a logic of non-exclusive opposites and permanent contradiction that transgresses the monologic true/false, either/or forms of Western rationalism. This was in accordance with Bakhtin's claim to have identified 'the special logic revealed in Dostoevsky's works' which cannot be understood 'in the usual referentially logical, systematic plane' of ordinary philosophy (*DP* 299). Dialogism is not finite: it is open, and seeks neither final resolution nor synthesis. Its fundamental structure is one of alterity: poles stay apart, 'regulated by the co-ordinates I and another' (*DP* 299) as in Martin Buber's I–Thou relations. Dialogism, as Kristeva saw, should not be confused with dialectics (*WDN* 88–9, *RP* 110). A few years later Bakhtin himself obligingly spelt it out, describing the mechanism whereby dialogism is reduced to monologism in doing so:

> Dialogue and dialectics. Take a dialogue and remove the voices (the
> partitioning of voices), remove the intonations (emotional and indi-
> vidualizing ones), carve out abstract concepts and judgments from
> living words and responses, cram everything into one abstract con-
> sciousness – and that's how you get dialectics. (*SG* 147)[46]

Bakhtin came to attribute the 'special logic' of dialogism to the novel in general. For Kristeva, it was this discovery of 'a logic of distance, relativity, analogy, nonexclusive and transfinite opposition' (*WDN* 85–6) which constituted the particular significance of his work.

The novel

In a similar way, Bakhtin offers a very different theory of the novel from others in the Marxist tradition. Unlike most theorists since Lenin, he conceives the novel not as a reflection of society but as a site which heteroglossia 'enters'. He rewrites the orthodox imperative, 'the novel must be a full and comprehensive reflection of its era' accordingly: 'The novel must represent all the social and ideological voices of its era, that is, all the era's languages that have any claim to being significant; the novel must be a microcosm of heteroglossia' (*DI* 411). The novel doesn't actually take us into the streets but *represents* them, in a microcosm of the macrocosm. Bakhtin implies that all the different discourses and positions in society are necessarily depicted in the novel, speaking and contesting in the novel as in the world outside. Although he emphasizes at times that the novel presents a typified image of language (*DI* 336–7), at the same time there is also a constant implication that the novel in fact manages to avoid representation altogether because it merely stages, rehearses, or repeats the actual language of the everyday, which 'enters' the novel from the outside (if language is already a form of representation, it does not itself have to be represented in the novel). Thus Bakhtin characteristically tends to slide indiscriminately between the two, having it both ways, rather in the way that he often blurs the distinction between actual medieval carnivals and their representation in Rabelais' text.[47]

This breakdown of distinctions occurs at another level with the novel itself. This is because the novel, which alone of all the literary genres resists monologism through the dialogism of heteroglossia, is really a metagenre, strictly speaking not a genre at all, identified not so much with the novel's more usual manifestations on the bookshelf, but rather as a transhistorical form with a protean ability to synthesize and subsume other genres and discourses. The carnivalesque is also carnivorous: the novel is a carnivore, ingesting and devouring. Whereas most other genres constitute themselves through forms of exclusion, the novel alone incorporates all others as others and yet maintains its separate status as 'it fights for its own hegemony' (*DI* 4). The more carnivorous it is, the more it resists monologism, for like carnival, the novel is itself dialogical. It is thus an anti-authoritarian, democratizing art form which represents the multiplicity of conflict around representation in the life which it re-enacts, resisting all totalizing narratives or theories while itself being driven towards totalization by its ability to absorb and re-stage the heteroglossia of society as a whole.

The idea that language in society, as in the novel, is heteroglot and fully represents 'the coexistence of socio-ideological contradictions' allows no space, however, for what a novel does not say, for things which cannot be said. Or to shift from Pierre Macherey to

Foucault, it assumes that there are no groups in society that are voiceless or silent, that none have been excluded from speech as such.[48] Carnival, as Stallybrass and White point out, in fact 'often violently abuses and demonizes *weaker*, not stronger, social groups – women, ethnic and religious minorities, those who "don't belong" – in a process of *displaced abjection*'.[49] In other respects Bakhtin is close to Foucault: for both thinkers, society consists of competing contradictory discourses (though as we have seen the presence of reported speech means that for Bakhtin discourses can never be as stratified as for Foucault), each of which expresses a different order of things that successively strive for and resist totalization. Both continue to endorse a broadly Marxist perspective in the argument that a dominant power structure will seek to impose monologism. In Bakhtin, however, instead of Foucault's total interdependence of power and resistance, we have the promise of an dynamic oscillation between the forces of totalization and detotalization.

Dialogism does not of itself offer any theory of power. Aside from his more metaphysical inferences, Bakhtin always explains the operation of the struggle between centripetal and centrifugal forces in terms of the heteroglossia inherent to language. According to Bakhtin, each of society's conflicting discourses attempts to dominate the others in order to produce a monologic unitary state. The drive towards 'concrete verbal and ideological unification' (*DI* 271) develops in intrinsic connection with the processes of socio-political and cultural centralization. Simultaneously, however, society's other linguistic stratifications work against this towards decentralization:

> Alongside the centripetal forces, the centrifugal forces of language carry on their uninterrupted work; alongside verbal–ideological centralization and unification, the uninterrupted processes of decentralization and disunification go forward. (*DI* 272)

Language always provides the fulcrum for such conflict of power, its diversity producing an irreducible antagonism that begins more to resemble Nietzschean conflictual forces than the class struggle or economic contradiction. If heteroglossia needs to be dialogized in the novel to become effective, there nevertheless seems to be a benign trust expressed here that whether individuals are aware of it or not absolute monologism is impossible, for heteroglossia will always ensure decentralization. At times this almost seems to imply that the diverse languages of different social groups will in effect do our politics for us.

Identity and the other

As we have seen, it was the Nietzschean aspect of Bakhtin that
Kristeva isolated as early as 1966 in her discussion of the negativity
of the carnivalesque. Beyond its well-debated qualities of ideological
subversion, she saw in carnival itself the consequences of Bakhtin's
dialogism of non-exclusive oppositions:

> A carnival participant is both actor and spectator; he loses his sense
> of individuality, passes through a zero point of carnivalesque activity
> and splits into a subject of the spectacle and an object of the game.
> Within the carnival, the subject is reduced to nothingness, while the
> structure of *the author* emerges as an anonymity that creates and sees
> itself created as self and other, as man and mask. The cynicism of this
> carnivalesque scene, which destroys a god in order to impose its own
> dialogical laws, calls to mind Nietzsche's Dionysianism. (*WDN* 78)

The carnivalesque dismembers the identity principle: the participants lose their identities and no longer coincide with themselves.
So too, if 'other voicedness' is always a condition for voice, then the
self is always constituted by the other, the otherness of discourse,
by the voices of the dead. 'It is customary to speak about the authorial mask. But in which utterances . . . is there a *face* and not a
mask?' (*SG* 152). A self must always already be internally dialogized
because it must always speak through another's mask, like the fools
and clowns at carnival time, except that in speech there can only
be an unending series of masks, for the other's mask itself speaks
through another mask, itself the mask of a mask *ad infinitum*.[50] There
is never an originary moment for speech or for the self, never an
original voice, which also means that there can never be proper
meanings, originary or final truths: only echoes, pastiches, paro-
dies, myths, ghostly and ghastly repetitions.

   As Bakhtin describes it: 'The limit of precision in the natural
sciences is identity ($a = a$). In the human sciences precision is sur-
mounting the otherness of the other without transforming him into
purely one's own (any kind of substitution, modernization, non-
recognition of the other, and so forth)' (*SG* 169). This suggests the
attractions of Bakhtin's work for certain forms of minority politics.
It opens up the possibility of an opening to the other which does
not construct it as an absolute other or transform it into the same.
In addition, heteroglossia offers a means of breaking up the dominant monological discourses of oppressive systems, be they patriarchal, colonial, or neo-colonial, and allowing other voices to speak.
Thus, for example, Bakhtin has recently been invoked optimistically

in anthropology, colonial discourse theory, minority, and subaltern studies, as having made available a way in which a dialogue can be set up so that while speaking to the other, the other can also speak and be listened to.[51] At this point it begins to seem that if Bakhtin's project resembles any other, it must be that of Lévinas, for its consistent ethical endeavour is to respect the alterity of the other and to resist the monological drive to incorporate it within the same. But for all their resemblances, particularly in the stress of both upon dialogue, Lévinas always assumes an authentic speech – which is the very possibility that Bakhtin undermines.[52]

The trouble is that the straightforward notion of dialogue in the sense of conversation remains within the very terms of the binary oppositions which Bakhtin's work also breaks down. Dialogism, Bakhtin even admits, 'cannot ultimately be fitted into the frame of any manifest dialogue, into the frame of a mere conversation between persons' (*DI* 326). All discourse will rather enact the more complex radical experience of the 'voiced otherness' which Bakhtin first isolated in Dostoevsky. To the extent that it overruns the identity principle, dialogism questions the very possibility of sameness and otherness as such in language. Here Bakhtin comes closer to Derrida than Lévinas – which is not to identify them, not because of any simple opposition between speech and writing but rather because any similarities are dislocated by the exotopy that necessarily enforces a radical exteriority between dialogism and deconstruction. Dialogism names voice as the basis of language's conflictual basis, its ambivalence and doubledness, its irreducible alterity which produces a 'dialogic correlation between identity and non-identity' (*SG* 159). There therefore can be no same and no other as such. Voice can only be achieved through other voices. Instead of allowing the self or the other to speak, dialogism refracts authorial intention, producing a 'mutual outsideness' (*SG* 168) of both same and other. This opens up 'the possibility of never having to define oneself in language . . . of saying "I am me" in someone else's language, and in my own language, "I am other"' (*DI* 315). '*Not-I* in me' (*SG* 146): dialogism cannot offer the ability, in Philip Lewis's formulation, 'to bespeak the other without compromising its alterity' but only because it must mean that there is no discourse of the other as such – for if there is no same neither can there be an other.[53]

This radical alterity makes Bakhtin tricky to use in conjunction with any conventional model of the other, because with him sameness and difference become implicated within each other. The same difficulty holds for theory. As David Carroll has stressed, representation, narrative, or theory cannot encompass dialogism without it becoming monological; in this sense they have the same function as poetry, against which the novel is defined, and will only reduce heterogeneity to sameness.⁵⁴ Unless, that is, they are themselves dialogized, in which case, those who saw a 'way out' in Bakhtin were in a sense right after all. Bakhtin's position may conflict with the central tenets of many an orthodoxy, indeed of the very project of 'theory' itself, but he does facilitate a move into the promised realm of the social. Not however by helping us to leave the academy to dance in the streets, but by breaking down the very dualism on which this opposition is predicated. For Bakhtin enacts in his work the process of exotopy: 'not merging with another, but preserving one's own position of *extralocality* [exotopy] and the *surplus* of vision and understanding connected with it' (*DP* 299). If Bakhtin enables and sustains this recognition of and identification with irreducible otherness, of sameness with difference, it also means that the social will not be recognizable as 'the social' any more. It will have rather become what Stallybrass and White identify as a form of 'the grotesque': 'a boundary phenomenon of hybridization or inmixing, in which self and other become enmeshed in an inclusive, heterogeneous, dangerously unstable zone' (193). The self has become other, and the social is a part of the self: since a Marxist criticism will always consider the self to be part of the social, this could even represent the resolution of the long-running argument that Marxism neglects the sphere of subjectivity.

Bakhtin, therefore, undermines the distinction between insides and outsides on which so much cultural criticism is predicated. He shows the operation of a conflict that has become even more complex than tracing the effects of social antagonism in the torn halves of culture, but at the cost of breaking down the divisions from which critique can be constructed. It is one thing to sustain unresolvable contradictions in the manner of an Adorno, another to operate a criticism as a form of the grotesque, dissolving all distinctions, and therefore any ground for criticism as such. The draw of the binary is too strong, its appeal too seductive. Without it, political positions, identities, even of cultural hybridity, seem unsustainable. Is it impossible to reconcile this requirement with the far-reaching consequences of dialogization? In short, does dialogism disable dialectics?

Although the diversity of languages will ensure that totalization never occurs, for Bakhtin political critique and intervention come with the added component of dialogization. At the same time, we have seen how Bakhtin also claims that the dialogic principle operates everywhere without specific voluntaristic intervention. His argument oscillates between the two. From the perspective of Adorno, it could be maintained that dialogism, in its primary form, enacts and stages the antagonistic conflicts within society itself. Its dynamism, derived from the diversity of languages, is the result of social conflict, and need not therefore rely on a philosophical principle. But even if it begins in this way, as we have seen Bakhtin insists that it does not operate dialectically. Indeed, not only does it not work towards a final resolution, it does not even sustain the conflict that is the product of its own generative social situation: dialogics work remorselessly towards ever greater decentralization and dispersion. At the same time, it is noticeable that Bakhtin never formally abandons the central antimony of centrifugal and centripetal forces, a structure of totalization and detotalization in some ways comparable to Adorno's dialectic of transcendent and immanent critique. But whereas Adorno stresses that for an effective cultural criticism the two must necessarily be deployed at once, sustaining each other even while each shows how the other is individually impossible, Bakhtin identifies only one of his torn halves as the basis for criticism, and then emphasizes the detotalizing force of dialogics to the extent that he begins to undo the original generative dialectic on which his argument was originally predicated. The over-reaching consequences of dialogism, operating within a dialectic of centripetal and centrifugal forces, but then turning against dialectics as such, meant that it apparently ended up by dissolving all boundaries so that conceptual distinctions as such became impossible to sustain. Dialogism, in other words, when pushed to its logical conclusions, seems to go too far, to make criticism impossible.

The question that remains, however, is whether its operation within the dialectic of centripetal and centrifugal forces means that dialogism sustains or dissolves the tension between them. The whole 'struggle over Bakhtin', between apparently incompatible different versions of his work, suggests that *dialogism is itself dialogical*. In other words, dialogism is also two-faced, two-voiced: a 'double-accented, double-styled *hybrid construction*' (*DI* 304); it does not merely describe such doubling, it stages and enacts it in its full incompatibilities. Dialogism works as an internally riven economy, whereby in one domain it consists of the benign openness of intersubjective exchange between multiple voices, while in another it also enables a critical, subversive, contestatory challenge to monological, hegemonic forms of authority which it shows can be transgressed and contested. Dialogism thus itself involves a dialogic hybridity: of a dissonant heterogeneity which retains a critical, dialectical cutting edge. Its own antimonies, which seem always on the brink of dissolving each other, operate within an oscillating dynamic of centripetal and centrifugal forces not as the irresolvable flux of a Nietzschean *agon* but in a dislocating fissure that is simultaneously contrapuntal and antagonistic: sameness and difference, dialogue in one sphere, contestation in another. Its irreducible conflictual structure operates from that very differential, reversible fulcrum which, Adorno argued, enables effective cultural critique.

(1985)

Notes

1 This chapter has been overshadowed by the death of Allon White in 1988. My interest in Bakhtin developed in a spirit of friendly though always polemical dispute with Allon – a dialogue which began with his interventions at the first Southampton 'Theory and Text' Conference of 1981 (see, for example, *Oxford Literary Review* 5 (1982), 74–5). 'Back to Bakhtin' marked a return intervention at Sussex, where Allon worked; it was first given as a seminar paper there in 1984. A shorter version was published in *Cultural Critique* 2 (1985–86), and produced a vigorous response from Allon, 'The Struggle Over Bakhtin', which set out his later position. With Allon's tragic illness all desire for continuation of our debate ceased on my part. In revising the article for inclusion here, I have removed the critique of his work, but have not wanted to excise all evidence of our altercation, to turn his death into a silence without trace. This chapter is dedicated to his memory.

2 This passes over a third political position, namely of Trotskyism. It is a moot point, however, whether the Fourth Internationalists can ever claim to have established a literary critical position. For an example of an attempt, see Slaughter, *Marxism, Ideology and Literature*, and certain moments of post-Althusserian revolutionary enthusiasm in the writings of Terry Eagleton, particularly *Walter Benjamin*.

3 Today the History Workshop conference continues to thrive, while the Essex Conference, after a lapse of many years, has recently been revived – but now defensively takes place behind closed doors, by invitation only. For the arguments between the two camps in the 1970s see Thompson, *The Poverty of Theory*; Nield and Seed, 'Theoretical Poverty or the Poverty of Theory'; Hirst, 'The Necessity of Theory'. For the autocriticism see Rancière, *La Leçon d'Althusser*; Althusser, *Essays in Self-Criticism*; Hindess and Hirst, *Mode of Production and Social Formation*; Cutler, Hindess, Hirst, and Hussain, *Marx's 'Capital' and Capitalism Today*; Hirst, *On Law and Ideology*; and Benton, *The Rise and Fall of Structural Marxism*. In *White Mythologies*, I suggest that Hindess and Hirst's critique, which effectively ended British Althusserianism, was based on a serious misreading of his argument.

4 Widdowson, *Re-Reading English*. For a more extended discussion of this book see my 'Re. Reading *Re-Reading English*'.

5 For further discussion of the problem of Marxism and history, see my *White Mythologies*.

6 Hoyles, 'Radical Critical Theory and English', in *Re-Reading English*, 44–5 (my emphasis).

7 Williams, *Marxism and Literature*, 35–42 (Williams invokes Voloshinov's theory of language for his new 'cultural materialism'); Bennett, *Formalism and Marxism*; Eagleton, *Walter Benjamin*, and 'Wittgenstein's Friends'; Forgacs, 'Marxist Literary Theories'; White, 'Bakhtin, Sociolinguistics and Deconstruction'.

8 Pechey, 'Bakhtin, Marxism, and Post-Structuralism', 237. Pechey's argument differs, however, from those cited in notes 6 and 7 in so far as he recognizes the complicity between Bakhtin and poststructuralism rather than suggesting that the one constitutes an answer to the other.

9 Jameson, *The Prison-House of Language*. Jameson first mentions Bakhtin, in a discussion of the relation of the carnivalesque to modernism, in 'Wyndham Lewis as Futurist', 303–6.

10 Bennett, *Formalism and Marxism*, 95. The most sustained treatment of Bakhtin in relation to Russian Formalism is that of Frow in *Marxism and Literary History*, 125–69.

11 Lodge, 'Double Discourses; Joyce and Bakhtin', 1. For further thoughts see Lodge's *After Bakhtin*.

12 Booth, 'Freedom of Interpretation'; Carroll, 'The Alterity of Discourse'; de Man, 'Dialogue and Dialogism'; reprinted in *The Resistance to Theory*, 106–14; LaCapra, 'Bakhtin, Marxism and the Carnivalesque', in *Rethinking Intellectual History*, 291–324. For special issues on Bakhtin see *Critical Inquiry*, 'Forum on Bakhtin', reprinted with additions as *Bakhtin: Essays and Dialogues on his Work*, ed. Morson; *Etudes françaises*, 'Bakhtine mode d'emploi'; *Studies in Twentieth Century Literature*; and *University of Ottawa Quarterly*. For a comprehensive survey of Bakhtin criticism in English, see Hirschkop's 'Critical Work on the Bakhtin Circle: A Bibliographical Essay', in Hirschkop and Shepherd, eds, *Bakhtin and Cultural Theory*, 195–212.

13 de Man, 'Dialogue and Dialogism', 104.

14 Weber, 'The Intersection', 111. For other discussions of the relation between Bakhtin and Derrida see Holquist, 'The Surd Heard: Bakhtin and Derrida', in Morson, ed., *Literature and History*, 137–56, and McCannell, 'The Temporality of Textuality'. For Bakhtin and Derrida on 'context' see Sprinker, 'Boundless Context'.

15 Bakhtin, *Speech Genres*, 161. Bakhtin's objection to structuralism, 'I am against enclosure in a text' (169) also seems similar to Derrida's, until we remember that the latter rather demonstrates how the closure necessary for structuralism's system can never in fact be achieved. Clearly many of the comparisons that are drawn between the two are fairly impressionistic. For a detailed critique of the strategies of the humanist appropriation of Bakhtin, see Hirschkop, 'A Response to the Forum on Mikhail Bakhtin', in Morson, ed., *Bakhtin*, 73–9. Bakhtin's work, together with that of Medvedev and Voloshinov, will be cited as follows: *MPL*: Voloshinov, *Marxism and the Philosophy of Language*; *FMC*: Voloshinov, *Freudianism: A Marxist Critique*; *FM*: Medvedev, *The Formal Method in Literary Scholarship*; *DP*: Bakhtin, *Problems of Dostoevsky's Poetics*; *RW*: Bakhtin, *Rabelais and His World*; *DI*: Bakhtin, *The Dialogic Imagination*; *SG*: Bakhtin, *Speech Genres*.

16 Eagleton, *Walter Benjamin*, 150.

17 *DI* xxii–xxiii. For discussion of Bakhtin's relation to Husserl and Heidegger see de Man, 'Dialogue and Dialogism', 103–5.

18 Hirschkop has suggested (private communication) that such a transformation depends 'in large part on confusing a neo-Kantian and phenomenological

critique of the formalist position with a lame humanist denial of anything remotely "scientistic"'. As evidence, he cites the fact that the one essay from *Vosprosy* not translated in *The Dialogic Imagination* is the heavily phenomenological/neo-Kantian article on Formalism: 'the danger is that a very technical philosophical Bakhtin, mired in German epistemological speculation, would be every bit as "theoretical" and frightening to the Anglo-American humanities as structuralism'.

19 The authorship question – which makes one aware that the history of Bakhtin's reception in the Soviet Union has been even more complicated than in the West – was initiated by V. V. Ivanov in 1973 (translated as 'The Significance of M. M. Bakhtin's Ideas on Sign, Utterance and Dialogue for Modern Semiotics', in Baran, *Structuralism and Semiotics*, 186–243). For a detailed discussion of the issues, see Todorov, *Mikhail Bakhtine*, 13–26, or *Mikhail Bakhtin: The Dialogical Principle*, 3–13. See Hirschkop, 'Critical Work on the Bakhtin Circle', for bibliographical references for the whole debate.

20 Holquist, 'The Politics of Representation', in *Allegory and Representation,* ed. Greenblatt, 171, 173.

21 Clark and Holquist, *Mikhail Bakhtin*.

22 Hirschkop, 'Critical Work on the Bakhtin Circle', draws attention to the editorial preface of a Russian reprint of *The Formal Method* where this hypothesis is advanced. The story of Bakhtin staying gnomically silent while his wife tells a visitor that Bakhtin himself wrote the Voloshinov/Medvedev books seems to be a piece of Russian urban mythology.

23 Discussions of the contributions of Voloshinov's *Marxism and the Philosophy of Language* (1929, English translation 1973, French translation 1977) can be found in Williams's *Marxism and Literature*, 35–42 (the earliest sustained analysis of Voloshinov by a British Marxist), and in Houdebine, *Langage et Marxisme*, 161–73.

24 Eagleton, 'Wittgenstein's Friends', 78. Further references will be cited in the text.

25 In fact Eagleton himself dismisses carnival eleven pages later as 'no more than a compliant, containable libertarianism' (90).

26 White, 'The Authoritative Lie', 312. A contemporary example of such academic carnivalesque inversion would be Sharratt's *Reading Relations* (1983) which interrogates the claims of Marxist criticism through a parody of Eagleton's *Criticism and Ideology* (1976).

27 'The Authoritative Lie', 312. The status of Bakhtin's own language is also discussed by Kristeva in her introduction to *La Poétique de Dostoievski*, 21 ('The Ruin of a Poetics', 116–17; further references will be cited in the text as *RP*).

28 Holquist, 'The Politics of Representation', 171.

29 For a full discussion of the implications of Saussure's distinction, see Attridge, 'Language as History/History as Language: Saussure and the Romance of Etymology', in Attridge, Bennington, and Young, eds, *Post-Structuralism and the Question of History*, 183–211. For the most sophisticated analysis of Voloshinov, see Weber's 'The Intersection'.

30 Cf. 'Discourse lives outside itself, in its living directedness towards the object; if we detach ourselves completely from this directedness all we have left is the naked corpse of the word, from which we can learn nothing at all about the social situation or the fate of a given word in life. *To study the word as such, ignoring the directedness that reaches out beyond it, is just as senseless as to study psychological experience outside the context of that*

real life toward which it was directed and by which it is determined' (*DI* 292, translation modified).

31 Pechey, 'Bakhtin, Marxism, and Post-Structuralism', 241. Weber here contrasts Voloshinov to Habermas whose theory of communicative competence 'proceeds from a concept of the subject which remains largely unproblematized' ('The Intersection', 97).

32 *MPL* 90. With Voloshinov's idea of the unconscious as an encrypted foreign body in the psyche, compare Abraham, 'The Shell and the Kernel', and Derrida, 'Fors'.

33 It might be tempting here to identify the sign with the tropes of allegory or metaphor. Bakhtin, however, always argues for the separation of trope from dialogism; see de Man, 'Dialogue and Dialogism' 105, for the argument that this reveals 'the metaphysical *impensé* of Bakhtin's thought'.

34 Todorov, *Mikhail Bakhtine*, 165. In *The Dialogic Imagination* Bakhtin remarks that even monoglossia's 'perception presumes heteroglossia as a background, and even it interacts dialogically with various aspects of this heteroglossia' (*DI* 375).

35 Bakhtin, 'Rabelais and Gogol', 46.

36 A tendency noticeable in Jameson, Eagleton, Pechey, and Allon White. Bennett and Forgacs are the exceptions.

37 Smith, *The Wealth of Nations*, V.i.g.15.

38 Eagleton, 'Wittgenstein's Friends', 89–90; the same point is made in *Walter Benjamin*, 148. White's subsequent defence of its political effectivity does not altogether succeed in answering Eagleton's objections. White puts forward the GLC (Greater London Council's) 'people's festivals' as a contemporary instance of carnival as a form of effective political opposition ('The Struggle Over Bakhtin', 240). The problem with this example, however, is that the GLC, though at that time enjoying a socialist majority, was nevertheless itself a State apparatus which employed its festivals as an oppositional tactic. Once the GLC had been abolished by Mrs Thatcher – despite its carnivals – the so-called people's festivals ceased. By contrast it is striking that in all their discussions of the politics of carnival neither Eagleton nor Stallybrass and White ever mention London's annual Notting Hill Carnival – the second largest carnival in the world (after Rio) which involves up to a million participants. For a full history, see Owusu and Ross, *Behind the Masquerade*. An altogether different view of carnival is advanced by Kristeva who contends that its laughter is serious, 'the only way that it can avoid becoming either the scene of the law or the scene of its parody, in order to become the scene of its other' ('Word, Dialogue, and Novel', in *Desire in Language*, 80), hereafter cited as *WDN*.

39 Stallybrass and White, *The Politics and Poetics of Transgression*, 19.

40 Eagleton, 'Bakhtin, Schopenhauer, Kundera', in Hirschkop and Shepherd, *Bakhtin and Cultural Theory*, 178–9.

41 For a comparison of 'the Bakhtinian programme' with that of Habermas, see Hirschkop's 'Bakhtin and Cultural Theory', in Hirschkop and Shepherd, *Bakhtin and Cultural Theory*, 1–38.

42 Discussions of the status of history in Bakhtin include Anchor, 'Bakhtin's Truths of Laughter'; DeJean, 'Bakhtin and/in History'; and Howes, 'Rhetoric of Attack'.

43 Eagleton, *Walter Benjamin*, 150 (following White).

44 Jameson, *The Political Unconscious*, 84. A less restricted reading is briefly suggested at 285.

45 *SG* 162. Cf. Todorov, *Mikhail Bakhtine*, 160.

46 Bakhtin's formulation here can be usefully compared to Kristeva's redefinition of the object of linguistics (which is obviously as much indebted to Bakhtin as to Roman Jakobson) in 'The Ethics of Linguistics', *Desire in Language*, 24–5. Some have criticized Kristeva's reading of Bakhtin, particularly her strategy of withdrawing 'the kernel which links up with the most advanced contemporary research' from the 'worn-out ideological husk' that surrounds it. What remains extraordinary, however, is that as early as the 1960s, she recognized Bakhtin's work as 'a hitherto unknown precursor, unaware of its role', of a movement that had hardly begun and had certainly yet to be termed poststructuralism or deconstruction (*RP* 107). At the end of her first essay on Bakhtin, she predicted the growing importance of a movement concerned with isolating and exploring the extensive implications of that different kind of logic of alterity:

> The path charted between the two poles of dialogue radically abolishes problems of causality, finality, et cetera, from our philosophical arena. It suggests the importance of the dialogical principle for a space of thought much larger than that of the novel. More than binarism, dialogism may well become the basis of our time's intellectual structure. (*WDN* 89)

47 Stallybrass and White discuss this problem in *The Politics and Poetics of Transgression*, 59–61; they themselves sharpen up Bakhtin's method considerably through their use of Babcock's notion of 'symbolic inversion' (17).

48 Macherey, *A Theory of Literary Production*; Foucault, 'The Order of Discourse', trans. Ian McLeod, in Young, ed., *Untying the Text: A Post-Structuralist Reader*, 48–77; Foucault, *The History of Sexuality*. See *SG* 133–4, however, for some comments on the relation of silence to speech. In comparing Bakhtin to Foucault it should be noted that, with the possible exception of the Rabelais book, Bakhtin does not analyse the operations of power according to the sovereignty model of repression that Foucault criticizes.

49 Stallybrass and White, *The Politics and Poetics of Transgression*, 19.

50 Compare Descombes' account of Klossowski's 'liquidation of the identity principle', *Modern French Philosophy*, 183.

51 See, for example, Bauer, *Feminist Dialogics*; Pechey, 'On the Borders of Bakhtin', and Clifford, 'On Ethnographic Authority', in *The Predicament of Culture*, 21–54. Bhabha, on the other hand, in 'Signs Taken for Wonders', in *The Location of Culture*, 102–22 employs the concept of hybridity in order to suggest the complex movements of alterity in the colonial text. For Bakhtin's and Bhabha's use of 'hybridity', see my *Colonial Desire*, 20–6.

52 For a more extended account of Lévinas's position, see *White Mythologies*, 12–18.

53 Lewis, 'The Post-Structuralist Condition', 14.

54 Carroll, 'The Alterity of Discourse', 78.

3..

Poststructuralism – the improper name

Bakhtin thus operated as something of an elusive third term in the conflict between Marxism and poststructuralism, a struggle between transcendent and immanent critiques. Bakhtin was transformed into a discrete object of desire as each sought for a subsuming position, but he could only be used to show what the other lacked – a move which always incurred the risk of turning the original position inside out. In the institutional prevarication between insides and outsides, you cannot escape from either by recourse to its opposite – for each, in Stallybrass and White's terms, can always become a symbolic inversion of the other. The vacillation between them points to the operation of an anxiety, the entangling alterity of that which is outside the institution and which constitutes the condition of institutional production.

The pressure for criticism to get outside its object determines the paradigms of contemporary theory which mirror and reproduce such compulsion at a theoretical level. The dichotomy of inside and outside is transformed into an interminable drive for theory to get outside itself, to step outside its own skin. Take, for example, the 'postmodernism' which has become the topic of such profuse discussion in the past ten years or so. Who felt the need to introduce the concept as a rival to modernism, which had virtually been forgotten about anyway, and why? What is the relation of postmodernism to the poststructuralism that preceded it, but which now constitutes a minor theoretical aspect of it? And what is its relation to that other more recent 'post' of contemporary theory, 'postcolonialism'? To say nothing of the notion of 'postfeminism'. Some such as Gerald Graff have argued that these movements involve a meaningless repetition of new theories versus old, meaningless because their only necessity is that they be new.[1] By defining itself against a past but also in a sequence of modernity, the new certainly marks a relation to history.[2] But it could also be maintained that the addition of the 'post' is symptomatic of the increasingly insistent institutional compulsion always to put oneself on the out-side, the beyond: 'post', 'neo', 'new' are the names for the outside of (the other) theory, for theory being outside itself, attempting to put boundaries between itself and its putatively surpassed other. In Jameson's terms, they are themselves a symbolic displacement for critical distance, substituting a relation of time, of postness, of newness, for the lost relation of space. But even if time enables a distance, this postness is still always a self-reflective critique, that is, a difference between theories rather than a different critique of culture as such. The succession of modernities in theory betrays symptomatically the lost critical relation between criticism and the world. In its absence, criticism turns in on itself to produce an endless succession of narcissistic, self-critical perspectives.

A larger version of this structure would be the claim that postmodernism can be defined by its critical and self-reflexive atti-tude to the Enlightenment project. Zygmunt Bauman, for example, argues that postmodernism represents a break with modernism, a reflection on its goals, a critical self-consciousness about it and to that degree a revision of it.[3] This, roughly speaking, squares with Habermas's account, except that for him it amounts to a betrayal of the Enlightenment and its principles. The question that emerges here is whether postmodernism can be said to exist as such as a separable movement from modernism: the argument set up by Habermas, and increasingly followed by those sympathetic to critical theory, is that postmodernism far from being something new merely represents a negative reversal – Habermas's 'neo-conservatism' – that seeks to undermine the original emancipatory Enlightenment project of which Marxism is the most fully developed example. This assumes a view of the Enlightenment as 'a project', that is, a move-ment with a unified intention that was not in any way ambiguous, or divided against itself.

The dispute about whether postmodernism can in any mean-ingful sense be conceded as a separate conceptual entity exactly parallels the discussions that took place in the 1980s about whether poststructuralism was in any real respect different from structural-ism. Today the argument might equally go the other way, namely, we might wonder whether structuralism was ever different from poststructuralism.[4]

So-called poststructuralism

If the problem with Bakhtin was whether there was a real Bakhtin, the question with poststructuralism was whether it existed at all. A parallel case would be Walter Benn Michaels and Steven Knapp's polemic 'Against Theory' which, while not directed against poststructuralism as such, rested its complaint on the key characteristic of theory's 'tendency to generate theoretical problems by splitting apart terms that are in fact inseparable':[5] in other words, making difference out of sameness, but a difference that is somehow a false one, because the same really is just the same and identical with itself. The reluctance to admit that there was any difference between structuralism and poststructuralism was strikingly marked by the repeated insistence by critics on referring to '*so-called* poststructuralism'.[6] Structuralism, like modernity, was not to be given up so easily. Which is not altogether unrelated to the way in which attention quickly focused on the issue of history. Rodolphe Gasché put it like this:

> As innocent as the prefix *post-* in front of *structuralism* may sound, it is burdened with the formidable task of blaming and overcoming structuralism's alleged ahistoricity. The mere linguistic event of a formation such as 'post-structuralism' alone suggests that history-in-person has come to belie the theoretical ambitions of the previous ahistorical doctrine. . . . Yet . . . it is, in practice, not very easy to distinguish poststructuralism from what precedes it.[7]

As Gasché observes, the 'post' of poststructuralism itself gives the lie to structuralism's fabled emphasis on the synchronic, to its apparent ahistoricity. Either the introduction of the 'post' constitutes an event which, at a stroke, dismembers the entire structuralist theoretical machinery – or it marks a historicity that had up to that moment lain concealed.[8] If the latter is the case, then the problem becomes the fact that the 'post' is entirely superfluous, excessive, in that it implies a real difference when in fact there was none. Interestingly enough, then, given its own obsession with the various versions of difference, when it first emerged as a term, poststructuralism was taken as the sign of a false difference, of difference where there was no difference. This would be comparable to more recent arguments about postmodernity.

In fact, paradoxically given its alleged ahistoricity, structuralism had always emphasized its own temporality. As early as 1964, Roland Barthes forecast the end of a movement that at that time had hardly even begun, declaring that

> Structural man is scarcely concerned to *last*; he knows that structuralism, too, is a certain *form* of the world; and just as he experiences his validity (but not his truth) in his power to speak the old languages of the world in a new way, so he knows that it will suffice that a new

language rise out of history, a new language which speaks him in his
turn, for his task to be done.[9]

And sure enough, the death of structural man duly took place,
doubtless to be laid in the grave alongside authorial man, whose
demise he had brought about. The new language which showed
that his task was done was that of poststructural woman – a bewil-
dering succession for most people who had scarcely begun to understand structural man's curious babble of signifiers and signifieds,
synchronic and diachronic, *langue* and *parole*, *sjuzet* and *fabula*,
enunciation, and enounced, etc. etc.

The relation between the two remains an open question. Were
they different or were they the same? Would structuralism have
been the same if poststructuralism had never existed? Or did
poststructuralism make it, retrospectively by a kind of deferred
action, different? The connection between them is hard to assess
because no one has ever really agreed on a definition of poststructuralism, which remains to this day conceptually elusive, no more
perhaps than an 'order word', in Deleuze and Guattari's term.[10] But
then what, for that matter, was structuralism? And how is it that it
seemed to involve many of the same thinkers – who subsequently
reappeared as poststructuralists?

Post it

The genealogy of the word 'poststructuralism' is itself instructive.
It's interesting to note that the appearance of the word was preceded
by talk of 'The End of Structuralism' (Jean-Marie Benoist, 1970), of
'Structuralism: The Aftermath' (Eugenio Donato, 1973), or the highly
symptomatic renaming of the 1970 volume, *The Languages of Criticism
and the Sciences of Man* as *The Structuralist Controversy* in 1972.[11] It
is now widely agreed that Derrida's appearance at the original 1966
Symposium with a paper entitled 'Structure, Sign, and Play in the
Human Sciences', constituted the decisive intervention that in the
USA produced a new critical relationship to structuralism.

Credit for this historic intervention must also in certain respects
go to Eugenio Donato, who appears, from his paper, to have been
the only speaker who had understood the significance of Derrida's
two articles 'De la grammatologie' that had appeared in the journal
Critique in December 1965 and January 1966. Donato writes:

It should be possible to see, for literature, both the necessity and the
dilemma of an enterprise such as [that of] Derrida, in as much as

language in its being is difference, yet it cannot escape the tyranny of the linguistic sign; that is to say, identity and presence. It has the constant and interminable task of demystifying itself, but it can only do so from a position which it can never occupy.[12]

There has scarcely been a more succinct summary of the deconstructive premise – in which Donato emphasizes the way in which difference may undo identity but cannot escape it either.

It was only in the Preface to the renamed version of the Johns Hopkins Symposium, written in November 1971, that the editors Macksey and Donato concede a decisive indication that something had changed in their perception of the structuralist activity, beginning their Preface with the comment that 'the republication of a symposium connected with structuralism perhaps deserves a word of explanation' (ix). The assumption in the English-speaking world that structuralism was an avowedly scientific project has now to be qualified. They observe that Roland Barthes, whose name was one of the first to be linked with the concept of 'structuralism',

> has left little doubt in his recent works that the avowed scientific end which Parisian structuralism had assigned itself constitutes more a strategic moment in an open-ended process than an attainable goal. Although the intellectual inheritance was clear, with its preoccupation with articulated sign-systems and the repudiation of the hermeneutic enterprises of the last century, evidence was already available in the Johns Hopkins symposium of the ensuing moment of theoretical deconstruction. (ix)

For Macksey and Donato that act of 'theoretical deconstruction' takes the form of the decline in methodological importance of linguistics – that is to say, Saussure – and the replacement of Hegel by Nietzsche in the central position of French thought. Declaring that the deconstruction of structuralism does not just take the form of a change in the pantheon of intellectual gods, Macksey and Donato note a new element of negativity, of 'philosophical metaphors of defeat':

> Today's task for thinkers within this climate thus seems to reside in the possibility of developing a critical discourse without identities to sustain concepts, without privileged origins, or without an ordered temporality to guarantee the mimetic possibilities of representation. (xii)

What is striking here is the way in which the end of structuralism is not associated exclusively with Derrida and deconstruction, but equally with the work of Foucault and Deleuze; Macksey and Donato's ensuing description develops into a distinctly Foucauldian discourse which stresses the event, 'adrift in radical discontinuity', and singularities, the 'fundamental entities of such systems'.[13] It is the Nietzscheanism of Foucault that constitutes the way of the future. Ominously, this already seems to produce a sense of futility and disempowerment. At the same time, the title of their Preface, 'The Space Between', implies that it is written at a time (1971) that comes after the strategic moment of structuralism, but before its successor can be imagined. 'We are left', they announce, 'with the necessity of articulating what Said has called "the vacant spaces between things, words, ideas".' It is as if they are waiting for some terrifying monstrosity to arrive. Macksey and Donato are left adrift in the interval, unable to posit a new moment of comparable definitiveness, unable to *comprehend* that which is to follow: 'the times are not propitious', they announce, 'to another symposium which would attempt to *circumscribe* this new topology' (xiii, my emphasis). Circumscribing what followed would always be the difficult thing.

Seven years after 'The Space Between', twelve after the original symposium, Josué Harari was preparing an anthology of contemporary criticism, to be called *Textual Strategies: Criticism in the Wake of Structuralism*. When it appeared the next year, 1979, however, its subtitle was changed to read *Perspectives in Post-Structuralist Criticism*.[14] The first announcement of the advent of poststructuralism had been made. The new topography had arrived. Or had it? If we allow that with Harari's title, poststructuralism had at least appeared *de facto* if not *de jure*, let's look at his definition of what his anthology was about. What is most noticeable is Harari's uncertainty as to whether he is discussing anything specific at all. Beginning with a lengthy discussion of structuralism, he concludes that 'there is no unified view of structuralism' and that as a movement it is 'most clearly defined on the basis of the transformations it has wrought in the disciplines it has affected'. He then asks, 'what is poststructuralism?', which begs the question to the extent that it already posits its existence. Perhaps this is why a hesitant note immediately follows: 'the question is less ambitious than it may appear; it does not seek a clear or unified answer, but only tentative answers that may perhaps be reduced, in the end, to nothing more than a panorama only slightly different from that offered by structuralism' (27). Despite this qualification, Harari then offers the following definition:

> The fundamental difference between the structuralist and poststructuralist *enterprises* can be seen in the shift from the problematic

of the subject to the deconstruction of the concept of representation. I refer here to Jacques Derrida, whose work constitutes a systematic critique of structuralism. (29) [my emphasis]

A shift from the critique of the subject to the critique of the sign: in other words we are dealing here with a thematic change, a conceptual and temporal shift, as well as a change of analytical object.[15] Whereas structuralism, according to Harari, had problematized the subject, poststructuralism has moved to a 'deconstruction' of representation. Poststructuralism, it is implied, had developed as a response to Derrida's critique of structuralism in 'Structure, Sign, and Play': the deconstruction of structuralism produced poststructuralism, which would explain why in the early years, the distinction between poststructuralism and deconstruction was often hard to gauge. However, as Philip Lewis was to point out in an important review article of Harari entitled 'The Post-Structuralist Condition' (1983), in many ways structuralism was still subject-centered, and was 'even in its tamer forms' 'already well along with the deconstruction of representation'.[16] Which doesn't leave much change out of Harari's definition – except, importantly, the name, and work, of Derrida.

Yet it was still widely felt that structuralism could not be thought of in the same ways any more as it had been in the scientistic days of the 1960s and 1970s. This is the argument of my Introduction to *Untying the Text: A Poststructuralist Reader* (1981), where I defined poststructuralism as structuralism's difference from itself, the wrinkling on structuralism's Apollonian brow; not a development of structuralism or something that can be defined in terms of a conceptual chronology so much as a displacement, a transforming of structuralist concepts by turning one against the other, so as to emphasize their difference rather than their sameness.[17] This process of decomposing structuralism was related to its characteristic autocritical mode which allowed Derrida, Jacques Lacan, and Foucault to push the implications of 'difference' beyond structuralism's own conceptual limits. The emphasis on an autocritical effect represented a similar argument to that which Bauman has more recently proposed for postmodernism in its relation to modernism. But Philip Lewis was equally sceptical of this idea:

One may then wonder if Derrida, by pursuing those implications, does not become, complicitously, more structuralist than the structuralists, if his poststructuralism is not finally an arch- or hyper-structuralism. If poststructuralism is nothing more than the advent in due course of structuralism's auto-critical moment, its pursuit of its own integrity, what sense does it make to insist on the notion of *post*structuralism? Why denominate a new outlook, promote concerns about a new wave of Gallic infiltration, if we simply confront an inherent evolution, a predictable change of accent or key? (5)

Lewis's objection demonstrates the difficulties in describing the difference between the two in terms of 'evolution', and yet the prefix 'post' suggests exactly that kind of evolutionary progression.

In an article published in 1982 I emphasized the argument about poststructuralism as a form of displacement even further, suggesting that the 'post' in poststructuralism could operate as a form of space as well as time:

In relations of time, the prefix 'post' implies subsequently, or 'coming after', as in postpone. But oddly enough in relations of space – and if we switch to space we are switching to structuralism's own visual metaphor of a geometric or morphological structure – we find that the prefix 'post' now means 'behind' – as in 'post-jacent', 'post-scenium', or 'post-oral'. This uncanny antithetical doubling is rather humbly embodied in the word 'posterior', which means both coming after, later in time, as in posterity, as well as 'situated behind' – and hence its familiar use in the decorous British euphemism.

So 'poststructuralism' suggests that structuralism itself can only exist as always already inhabited by poststructuralism, which comes both behind and after. It is always already unfolding as a repetition, not of the same but as a kind of *Nachträglichkeit*, or deferred action. In this sense, poststructuralism becomes structuralism's primal scene – as Barbara Johnson describes it, 'the first occurrence of what has been repeating itself in the patient without ever having occurred'.[18]

This suggestion of a *beyond* which is also a *before* is reinforced, as Geoffrey Bennington has remarked, by the so-called 'materiality of the signifier' in the word 'poststructuralism' itself, for which the *post* is ineluctably *pre*: 'it is a prefix, it thus comes before and not after. The post is at the beginning, it precedes, in a certain linear order of the signifier, that which it comes after'.[19] There is, in other words, a paradox in the prefix 'post', the same paradox that Derrida has elaborated in his well-known discussion of the Preface: that which comes after comes before. As Bennington suggests, the notion of the 'post' in poststructuralism as a beyond which is also a before, comes close to a definition of 'postmodernism' given by Lyotard in 1982 in the article 'Response to the Question: What is Postmodernism?' Here Lyotard seems more or less to abandon the emphasis on grand narratives of *The Postmodern Condition* for an entirely different description of postmodernism which also forsakes any idea of a simple temporal progression between modernism and postmodernism. Lyotard argues that: 'A work can become modern only if it is first postmodern. Postmodernism thus understood is not modernism at its end but in the nascent state'.[20] The 'post' thus here becomes before, and the '*post modern* would have to be understood according to the paradox of the future (*post*) anterior (*modo*)' (81). We recall Gasché's observation of the way in which the 'post' of poststructuralism problematizes the relation to history, now not only introducing the trace of its wake but disconcertingly making what should come after come before, turning narrative into a labyrinth of discrete impossible events.[21] As time and space begin to turn each other inside out, it begins to seem that, like the joke or the uncanny, poststructuralism can best be defined not so much by any intrinsic content as by the deferred action of its effect.

Spaced-out

As Jonathan Culler has pointed out, in the USA poststructuralism virtually did precede structuralism. This is because in many respects poststructuralism (a word that has begun to be used in France only recently) represents the American translation of that nonscientistic form of structuralism that Culler himself separated off from structuralism proper in his highly influential *Structuralist Poetics* (1975). The chapter on *Tel Quel* is called 'Beyond Structuralism', which perhaps made it inevitable that those whose work fell under the rubric of structuralist poetics (Lévi-Strauss, Roman Jakobson, A. J. Greimas, Gérard Genette, certain works of Barthes, Vladimir Propp, Todorov) would be called structuralists, with those treated in this chapter (later writings of Barthes and Kristeva, together with Derrida) as beyond or 'post' structuralists. Those whose work evidently found little place in Culler's scheme – Lacan, Deleuze, Foucault, Luce Irigaray etc. – naturally tended to be placed into the second category as they were gradually discovered by Anglo-American readers. Poststructuralism, in this case, would amount to a form of translation, of metaphoricity, its 'post' denoting the crossing of national and conceptual frontiers that had served to separate structuralism from itself. Nevertheless, what Culler had done in dividing up structuralism in *Structuralist Poetics* was to detect a certain tension within structuralism as such.[22] Culler himself declined to pursue this further: at the beginning of *On Deconstruction* (1983), he introduced the question only to conclude that 'the distinction between structuralism and post-structuralism is highly unreliable'.[23]

At this point, it is worth returning to Lewis's argument that despite everything structuralism and poststructuralism really amount to the same thing. How does he deny their difference? Naturally by arguing that structuralism itself is best defined in terms of certain differences. Lewis takes the tripartite definition that Vincent Descombes offers in his *Modern French Philosophy* (1980), where structuralism is delineated as

1 The method of structural analysis
2 the semiological account of meaning and communication
3 the philosophical critique spawned by structuralism, which targets semiology as well as phenomenology.[24]

Pointing out that 'the critical revisionary strain of structuralist theory is subject to entrapment in the positions and models it challenges', Lewis then produces the following redefinition of Descombes' definition:

1 a concept of structure and method of comparative analysis
2 a disciplinary base in semiology that furnishes models for the pursuit of interdisciplinary enquiry
3 a critical orientation or strategy alert to the anomalies of theory and ultimately sceptical of its own theses. (9)

In terms of this scheme, Lewis suggests, the majority of essays in *Textual Strategies* could pass for orthodox structuralist texts.[25] A separate poststructuralism would have to depend on the relation of no. 3, critical structuralism, to the basic, orthodox structuralism of 1 and 2. The question, says Lewis, is 'whether the auto-critical, counter-theoretical impulse we have encountered in no. 3 has developed to the point of taking us out of the structuralist arena into distinctly different territory' (10). As we have seen, Lewis argues that it has not. Poststructuralism has not separated itself from structuralism, has not crossed any frontiers.

It is noticeable, however, that the schema which Descombes sets up, in which 3 is critical of 1 and 2, and yet depends on them, closely corresponds to a conceptual effect often articulated in deconstructive analyses, namely 'a displacement that indicates an irreducible alterity'.[26] Derrida calls this 'spacing', which, he argues, consists in 'the impossibility for an identity to be closed upon itself, on the inside of its proper interiority, or on its coincidence with itself'.[27] The problem with structuralism begins with this impossibility, and the conflict between the identity and difference of structuralism

and poststructuralism can be seen to correspond to a certain temporal and spatial movement indistinguishable from spacing as such:

> spacing is a concept which also, but not exclusively, carries the mean-
> ing of a productive, positive, generative force. . . . It marks what is set
> aside from itself, what interrupts every self-identity, every punctual
> assemblage of the self, every self-homogeneity, self-interiority.[28]

If structuralism, on this analogy, has less a homogeneous identity
than a differential one, it's important to emphasize that this is not
difference in any static form, nor even just an internal difference,
its difference from itself, but a conflict of forces in a movement of
setting aside that is the product of non-identity. This paradoxical
structure describes much more effectively than any binary opposition the relation of structuralism and poststructuralism. The difference between them cannot be grasped in terms of opposites, or in
terms of any interval between objects. Both terms exist, in Samuel
Weber's words, in a state of 'irreducible dislocation' in which 'the
other inhabits the self as its condition of possibility'.[29]

Since, as Weber puts it, 'the identity of a theory is determined
by the objects it constructs', then we would expect poststructuralism to include within itself the dynamic of conflict that it isolates.
Such a dynamic, in fact, could be said to constitute the identity of
poststructuralism as such. Poststructuralism eludes definition because it cannot be defined through a certain conceptual content,
but only through its insistently deranging pressure. Poststructuralism
comprises nothing less than 'the form of which it speaks': any definition must isolate the particular logic which it enacts, whilst no
definition will be adequate while it uses the very categories and
forms which poststructuralism subverts.[30] This enforcing power of
dislocation explains why structuralism can be said to have been
always already inhabited by the tension of poststructuralism; and
why neither can be disassociated from the other. At one and the
same time they *appear to be different and to be the same thing*. It is
impossible to separate the two.

The relation between structuralism and poststructuralism can
best be understood through the operation of these ambivalent
conflictual forces. There is such a thing as poststructuralism, if
we choose to name that difference. If we consider such difference
in conventional terms, however, by asking, as Lewis does, 'whether
the auto-critical, counter-theoretical impulse . . . has developed to
the point of taking us out of the structuralist arena into distinctly
different territory' – that is, attempting to define its status according

to notions of evolution and topography, of insides and outsides, of differences between rather than within – then inevitably any significant distinction will be lost. Both structuralism and poststructuralism can articulate themselves only in a relation in which each can neither altogether incorporate nor fully detach itself from the other. Each can only define itself in contradistinction to the other, but cannot entirely separate itself from that other, continually bringing to light the traces of the other which should have remained hidden. Poststructuralism may in certain respects undo structuralism, but it cannot escape it either: each persists as the haunting difference within the other.

It turns out then that poststructuralism is indeed 'so-called', its very activity a form of impropriety (a word which, suitably enough, finds its place in OED's 'List of Spurious Words'): poststructuralism is, quite properly, an improper name – which is what, almost, everyone said about it in the first place.

Poststructuralism, culture and hybridization

And after all, what does poststructuralism consist of but an improper melange of all kinds of different discursive practices, of philosophy, psychoanalysis, criticism, semiotics, history, Marxism, anthropology, translated into a kind of illegitimate, hybrid philosophy? – which explains, perhaps, its frequent conflict with other disciplines within the institution. Whereas structuralism's great appeal was that it was a method that could be used with spectacular success by all these different disciplines, poststructuralism turned this round and juxtaposed them, jeopardizing and exceeding the limits of disciplinary boundaries. The predictable reaction to this was a widespread attempt to *exclude* poststructuralism, to put it outside the academy (on to the very streets which according to its critics poststructuralism itself excluded), and it was doubtless for this reason that resistance to poststructuralism often attempted to use institutional power rather than intellectual authority.[31]

If poststructuralism's hybridity means that it must also remain in its own way internally flawed, permanently stalked by its tragic differential error, as Adorno has shown, this situation of torn halves that don't add up need not necessarily be a cause for concern or dismissal. This impropriety may help in an understanding of the politics of poststructuralism. For poststructuralism has also enabled a new kind of ability to cross disciplinary and cultural boundaries, to make innovative and disconcertingly improper connections, that can also be called 'the political'. The question of the political when posed to theory is characteristically situated from the outside, in terms other than its own, which means that it can always be rejected on the grounds that it only offers a challenge on the basis of its having posited a second incommensurable term. In other words, 'the political' generally takes the form of a transcendent critique. What we find in poststructuralism is not an antithetical immanent critique, although at times literary accounts of 'textuality' have certainly fallen into this trap. Rather it consists of an improper discourse which poses its questions from outside as well as inside, from the outside operating within the inside, and the inside on the out. Those questions should inevitably involve the political, because they will always be ones that transgress boundary divisions, and therefore pose a challenge in the terms of the other. But they cannot simply be dismissed because they come from the other, because by definition they are never entirely other either. Poststructuralism, in other words, is about the breakdown of the very dialectic of immanence and transcendence.

Poststructuralism has always been distinguished by the heavy premium which it has placed on alterity, inverting structuralism's tendency to put theory itself into the transcendent position of scientism, authority, and mastery of theory. But in its breaking down of conventional inside–outside oppositions, it has generally been the critics of poststructuralist theory who have demanded to know its relation to, and implications for, political practice, and who have reasonably refused to be satisfied by demonstrations of the difficulty of grounding and legitimating political action in language. For a long time, the conceptual undoings and complexities characteristic of poststructuralism were held by those on the Left to involve problems for identity politics, as it was assumed that all politics had to be predicated on a form of agency that required an undivided subjectivity. More recently, it has become clear that such a structure while problematizing assumptions about political agency, in fact corresponds to certain forms of contemporary identity: it best describes the situation of all those, commonly though not necessarily accurately described as 'minorities', who find themselves simultaneously inside and outside a community or a culture. They are included but excluded, their identity not simply a question of double consciousness, of a grafting of two cultures on to each other like a well-cultivated vine or apple tree, but rather one of diaspora, of permanent spatial and temporal dislocation, of hybridized identification with two or more cultures each of which dwells within the other both as its disavowal and as its condition of possibility and of potential. Suddenly it becomes apparent that poststructuralism's abstract theorizing, apparently divorced from the social and from history, in fact catches most accurately the forms of certain contemporary political and social situations relevant to the new radical democratic movements. If politics of the Left has tended to presuppose and invoke forms of identification, the most significant political argument that has come out of poststructuralism is that identity does not have to be absolute: *it is possible to be both the same and different at once.* Another way of putting this would be to say that the fundamental basis of language in metaphor, the assertion of identity between two things that are unlike, can extend into identities and other forms of conceptualization. Its enabling conundrum has had far-reaching consequences for contemporary politics, particularly in the spheres of race, ethnicity and sexuality. It is not, of course, that Marxism itself had not perceived this possibility. Indeed the very basis of Marxist economic theory, that of exchange-value, is precisely predicated on the assumption that two unlike things can in certain respects be the same. At the moment of the exchange itself, they are indeed both equivalent, of equal value, and different (otherwise there would be no point in exchanging them in the first place). The radicalism of this analysis of the exchange process can be seen to the degree that it exists in fundamental antithesis to the traditional law of identity, whereby an object cannot be A and not-A at the same time. But while the Marxist analysis of value was predicated on the ramifications of the fact that, in exchange or when metaphorized through money, objects can indeed break this law of identity, the fact that the same violent process, of yoking unlike things together and asserting an identity between them, occurs altogether effortlessly and uncontrollably in the linguistic realm was overlooked. To recognize the effects of this constitutive structure of metaphor, and therefore of conceptualization, involves a fundamental revision of the logics of, among many other things, human and political identity. Poststructuralism could be said to be the theory of such a different logic.

This identity of sameness and difference also holds for the relation between modernism and postmodernism, and even for that between postmodernism and poststructuralism. In *White Mythologies*, I argued that postmodernism involves the deconstruction of the cultural and historical hegemony of 'the West'. Postmodernism thus implies a certain relativity, problematizing the relation of Western to non-Western cultures. Poststructuralism, by contrast, addresses this question less overtly because it is concerned with a critique of the Eurocentric premises of Western knowledge. Unlike postmodernism, it does not privilege the diasporic standpoint of the periphery in order to achieve its critique of 'the West', but rather uses the alterity of Western culture to work critically against itself. Postmodernism and poststructuralism are therefore positioned against each other as forms of transcendent and immanent critiques of their own culture. This is not to say that they are themselves individually totalized entities, which helps to explain why the productive relation to other cultures that is so marked a characteristic of postmodernist culture, is also accompanied by their ruthless economic exploitation: so the West continues the long process of commodifying them, turning the primitive into an object of aesthetic consumption, deploring the loss of its purity, while producing its modern Westernized hybrid forms. Today this process has entered a new phase in Western societies with the commodification of ethnicity.

And what of that other 'post' with which we started, the postcolonial: does it too share the disoriented hybrid structure of its companions, poststructuralism and postmodernism? If 'post' indicates a displacement of time and space, the 'post' of postcolonial also includes the extremities of the outpost, the frontier territory which determines the identity of the metropolitan imperial culture even while it is simultaneously excluded from it. The inside–outside structure of institutional thinking is thus re-enacted in its own theoretical paradigms which produce the division between home and empire, the North and South, or 'the West' and the 'Third World'. But each inhabits the other despite the conceptual partition which separates the world into an inside and an outside. With the disappearance of the Second World, the description 'Third World' is now no doubt even more of a disempowering anachronism. The current tendency to simplify the division into the gap between the North and the South fails, however, to register the ways in which the postcolonial world is not simply positioned on the outside of the West but is also turned inside out. A postcolonial culture, which has been at the very minimum twice deterritorialized and reterritorialized in the doubled movements of colonization and decolonization, will be severely riven, set against itself, in a productive, generative but difficult pattern of competing, intertwined cultures and histories. This is not only a question of the present-day consequences of the colonialism of the past. Today emigration and immigration, the effects of neo-colonial economic investment, control and exploitation, of two-week packages of transcultural colonization (tourism), mean that such countries are simultaneously set up as inside and outside the First World, that they are living the dislocation of themselves by the West every day. It remains an open question whether the postmodern hybridization of the West as it draws its peripheries into itself will ever generate a comparable transformative force.

(1986)

Notes

1 Graff, *Professing Literature*.

2 Cf. Lyotard, 'Reply to the Question: What is Postmodernism?', in *The Postmodern Condition*, 71–82; Habermas, 'Modernity: An Incomplete Project', and *The Philosophical Discourse of Modernity*.

3 Bauman, *Modernity and Ambivalence*.

4 However, concerned as it is with the relation between the name post-structuralism and contemporary attempts to conceptualize what it was, this account does not discuss recent historical assessments of post-structuralism, such as Easthope's *British Post-Structuralism Since 1968* which argues persuasively for a non-deconstructive British version.

5 Michaels and Knapp, 'Against Theory', in Mitchell, *Against Theory*, 12.

6 For example, Gasché, 'Of Aesthetic and Historical Determination', in Attridge, Bennington, and Young, *Post-Structuralism and the Question of History*, 139; Zizek, *The Sublime Object of Ideology*, 1.

7 Gasché, *ibid.*, 139.

8 For extended discussions of the question of historicity in poststructuralism see Bennington and Young, 'Introduction: Posing the Question' in *Post-Structuralism and the Question of History*, eds Attridge, Bennington and Young, 1–11; and Young, *White Mythologies*.

9 Barthes, 'The Structuralist Activity', 154.

10 Deleuze and Guattari, *A Thousand Plateaus*, 107–110.

11 Benoist, 'The End of Structuralism'; Donato, 'Structuralism: The Aftermath'; Macksey and Donato, *The Languages of Criticism and the Sciences of Man*; *The Structuralist Controversy*. Bennington cites a first appearance of the word, unexpectedly in French, from 1973 (Bennington, *Dudding*, 17). See also his discussion in 'Postal Politics', in Bhabha, *Nation and Narration*, 122–4.

12 Macksey and Donato, *The Structuralist Controversy*, 95.

13 Their focus on Deleuze and Foucault is also indicated by the way in which, when attempting to indicate at the beginning of their Preface the common denominator of French intellectuals, they resort to Deleuze's description of Foucault (x).

14 Harari, *Textual Strategies*.

15 Cf. Harari, 'Changing the Object of Criticism'.

16 Lewis, 'The Post-Structuralist Condition', 7–8, 11. Interestingly enough, Lewis's attack on Harari is the product of second thoughts, for to support his argument about poststructuralism, Harari cites Lewis's earlier remark that in poststructuralism 'Structuralist methods of analysis and modes of

critical thinking continue to be employed, but with a difference: deployed at the expense of basic concepts and presuppositions that structuralism mobilized in its formative stages' (31). So when Lewis later takes the opposite course of denying that there is any difference between structuralism and poststructuralism, he does so where he has, significantly enough, himself already introduced difference.

17 Young, 'Post-Structuralism: An Introduction', in Young, *Untying the Text*, 1–28.

18 Young, 'Post-Structuralism: The End of Theory', 4. For a discussion of this essay, see Easthope, *British Post-Structuralism*, 166–72.

19 Bennington, *Dudding*, 19.

20 Lyotard, *The Postmodern Condition*, 79.

21 This disordering of temporality in which the event disrupts the system, constitutes, it will be recalled, the basis for Derrida's essay, 'Structure, Sign, and Play in the Discourse of the Human Sciences', in Macksey and Donato, *The Structuralist Controversy*, 247–65, that was to disrupt the mimetic possibilities of structuralism.

22 For Culler's later re-assessment of his characterization of structuralism in *Structuralist Poetics* see *On Deconstruction*. It is striking that when those who came 'beyond structuralism' were subsequently assimilated into the American academy it became equally popular to denounce the emasculation of this second importation as 'American deconstruction'.

23 Culler, *On Deconstruction*, 30.

24 Lewis, 'The Post-Structuralist Condition', 6, citing Descombes, *Modern French Philosophy*, 81.

25 It is noticeable that Marxism or feminism are given no place at all in Harari's *Textual Strategies*.

26 Derrida, *Positions*, 81.

27 Derrida, *Positions*, 96.

28 Derrida, *Positions*, 107.

29 Weber, *The Legend of Freud*, 33. In his book, Weber isolates this impossible, incompatible structure as the constitutive moment of the unconscious: 'If the unconscious means anything whatsoever, it is that the relation of self and others, inner and outer, cannot be grasped as an *interval between polar opposites* but rather as an irreducible dislocation of the subject in which the other inhabits the self as its condition of possibility' (32–3). As Weber puts it when describing the relation of the ego to the id, for each 'to define itself, it must simultaneously set itself apart from what it is not' and yet remain 'ineluctably haunted by what it seeks to exclude' (33).

30 Weber, *The Legend of Freud*, 19; Derrida, 'Structure, Sign, and Play', 257.

31 The two Cambridges provide two famous examples: the MacCabe affair at Cambridge, and W. J. Bate's notorious article calling upon Deans to deny poststructuralists tenure (Bate, 'The Crisis in English Studies').

4..

The politics of 'the politics of literary theory'

> A revolution is not a dinner party, or writing an essay.
> Mao Tse-Tung

The politics of the politics of ...

'The politics of . . .': what kinds of restrictions are imposed from the outset by the coupling of 'politics' with 'theory'? Such a juxtaposition constitutes a demand for a politics: and a politics involves a supposition that something will be delivered: here, that 'theory' should be able to produce a political effect, that it should realize the sorts of ends that are expected in politics.

Could such a demand be restrictive? The yoking of 'politics' to theory assumes that politics is already known, that it is self-evident what it involves, that it is positioned outside theory, so that theory can have nothing to say about it – whereas on the contrary politics can have a lot to say about theory: that it can judge it, identify it, according to protocols that have, by implication, been thought through elsewhere, somewhere beyond theory.

Its formulation thus implies that it is posed from the outside, that the question of politics frames theory with the invocation of more powerful necessities. If the political is invoked as an outside against which theory must be judged, then it is being used in its primary meaning where 'the political' describes anything that affects the State or public affairs – something that Literature, or literary theory, or even plain theory, is not generally noted for doing. But this is how 'the political' works in practice as an objection made against theory that is not political enough.

The degree of fury attached to the question of politics and theory seems at times to be in almost direct relation to the relative political ineffectivity of literary and cultural criticism. Critics continue to entertain the fantasy that their work has the power to bring about a major political revolution – as is maintained by books with subtitles such as *Towards a Revolutionary Criticism*. The more extravagant the claim that is made, the more obvious the complete lack of relation between political utterances by literary critics and political effects becomes. The political criteria of engagement with the 'realities' of the 'world outside' that such critics bring to bear against their opponents seem often to be equally applicable to themselves. Eagleton, for instance, in his book of revolutionary criticism remarks of Derrida's apparent silence on the subject of historical materialism: 'It is not certain that Marxists should be too tolerant of this stance: in a world groaning in agony, where the very future of humankind hangs by a hair, there is something objectionably luxurious about it'.[1] Setting aside the interesting question of exactly whose hair it is from which the world hangs, would this objection not also apply to all literary criticism, revolutionary or otherwise? Can Eagleton, a literary critic, really pose as the much needed (Charles) Atlas who can save the whole world from dropping?

As Eagleton's Archimedean perspective here suggests, 'the political' often takes the form of a strategy of containment. Perhaps the current pressure for theory to deliver a politics itself constitutes a response to the reformulation by theory of the concept and operation of the political. As with the call for 'history', it can be used to reintroduce the very formulations that theory has been concerned to recast: the call for the political in itself seeks to reinstitute or reground the link between representation and reference that has been questioned by the semiotics of the past twenty years. If the representation of the literary text to the world becomes problematic, then that link can be reinvoked by the introduction of political criteria in criticism which re-establish at a stroke the supposedly lost connection with ethics, action, and 'the world'. Such a move has a moral rather than a conceptual authority, but is limiting to the extent that it side-steps rather than attempts to address the theoretical difficulties that are at stake. Meanwhile, all such inferences about politics and theory assume that politics remains unaffected by any rethinking by theory of 'the political'.

And what, beyond that, is this 'literary theory' anyway that can, as an entity, possess a politics? Is there a 'literary theory' as such? It's doubtful, but this problem will have to be untied elsewhere: let us assume for now that at the very least there can be literary theory in the sense of literary theories.

Some clichés: 1

First cliché: 'the politics of literary theory'. Even as a phrase, it is already not altogether obvious what this means. Does it signify 'the

political positions which literary theories enounce', that is the political principles of literary theories – or, if they are not articulated
as principles as such, then the political positions which can be
ascribed to them? Or does it mean 'the political effects of literary
theory', context unspecified; or 'the politics that go on within literary theory' in the sense of the political affairs of literary theory and
its political life in relation to literary criticism, Literature, and their
institutions; or finally does it mean the form or process of organization of literary theory – the science and art of its government? In
practice the phrase includes all these different implications, which,
together with the fact that the politics implied in each are not necessarily of the same kind, may account for its ubiquity and the ease
with which it can be invoked.

What the different meanings of 'the politics of theory' do all
share is that possessive 'of' – meaning that literary theory whatever
it is, has or possesses a politics, a politics that can be ascribed to
it and for which it can be called to account. This assumes that
literary theory can somehow be isolated, that its politics is intrinsic
to it and not the product of any situation that it might find itself in
or with which it might be confronted. On the other hand, as we
have seen, the phrase 'the politics of' implies that politics as such
is also somehow outside theory: the phrase itself could therefore
be said to be self-contradictory, suggesting both that politics is
essential to theory, and thus exclusively interior, and at the same
time that politics constitutes a realm outside theory which is entirely exterior to it.

In the same way, the political effects of theory apparently only
take place in a realm that is outside it, that of 'the political'. But do
political principles necessarily tie up with, or cause, analogous
political effects? Not necessarily. If, as much contemporary criticism
argues, texts do not possess an intrinsic meaning then that must
also mean that they do not possess an intrinsic politics. If meanings
can change historically, then so must their politics. Indeed, as
deconstruction has shown, there is no text so politically determined
that a clever reading cannot show how it simultaneously undermines its own strategy, thus allowing the text to be claimed for an
opposing point of view. Strictly speaking, however, such a claim
would be at variance with deconstructive practice which would
show that the text puts forward incompatible positions, but would
not claim that any one was representative of what the text 'really'
said. In practice, though, deconstructive criticism tends to argue
against the reading that has been institutionally validated.

For the same reasons it is obvious that no critical position can be intrinsically political either. Criticism, like Literature, remains uneasily poised between subversive and repressive functions. And such forms of criticism as Marxism, feminism or deconstruction are capable of being both radical and conservative according to variations within each position. Arguments that claim that they can be generically identified one way or the other in the abstract must always be essentializing. Each critical position includes those who simply use a position in order to offer a new 'approach' to the already constituted object, Literature; but each also includes those who are trying to change that object and to produce a new configuration, thus redefining the discipline, its activity, and its rationale. This means that in spite of its claims it is possible for 'the political' to bear little relation to political effect. Certain forms of Marxist or even feminist criticism would be a case in point; it has been widely argued that as long as they continue to address the constituted cultural object, Literature, then they will never achieve political effects of any consequence.

Some clichés: 2

Second cliché: 'the crisis in English Studies'. This seems to have been going on for rather a long time. It might be taken to imply that criticism has got into a state where it is in danger of running out of steam, of dying out altogether, that it is undergoing a liquidity crisis of some sort. In fact the opposite is the case: in terms of production, popularity, and the general interest that it arouses, criticism has never been so vigorous, and critics have never believed so enthusiastically in the importance of their own enterprise. The 'crisis' comes not from too little criticism, but too much, from the fact that literary theory has shifted criticism from a secondary to a primary activity, from the fact that it threatens to engulf Literature altogether.

The crisis was felt because traditional criticism appeared so defenceless. Certainly there was extraordinarily little argument at a theoretical level from theory's opponents. This is largely the result of the fact that in order to argue against the positions of the theorist, the traditional critic who, in the Leavisite manner, eschews theory would be obliged to involve herself or himself in theoretical arguments – which he or she cannot do because it is the very need for theory and theoretical arguments that is at stake. The result of this situation has been that in Britain traditional critics ceded the intellectual battle with virtually no contest, contenting themselves with 'common-sense' objections or occasional denunciations in the popular press or literary weeklies.[2]

So much for the intellectual arguments. The institutionalization of literary theory, on the other hand, poses a real threat at the level of institutional power. That struggle will no doubt continue for some time although its outcome, aided ironically by the Thatcher government programme of early retirement for older academics, is not in doubt. The 'crisis' in this sense, is really only a process of the transfer of power, a *Fall of Hyperion* of the critics, an event of indisputable historical but little theoretical interest, merely, as de Man puts it, 'a passing squall in the intellectual weather of the world'.[3] The event of real intellectual interest is the crisis that occurred for theory as a result of its institutionalization, a process which articulated the diversity of positions within the theoretical domain that were formerly raided at random and eclectically homogenized. At this point, the traditional critic's 'crisis' became the theorist's 'the politics of'.

This crisis was the result of theory's very success: while theorists were contesting the precepts of traditional forms of criticism, that in itself gave any form of theory a political purchase. Against the ruminations of *belles-lettres*, or the unquestioned assumptions of most of what goes by the name of historical criticism, even the strictest formalist could be said to be making a political intervention. Now, however, the formalist critic, safely ensconced within the institution, lost her or his former political lever. 'Theory' was no longer political *per se*. And that is one reason why literary theorists turned to ask the question: what is the politics of theory itself, that is what are the political principles of the different areas of literary theory? What are their political effects?

Though 'literary theory' may appear as a homogeneous entity to its opponents, it is not self-identical but set against itself: the real arguments are not between theory and its opponents, but between competing theoretico-political positions. The crisis consequent upon its institutional success was accompanied by an outbreak of internal conflict which took place in Britain for the most part between three forms of theory – which for the sake of argument I shall characterize as Marxism, feminism, deconstruction – that comprise a triad of differentiated positions each of which makes political claims to the exclusion of the others. Crucial differences are now marked out: after all, heresy is a more serious matter than disbelief. The absence of any serious contestation elsewhere has meant that a new fifth column enemy has had to be constructed in the mask of the old: the charge is made that certain theoretical positions merely repeat and sustain the traditional forms that they have nominally opposed and superseded.

This argument runs as follows: the success of deconstruction, the ease with which it has been accommodated, and turned into a version of New Criticism in the United States, shows that to all intents and purposes it is hardly different from its critical predecessor. Both forms of criticism, it is suggested, concur in eliminating the social and historical, and hence the political; only a politicized form of criticism can offer real resistance to the literary institution as it is constituted. The problem with this argument is that it does not account for the historical conditions in which it is made, namely, the acknowledged crisis. The contradiction here is that deconstruction, and more generally theory in the form of poststructuralism, produced a political disruption in the institution at least as great as any form of 'politicized' criticism achieved in the past; yet, paradoxically, it was then accused of being apolitical while 'politicized' criticism attempted to capitalize on the political crisis that it was itself unable to produce.

Clearly a more complicated economy is at work. For a long time Marxism exercised a virtual monopoly over the political and theoretical work done in Britain, but today this is no longer the case. The threat of current theory to the institution of Literature and to Marxism itself has meant that the call for the political has also at times become a defensive gesture to protect both. In the United States the recent rise of Marxism in the literary sphere – in direct antithesis to its political and intellectual decline in Europe – could also be accounted for by the fact that it is felt to constitute the only viable defence against the success of deconstruction: but the lack of a Marxist political tradition since its extirpation in the 1950s means that this Marxism remains a very literary one which, unlike British Marxism, has few links with the social sciences or with a political base in the public sphere. You can make almost any political claim you like: you know that there is no danger that it will ever have any political effect.

At the same time, the pressure of feminism, and more recently Black Studies, has meant that today the political cannot be ignored by anyone, and may be responsible for the white male retreat into Marxism. Marxism can compete with feminism and Black Studies in so far as it offers to return literary criticism to its traditional moral function, but can, more covertly, also act as a defence against them.[4]

If the tendency now is to highlight politics at all times, the current call for the political is not merely a trend to be applauded or deplored as it is for William Cain in his *The Crisis in Criticism*.[5] If there is a crisis in theory which erupts as a question of politics then it may be the result of the institutionalization of theory in an institution that embodies the very presuppositions at issue, producing a dissension within theory that has yet to recognize the conditions of its own operativity. The result is that the very terms of what constitutes 'the political' are now being questioned. This means that the crisis is not so much about the institutionalization of theory as about the question of what comprises the political, how the political is established, and how competing political positions are judged or reconciled in relation to one other.

Model politics

What is the politics of theory – in the sense of how are its debates conducted, its objectives fought for and won? How are the different positions legitimated? There are two dominant forms according to which debate operates in current academic practice, neither of which, however, is adequate to the demands that current literary theory places upon them.

Politics, in Aristotelian terms, consists of the science and art of government, of supervising and reconciling the varying interests within a State. This model is endorsed in one practice of literary politics, and constitutes nothing less than the founding ideology of the American academic institution. So, for instance, we find the editors of the Modern Language Association's prestigious journal *Profession* affirming in their 1984 editorial that 'since Jefferson's time, our colleges and universities have . . . reflected American principles of democracy'.[6] This might be well termed the 'liberal' position, and can be found embodied in institutional form in the Modern Language Association's annual conference. To a European what is most remarkable about such an event – even more remarkable than the vast diversity of topics of papers for which it is famous – is the almost limitless politeness accorded, at least in public, to virtually every paper, whatever it may be saying. (An extreme example of this practice occurred at a conference I attended in which someone gave as their paper a chapter out of someone else's book. Not even the author, who was sitting in the audience, said anything. Polite questions concluded the session.) A democratic society requires and encourages a diversity of 'approaches' to Literature: everyone is allowed their own point of view without challenge. This means in effect that there is no position so radical that it will not be taken up and endorsed by the institution as a valid minority view. It is therefore in a sense almost impossible to be oppositional. On the other hand, this attitude has undoubtedly worked to the advantage of the institutionalization of theory, and in general it might seem reasonable enough, the epitome of the civil tolerance that the humanities are supposed to embody and sustain in our society.

Certain presuppositions, however, are at work here and show that the freedom of conscience allowed in such a 'diversity of approaches' model is itself a position – not simply a toleration of all positions. This explains the paradox that on occasion those most committed to such humanitarian ideals turn out to be most intolerant of contemporary theory.[7] In the first place, the liberal model implies that criticism is a matter of individual sensibility, even of quasi-religious conviction necessitating a version of religious tolerance, rather than an intellectual activity that needs to be argued out in a specific fashion. In the second place, it assumes without question that in the midst of the diversity of individual sensibilities stands the common object of appreciation, Literature, the status of which is not in question. Though the canon may have to be extended or modified under pressure from minorities in order to preserve its status as the common object, the status of Literature as such is not in doubt. All 'approaches' share the aim of getting close to the object, Literature, each competing with the other in order to extract more ore – in the form of books and articles – from its seemingly limitless mine. For the 'plurality of approaches' model depends on the Shelleyan idea that Literature is like Truth itself: its veil, however often torn, simultaneously remains miraculously intact, always ready to divulge more riches to the next reader. At the same time, as one might expect, such a liberal approach masks a drive for possession and a competitiveness that provides the very energy of the whole economy: for each reader reads with a secret wish and fantasy that her or his approach will at last see the literary object as it really is, finally get to it, seize it and carry it off – that her or his reading will be so complete, so final, so irrefutable, as to render all future readers powerless and dispossessed. While the liberal model, therefore, can easily accommodate, and indeed requires, competing positions, it cannot allow any questioning of Literature itself, and this goes some way to explaining the extent to which an unquestioned privileging of the literary can be found even among many of the most 'advanced' American critics.

    In Britain, as one might expect in a less democratic social and
political system, there is far less of the ideology of pluralism. It is
no surprise to find that in Britain there is no equivalent to the
Modern Language Association; nor is there a general conference of
'the profession' which everyone attends – broadly speaking, confer-
ences divide along political and theoretical lines. The general representatives of the profession to the university administrations
and the Government are, significantly, the trades unions, who take
no responsibility for 'Literature' as such.[8] The traditional form
of criticism in Britain, however, of scholarship as a labour in the
accumulation of knowledge, is really only the reverse image of the
'diversity of approaches' extraction model: here, Literature instead
of being a mine is itself the jewel, the aim of scholarship being to
overlay it with the encrustations of marginalia, glosses, and foot-
notes. The object of this labour of historical criticism is to create
a setting for the jewel, to force the text into the position of being
available only to a single, correct interpretation. This means that
other methods of criticism must simply be wrong. At the same time,
the 'diversity of approaches' model is equally dismissed by those
who oppose this scholarly historical view and who, generally speaking, are on the Left. Politics is a matter of commitment and demands; the liberal model, therefore, is quickly dismissed: 'all these
approaches and so few arrivals'.

    Effectively, the British model comprises antagonistic groups
who are already entrenched explicitly or implicitly according to
the political divisions operating in the country at large. Here the
institutional control and deployment of power is a good deal more
obvious. In this much more politicized situation, the explicit invocation of politics is, paradoxically, often attacked on the grounds
that it involves an intolerance, an unwillingness to countenance
opposition. Analogies are then implied with the politics of totalitarian regimes with which, it is suggested, certain critics have political
sympathies. But even those who attempt to occlude the political
are not really interested in tolerating their opponents, and certainly
see little reason to allow them even representative status within
their own institutions. They are, after all, a threat to everything that
Literature is supposed to stand for – including, apparently, tolerance, with the result that such critics must be intolerant themselves, and betray the very value with which they rationalize their
own behaviour. The differences are entrenched: denunciation rather
than dialogue forms the mode of exchange between the parties.
Competing approaches are simply regarded as incompatible, and

institutional power is utilized to prevent the bearers of radical views from being academically successful or employed at all.

Unpleasant though such mutual intolerance might appear, it could be argued that there is more of a rationale to this situation than might at first appear. It could be that differences have intellectual grounds rather than merely being a matter of individual sensibility. Any argument that can be made must necessarily involve incompatibility with other arguments, just as it would in philosophy or physics. The 'variety of approaches' model implies that none of them has a justifiable intellectual rationale, that none of them can be shown to be inadequate, based on fallacious presuppositions, or simply incoherent – or, on the other hand, to be coherent and irrefutable. In this sense, it has to be acknowledged that intellectual arguments are not liberal; they cannot be mapped by analogy on to the model of a democratic system.

We might call this second model, in which arguments are marshalled and opposed on rational grounds, the 'logical' or 'rational' model. It does, necessarily, involve a form of intolerance, for those who have been convinced by one argument have also decided that alternative arguments are erroneous, fallacious, or simply ineffective or inappropriate. Such a model may not constitute a satisfactory form of politics, but this only suggests that there is no reason why intellectual argument should be conducted according to the model of political and religious tolerance. This is the beginning of the conflict between the realms of knowledge and politics.

Although the logical model is ostensibly the framework within which debate is conducted in Britain, it remains the case that the lack of liberalism towards opposing positions is as likely to be predicated upon unargued presuppositions derived from existing politico-philosophical sympathies as upon the results of rational argument. Political commitment always presents its arguments as a simulacrum of the logical model, but the feint can be distinguished by the fact that where it operates no debate actually takes place. This goes towards explaining why, as has already been noted, there has been strikingly little discussion between traditional critics and contemporary theorists in Britain. No 'Limits of Pluralism' exchange can be found in any British journal – indeed there is no British journal that even attempts to represent competing points of view. The only intellectual exchange takes place among the multifarious positions within the theoretical domain.

The idea that any intellectual debate can operate entirely within a forum where speakers operate according only to the dictates of reason rather than, at least to some extent, according to historical and social positioning, is a pure fantasy of reason itself, as Derrida's analysis of Kant's *Conflict of Faculties* illustrates.[9] This is also the substance of Wittgenstein's critique of analytical philosophy. The logical model denies the operation of context and conditions and will thus tend to be determined by them, rather as the liberal model ends up by promulgating the very intolerance to which it is nominally opposed. It is curious, therefore, that even the debates within theory, especially discussions of the politics of theory, continue to operate according to the logical model's assumption not only that there is one correct position which could be universally valid but also that it should form part of a total system of knowledge. This impulse towards a complete system is itself illogical to the extent that it is derived from fantasy: paranoic delusion, Freud suggests, is simply 'a caricature of a philosophical system' – and vice versa.[10]

Marxism offers a third model which claims to subsume both the liberal and the logical: its theory of conflict makes the tension between different positions productive while at the same time eliminating them by resolving the differences into a 'higher' form. The operation of such a Marxist model when confronted by the plurality of theoretical methods at work today has been most clearly described by Jameson:

> Marxism cannot today be defended as a mere substitute for such other methods, which would then triumphantly be consigned to the ashcan of history; the authority of such methods springs from their faithful consonance with this or that local law of a fragmented social life, this or that subsystem of a complex and mushrooming cultural superstructure. In the spirit of a more authentic dialectical tradition, Marxism is here conceived as that 'untranscendable horizon' that subsumes such apparently antagonistic or incommensurable critical operations, assigning them an undoubted validity within itself, and thus at once canceling and preserving them.[11]

At a political level, this generosity means something very specific as Jameson makes clear: the return to the dualism of class struggle, and the unity, solidarity and class consciousness of the working class. Other oppressed groups, among them women and blacks, are characterized merely as symptoms of the fragmentation of postmodernist late capitalism and must therefore be subsumed back into the collectivity of the higher form of class consciousness. The drive to totalization in a dialectical model, while certainly acknowledging the operation of differences, must always have as its ultimate aim their negation, be they regional, racial, cultural, sexual, or even economic. The refusal of the British Labour Party to allow black sections was merely a symptomatic example of the oppressiveness of such classism in practice. This means that although Marxism presents itself as a dialectical synthesis of the liberal and logical models, in its pre post-Marxist forms at any rate, it represents a more sophisticated version of the logical model.

The assumption that total systematization is both desirable and perhaps even utopically possible leads to many of the problems that occur in discussions about the politics of theory where it is assumed that theories should operate globally at all levels. But the drive for a totalization of theory, the attempt to achieve an ultimate theoretical purity in which all the questions will finally be sorted out for all time – 'you know', as Foucault puts it, 'that much-heralded theory that finally encompasses everything, that finally totalizes and reassures' – must itself be predicated upon a denial of the historical and institutional conditions under which those questions emerged. Theories are themselves historical – even if the historical is also a theory, a fact that has to be denied in the drive for a total theory, or for total compatibility between theories as if they were part of a purely synchronic system, all parts of which must fit together. Articulation between theories, it then follows, has to be absolute: either complete compatibility, or utter incompatibility.[12] Yet different theoretical positions can be shown to be compatible or incompatible depending on the questions asked and the issues under discussion. The drive to reduce positions to an essential compatibility implies that the speaker is always speaking from the same place, that he or she addresses an identical addressee, about an identical object or situation.

This poses the question of the difficulty of squaring politics with knowledge. The surprising idea is that they should both be in the same location: almost by definition, if theoretical enquiry is going to have anything to say at all it will tend to conflict with existing forms of thought, including political ones – if it doesn't, then it will merely be affirming what is already known. For its part, politics, though usually founded on ideas with some semblance of rationality, must also be guided by pragmatic considerations and the necessity for compromises; it must seek to persuade, often through fairly simplistic forms of rhetoric. This suggests that both theoretical enquiry and practical politics may often have to deviate from established political doctrine.

It is a contradiction in terms for intellectual inquiry to be contained by prior intellectual conclusions, even if they are politically validated. Thinking may on many occasions involve the abandonment of politically acceptable positions, but it must do so in order to lead to the formulation of new ones that are more effective. The risk is that such a thinker will end up by shifting to an alternative political position altogether, and this is often the accusation that is made about radical political theorists. But the ossification of political thought, formulated in different historical conditions, can be more damaging politically. A constant difficulty for socialism is that it finds it hard to recognize the difference between a betrayal of political principle and a change that is required because certain formulations of policy no longer correspond to contemporary circumstances. In spite of the frequent invocations of history, both Marxism and socialism share a constant tendency to dehistoricize their own theory. Capitalism, by contrast, is always at an advantage because, as Lyotard has pointed out, its disavowal of belief, principle, or theory in favour of pragmatic considerations means that it can always adapt immediately and ruthlessly to political needs.

To invoke 'the politics of theory', therefore, can easily be a form of repression, whereby the new is judged by the very formulations which are in the process of being rethought, and thought itself becomes a political impossibility. A recent example would be 'the question of the subject'. If Marxism led the way in the 1960s in instituting an attack on the ideology of humanism prevalent in bourgeois society, in recent years its critique of the subject and subject-centred knowledge has diminished in the face of a supposition that it is impossible to operate politically without such a notion, however bourgeois it may be. Some feminists have come to the same conclusion. Both therefore risk being reintegrated into the very ideology to which they are nominally opposed. This is the kind of moment when theory instead of retreating before the political could be called upon to reformulate it instead. Those involved in such rethinking would not be prevented from engaging in other kinds of political activity, even though it might be incommensurate in certain respects with their current intellectual work. This becomes a problem only when it is assumed that all political activities, knowledge, and forms of thought must be part of a general theoretical totality applicable to every situation for all time.

It could nevertheless be objected that this leaves unsolved the problem of the conflict between politics and knowledge to which the question of 'the politics of theory' is partly addressed. There seems to be a conflict between knowledge and the political: the one no longer seems to be available for the other but to inhibit it. Does this mean that we have to assume that the two are simply incommensurable? This would be the Lyotardian view, in which mutual incompatibility is simply recognized as a state of mutual incompatibility.[13] If Lyotard would solve the problem by abolishing the tension between them altogether by declaring them examples of the differend, by characterizing them as different language games, this dissociation is not helpful at the level of politics where the language games must play with or against each other: they may be incommensurable, but they still come into contact, are proposed as alternatives. The very possibility of incommensurability as a theoretical suggestion, however, is enough to produce Eagleton's immediate condemnation:

> Lyotard . . . has found his latest secret weapon in the ruptures, instabilities, and micro-catastrophic discontinuities of 'paralogical' science. It is to this, rather than the clapped-out narratives of classical emancipation, which we are advised to have recourse – a statement which was published in Britain just as the miners' trade union, led by revolutionary socialists, was hell-bent on bringing down Mrs Thatcher and replacing her with a workers' government.[14]

Eagleton's objection here seems a good example of the incommensurability to which he is objecting. The irony of the assertion is that Eagleton's statement was itself published just as such confrontational politics had singularly failed to bring down Mrs Thatcher, and had ended with the crushing of the miners' union. The 1984 strike, which attempted to reproduce the dualism of Marxist dialectical politics, did not bring down Mrs Thatcher; nor did it produce class solidarity, as the splitting of the miners' union during the strike indicates. What is required is a new form of politics, in which the demand for unity does not absorb all energy, produce debilitating self-inflicted wounds and end by crippling political action, in which different groups and movements can work together effectively according to the requirements of different situations through, as Laclau and Mouffe put it, 'hegemonic articulation with other struggles and demands'.[15]

What is needed is a model that can include conflict, in which incompatibility provides more than an aporia, and yet which does not require that such differences are subsumed – and dissolved – into the nostalgic notion of a collective unity. The acknowledgement of irresolvable but productive differences has in fact been proposed as a theoretical possibility in recent years. Writing of psychoanalysis and anthropology, for instance, Paul Hirst and Penny

Woolley comment: 'They are condemned for the foreseeable future
to coexist in tension. We should try to make that tension productive rather than sterile. Recognizing mutual incompatibilities and
limitations may be one route to doing so'.[16] But the problem with
the idea that mutual incompatibilities can generate a productive
tension is that, expressed as a moral prescription as it is here, it
easily reverts into the liberal model once more: we all have our own
points of view, they all add up to life's rich tapestry, etc.

Deconstruction, which includes a non-totalizing conflictual
perspective as part of its own theoretical argument, has also been
accused, by Eagleton among others, of being simply another version of the liberal model. It does not, however, merely *recognize*
mutual incompatibilities, but demonstrates how they can operate
in relation to each other in a productive economy. *Diacritics* notwithstanding, deconstruction is not a political position and cannot
even be said to offer a politics as such, but it does provide a way
of thinking through certain conceptual problems in politics and in
knowledge, including the relation of politics to knowledge. There is
no reason why it necessarily precludes identification with certain
political ambitions of either Marxism or feminism.

Deconstruction demonstrates that the liberal model works according to the necessity of inclusion, while the logical model works
through exclusion: together they repeat the general structure of
inside and outside which we have already detected in the coupling
of politics and theory. Such a coupling, therefore, far from posing
the question of 'the political', simply repeats its theoretical problem. In suggesting, as Samuel Weber puts it, that any position can
'articulate itself only in and through an ambivalent relation to
an other that it can neither fully assimilate nor totally exclude',
deconstruction argues that differential positions can be held only
through a continuing articulation with and against others.[17] It therefore offers an account of the operation of those terms of theoretical
debate for which neither liberal nor logical models can provide
adequate forms of understanding. This means that it can also sup-
ply a way of rethinking the problem of how to articulate different
political positions, such as Marxism and feminism. Attempts to relate
them usually work either by the liberal model which leaves their
relation untheorized – such as in the frequent invocation of 'gender
and class', with 'race' often thrown in for good measure, or by the
logical model which always works to a structure of incompatibility
or exclusion/inclusion so that one always ends up by subsuming
the others: class before gender or race.

Deconstruction is not itself in turn a totalizing model that subsumes all other models, because by definition it is a theory of nontotality. It offers a way of thinking through some theoretical problems of the contemporary politics of theory: in this context, the term 'poststructuralism' or, more generally, 'postmodernism', may be taken to describe the conditions of contemporary theory in which traditional models of argument through which we achieve and legitimate knowledge are acknowledged to be no longer adequate or effective. Poststructuralism is not in itself a position but a state of difficulty, a name for a conflict in which there is a dynamic but no necessary cancelling, preserving or final resolution between terms. It is impossible to get out of it simply by denying it, as even Jameson has acknowledged.[18] In short, 'the politics of theory' could well be a description necessitated by the exigencies of contemporary theory itself, with theoretical differences symptomatic of a conflict that constitutes the very mode of thinking that produces theoretical insight.

Deconstruction's own contribution concerns the proposal of new hybridized logics through which theory can operate. One aspect of the crisis in theory which erupts as a question of politics may be the result of the institutionalization of theory in an institution that embodies and presupposes the very logics in dispute, producing a dissension within theory that has yet to recognize that conflict as the condition of its own operativity. The question of the political in this sense could therefore be seen to be symptomatic of the institutionalization of theory as such, as theory itself becomes conditioned according to the apparent inside–outside dichotomies of the institution.

Inside stories

If 'the politics of theory' can be seen as a symptom of such a situation, then what about 'the crisis in English Studies'? While it was the very nebulousness of the concept of 'Literature' that facilitated a home for such a wide-ranging diversity of interests now called 'theory', theory's subsequent questioning of the boundaries of the literary domain was one of the major factors that precipitated the crisis in English Studies. But crisis as such is nothing new: any account of the discipline will show that its history amounts to little less than a successive series of them. This is hardly surprising in view of the fact that the discipline is never quite sure what constitutes its object or what its own relation to that object should be.

From this perspective, English Studies itself constitutes nothing other than a practice of crisis management.

What is less usual about the current situation, however, is that it is being made unusually explicit that the dispute is taking place over the object 'Literature' and the function of literary criticism – and that the projected revisions offer a very different alternative. When traditional critics accuse contemporary theorists of destroying Literature-as-we-know-it, in many cases they are perfectly correct. For many forms of theory the point is precisely not to produce a new 'approach' at all but to change the very activity and object of criticism. Even here, however, there are radical differences between different theoretical positions and political interests. While neither Marxists, feminists, nor deconstructionists wish to preserve Literature intact as it has been constituted to date, this does not mean that their objectives are identical. In addition, as we shall see, there are other needs for change that are at least as significant.

With these sorts of pressures, Literature might well seem in danger of dissolving altogether, as well it might, whether by apocalyptic flood as Wordsworth feared or by some other means. Its vulnerability stems from the fact that even though it is frequently suggested that Literature involves an essence of some kind, it has always tended to be defined in terms of exclusions on which, paradoxically but inevitably, it remains dependent. The excluded elements will always return to expose its precarious identity, and however much they are denied will refuse to leave it in peace. Central to this process is the attempt to mark out a literary domain unsullied by other forms of knowledge. At this point it is possible to see that Literature itself is in some sense already structurally constituted by the inside/outside opposition which the demand for politics repeats.

As recent historians of English Studies have shown, the denial of the relevance of non-literary methodologies or knowledges forms a part of the attempt to define literature as Literature, as a discipline within the institution in its own right. The denial of the extra-literary in the appreciation of Literature constitutes a professional as well as an aesthetic strategy. But the very hand that closes the door to the rest of the world at the same moment opens another to let it back in. This structure continues to determine critical activity of traditional and modern kinds while it apparently provides the grounds for the most radical differences between them; these can then be debated endlessly without fear of any recognition that each presents the same argument in reverse. Whereas Literature and

Leavisite criticism are constituted through a process of exclusion, the reverse is the case for theory, which depends upon the transfer of knowledges from other disciplines. Few theorists, however, have interrogated the problems involved when such knowledge, or methodologies, are invoked for and translated to a different problematic.[19]

Thus a traditional English criticism has always maintained that you should not 'impose' anything on a text: you should come to it with an 'open' mind, bringing no presuppositions, special interests, other knowledges or foreign disciplines to it. Reading is less a cognitive activity than an affair of feeling that operates according to I. A. Richards's stimulus–response aesthetics. Yet when a reader's sensitive sensibility has responded to the text – in an always original way – it turns out that Literature is about life, in fact about nothing other than all those things in the world that are the formal provenance of all those prohibited knowledges. The poststructuralist, by contrast, never reads a text alone, but always in the company of friends – philosophical, psychoanalytic, anthropological, linguistic, or whatever. The result of the vast array of learning that is required before the poststructuralist can begin to read or analyse a text is then the discovery that the literary text is no longer about the world, or life, or any of the formal disciplines that have been studied, but about itself and the problems of its own self-representation, a narcissistic speculation on the impossibility of knowing more than that it cannot know more than itself. In both instances, therefore, one side of the equation remains irreducibly blank: the blank simply changes sides. Its positioning constitutes the ground for furious argument, but meanwhile both parties are determined by the same structure of exclusion that constitutes the literary domain, and are therefore, in a sense, in complete agreement.

Nor are 'political' forms of theory immune from the operations of this structure. Take Marxism, for instance. Whereas there is, relatively speaking, little doubt about what Marxist politics involves at the level of the State, it is less clear how such politics can be accommodated at the level of literary theory. Marxist criticism faces a problem because by definition it has to rely upon the transfer of Marxist theory to the literary domain, adapted for application to literary texts. Any Marxist model has to be concerned with the process of reconciling the two. Generally speaking, literary Marxism depends upon innovation at the level of Marxist theory proper: produce a new theory of Marxism and it will eventually be used for a new theory of Marxist literary criticism. This structure of priority creates an imbalance in which Marxism always already has a prior knowledge: the literary text then can have little to say to Marxism except to confirm its theses. This is effectively a version of Augustinian hermeneutics in which the meaning precedes the interpretation. In so far as Marxism's political objectives remain outside the sphere of Literature and literary theory, there will always be a tendency for theorizing to accommodate itself to this end and to invoke the 'outside' sphere of Marxism proper as its ultimate context. Although this gives it an effective moral and rhetorical advantage in argument, it also makes it vulnerable to certain forms of intellectual critique which, for example, point to its dependence upon a model of reflection, a form of specularity that is only the inversion of the literary specularity that Marxists criticize in formalist criticism.

If theory, including literary theory, is seen by some feminists as unacceptably male, the problem for Marxist criticism by contrast is that it always positions Literature and literary theory as 'feminine', that is, as 'inside', as a domestic activity opposed to the real world of politics by which it should really be judged. As Lisa Jardine has argued, this could in part account for the Marxist argument that Literature should be body-built into the more macho world of Cultural Studies.[20] At first glance, feminism itself might however appear to be doing something not altogether dissimilar. At its most straightforward, that is in a feminist reading of a literary text, feminist criticism involves the transference of feminist interests and priorities to Literature. This might imply the terms of the same exclusion model according to which these interests are not regarded as already being a part of the literary. But for feminism, unlike for Marxism, the literary does not have to be attached to or invoked against the 'real' political world 'outside', whether by the reflection model or any other, for one of the most important arguments of feminism is that the notion of the political as it has been traditionally constituted is itself a patriarchal model that effectively marginalizes the domain of women according to an inside–outside, domestic/real-world polarity. For feminism, by contrast, Literature has always been one of the spaces where crucial questions, such as the social construction of subjectivity and sexuality, have been formulated and explored. This means that instead of being read off against an already constituted body of feminist theory, Literature and literary theory contribute significantly to the self-definition of feminism itself.

However, feminist theory is not entirely immune to the terms of this inside/outside critique. Forms of feminist resistance are in constant danger of being recuperated, whether by men, institutions, or both: debates within feminist theory have circled around the question of what theoretical positions genuinely resist patriarchy, and which putative forms of resistance in fact collude with it. It is difficult, in any particular area of feminist theory, to avoid someone else coming along and pointing out that though in local terms such work may seem to counter patriarchy, when looked at from a wider or more philosophical perspective, it really just operates according to its system. This is because theory, whether it be philosophy, history, psychoanalysis, or Marxism, can always be regarded as part of the system itself. If this has led some feminists to reject theory altogether, the problem with that is that it leaves it untouched, unmarked, and able to pursue its recalcitrant ways unimpaired. Yet once you try to work through theory, accusations soon follow: Marxist feminists sacrifice gender to class, psychoanalytic feminists are either implicated in Freud's phallocentrism or are deemed to have fallen into the trap of essentializing woman and therefore continuing the characterizations of patriarchy.

Each of these arguments depends upon the opening up of larger and more radical perspectives, and poses the question of which is the more political: is it the immediate, local, social, that can claim a direct political pertinence, or the larger philosophical perspective that presents itself as more radical, less collusive, capable of changing fundamentals and therefore, ultimately, more political and more effective? The answer must be that both are necessary in some form; the problem lies less with the alternative perspectives than with the need to see them as mutually exclusive choices, a structure that debates within feminism have been inclined to repeat even while feminism itself opposes the binarism of male–female hierarchies.

The 'Englishness' of English Studies

If this structure seems to echo *the politics of*'s invocation of an outside to theory's inside, it comes as no surprise that a similar paradigm occurs with the notion of 'the political' in relation to Literature. It is often suggested by humanist critics that political forms of criticism constitute an illegitimate activity because they add politics on to a Literature which otherwise operates in a space that is free from its taint. After all, is not Literature defined by its ability to rise above the particular to the universal? Any number of examples can be found of critics making such a pious claim (usually when faced with political texts). Politics, in the last analysis, is extrinsic to Literature: from this point of view even 'the politics of literary theory' would be a contradiction in terms if the phrase implies anything intrinsic to the literary. Yet recent studies of the history of English as an academic discipline have revealed the extraordinary extent to which, in Britain at least, English was a self-consciously political activity from the start, deliberately conceived, in the face of the declining influence of the national church, to produce harmony among classes, and a shared sense of national identity.[21] In this context it is clear that its constitution as English Literature was not only a reflection of the nationalism of the period but also of Literature's simultaneous function as an instrument for colonial domination: as Gauri Viswanathan has shown, before it was generally instituted in British universities, English Literature was developed for consumption in the Empire.[22] Central to these overtly political ends, as for any form of propaganda, was the concealing of any political purpose.[23] Ironically, F. R. Leavis, at one level among those most opposed to the literary establishment and the class interests that it represented, proceeded to place even greater emphasis on English Literature as the great tradition in which could be found the repository of Englishness itself. Essential to that Englishness was Leavis's implacable refusal of theory – which since Burke's critique of the French Revolution at least, has always been regarded as unpleasantly foreign.

Notwithstanding the curious way in which, as Eagleton has pointed out, 'English Literature' in the twentieth century has been largely written by Americans, Irish, Poles, and Indians, this nationalistic model of English Literature has continued to operate in the reaction to literary theory where it is often the sheer foreignness of theory that is objected to, the objectors not pausing to consider the rationale of why literary theory should operate upon the domestic basis of English Literature, or, conversely, why discussion at a theoretical level should only be relevant to one particular area of literature, defined not even by the language in which it is written but by the political and geographic boundaries of a State.[24] Conversely, the less xenophobic attitude towards Literature in the United States – where English Literature itself is foreign – has made literary theory much more readily acceptable; as Morton Zabel noted in 1951, the US has always had a history of importing its aesthetics from Europe.[25] But then, so does Britain: the only difference seems to be that it tends to disavow any knowledge of it. Virtually all forms of criticism that are practised in Britain today, including historical criticism, are derived from European sources.

It is a curious historical accident that the development of Anglo-

American philosophy had the effect of obscuring the origins of literary criticism in Romantic continental thought. The separate development of Anglo-American philosophy explains why, on the one hand, many literary critics remain so ignorant about the philosophical foundations of their own discipline, and, on the other, why deconstruction was so quickly recognized as impinging directly on many of the presuppositions of literary analysis. Its rapid take-up in the literary sphere was accompanied by a new realization of the deep affinities of literary aesthetics as they are practised by literary critics with continental philosophy. What was discovered was the startling fact that literary criticism had remained intellectually frozen, operating in a curious time-warp, cut off, by the rift between Anglo-American and continental philosophy, from the sources of its formation. An example of this phenomenon in operation would be Cleanth Brooks in *The Well Wrought Urn* (1941) still quoting Coleridge's plagiarism from Friedrich Schelling on the function of art as the reconciliation of opposites. This produces the paradox that while it is the height of critical respectability to quote Schelling via Coleridge, it is anathema to discuss the work of later writers such as Hegel, Nietzsche, or Heidegger, in the same tradition. It is no wonder that, when challenged, the literary critics of the Establishment have made so little attempt to justify their own critical practices on intellectual grounds.

That relation to European philosophy explains why it was those critics who had been brought up in its intellectual and political environment who were able to recognize such affinities and who were thus instrumental in rediscovering this lost tradition.[26] But when these theorists turned to examine it once more, one hundred and fifty years later, they had to announce, not surprisingly, that ideas had changed – as well as the fact that the idea of Literature expressing a national essence was, after Fascism, deeply problematic. This organic association of nationalism, language, and Literature, derived from the Romantics, impinges not only upon the criticism of the Right: it remains almost equally powerful on the Left.

The politics of culture

At this point we are in a position to ask how 'the politics of literary theory' relates to that other well-known phrase or saying 'the crisis in English Studies'. One refers to a general concept 'literary theory', the other a specific area: 'English Studies'. The former has a politics, the latter a crisis. How do the two clichés articulate with each other? Their dialectical product is none other than 'cultural politics'. Cultural politics represents a welcome modification of the political as an inside–outside opposition. But the concept of culture is not itself unproblematic.

In general any definition of cultural politics is concerned to distinguish between the bourgeois notion of high culture and the more radical analytic concept of culture as the whole system of social relations and artefacts. As Jonathan Dollimore and Alan Sinfield put it:

> The analytic [concept of culture] is used in the social sciences and especially anthropology: it seeks to describe the whole system of significations by which a society or a section of it understands itself and its relations with the world. Cultural materialism draws upon [this] latter, analytic sense, and therefore studies 'high' culture alongside work in popular culture, in other media and from subordinated groups.[27]

But what does this idea of culture itself enforce? Whose culture? How are its limits defined? For Dollimore and Sinfield, Cultural Materialism is identified as the study of popular culture alongside high culture, seeking to embrace both poles of the torn halves of the high/low antimony of culture through anthropology's account of culture as the analysis of the meaning of the practices through which a society is organized. Here we might draw a comparison with structuralism which contested the notion of an aesthetic always associated with a 'high culture' and initiated analyses of a much wider variety of cultural forms through the development of a common method derived from anthropology. But neither forms of analysis take on board the extent to which the object of anthropology, culture, is also itself the aesthetic product of European 'high' culture. What is also noticeable in Dollimore and Sinfield's statement is that the adoption of anthropology's systematic account of the functioning of a culture as a totality has had the effect – as it did in structuralism – of removing the critical edge ('and therefore studies "high" culture *alongside* work in popular culture . . .'), the point of leverage of a critical practice which focuses on the dialectical differential conflicts of the unequal antimonies of high and low.

In fact culture in its broad anthropological sense has been in general use for some time now, probably ever since the counter culture of the 1960s. If someone today talks about 'the culture of the BBC', he or she is unlikely to be referring to the opera and the classics. The popularization of culture as 'the culture of everyday life', however, marks the very point when the concept has itself begun to come under criticism. Martin Jay has demonstrated the degree to which both the Frankfurt School and Raymond Williams, from whose work the idea of 'cultural politics' to a large part derives, form part of a tradition which seeks solace for the disintegrative effects of individualism in the nostalgic realm of an organic culture.[28] James Clifford, among others, has pointed to the contested nature of the concept of culture in anthropology itself which relies, he argues, to a large extent on the same organic assumptions:

> For all its supposed relativism . . . the concept's model of totality, basically organic in structure, was not different from the nineteenth-century concepts it replaced. . . . Despite many subsequent redefinitions the notion's organicist assumptions have persisted. Cultural systems hold together; and they change more or less continuously, anchored primarily by language and place. Recent semiotic or symbolic models that conceive of culture as communication are also functionalist in this sense.[29]

If not altogether synchronic, the anthropological concept of culture at best offers a Burkean notion of slow organic change – an indication of just how post-Marxist an anthropologized 'cultural politics' has come to be. Clifford's conclusion is no more reassuring for a 'cultural politics' designed in opposition to supposedly apolitical theory: 'It is high time that cultural and social totalities are subjected to the kind of radical questioning that textual ensembles have undergone in recent critical practice (for example Derrida). . . . It may be true that the culture concept has served its time.'[30] Despite this intriguing suggestion that it is time for the apparently no longer dangerous concept of culture to be let out on parole, there is no question of suggesting an immediate replacement. As the case of English Studies into Cultural Studies suggests, critics should be wary of quickly appropriating another term that sounds more acceptable because it comes from another discipline. The point is that to shift Literature to culture only pushes it towards an even more unstable, and arguably, undesirable category that is itself currently being contested within its own discipline. As an academic subject, anthropology, and its object culture, incorporated in the nineteenth century the various forms of scientific racism, a disciplinary history that might cause us to pause before taking even its modern definitions of culture on trust. Is anthropology's history of complicity variously with racism and slavery, or its readiness to facilitate colonial governance, really preferable to the nationalism attached to the concept of Literature that has caused such disillusionment in

the past few years and increased the pressure to move from Literature to culture? Recall Lévi-Strauss's account:

> [Anthropology] is the outcome of a historical process which has made
> the larger part of mankind subservient to the other. During this pro-
> cess millions of innocent human beings have had their resources plun-
> dered and their institutions and beliefs destroyed, while they themselves
> were ruthlessly killed, thrown into bondage, and contaminated by dis-
> eases they were unable to resist. Anthropology is daughter to this era
> of violence.[31]

Culture has been used instrumentally for imperialism and nationalism just as much as, if not more than, literature. To have substituted one dubious disciplinary object for another may prove not to
have been such a progressive political move unless these histories
and these questions are addressed and reconceived.

As Jameson has observed, today 'some of our most cherished
and time-honoured conceptions about cultural politics may . . . find
themselves outmoded'.[32] The shift from an aesthetic to an anthropological definition of culture, society as a system, doesn't guaran-
tee the substantive change that gets the critic outside the historical
role of literary criticism. If culture has been switched from a category of art to a category of the social, from the academy's own
activities to its other, its outside, such cultural theory continues to
alternate within traditional inside–outside polarities. The move to
Literature's outside might seem to mark a loss of belief in the literary, the internal terms of the discipline itself; it would be more
revolutionary if it wasn't for the fact that this imperious expansion
into social criticism has also been a constant trope of the literary
in its most conservative tradition – that of Coleridge, Arnold, Eliot,
and Leavis. To that extent Cultural Materialism still operates within
the traditional parameters of its own abjured discipline.

The name itself, on the other hand, suggests something rather
different, that is an indication of the scaling down of the ambitions
of orthodox Marxism. 'Cultural Materialism', we could say, amounts
to a way of describing British ex-Marxists, tactfully removing the
suggestion of Marxism as such – the love that no longer dares
speak its name. This is the significance of the way in which traditional 'historical materialism' has been jettisoned in favour of the
anthropological 'Cultural Materialism' first developed by Marvin
Harris.[33] If so, this suggests that contemporary cultural theory marks
the appearance of a new consensus on the Left, a reformation of the

parameters of Marxist analysis in response to the intellectual and political challenges of the past fifteen years. To question the use of the concept of culture is not to suggest that a new concept is required to replace it, but rather to advocate its use through an articulation of those historical openings that already divide it from itself, re-emphasizing the forms of the conflictual stress that betray the signs of halves that don't add up. The point here is that whereas the history in 'historical materialism' was militantly dialectical, the anthropological concept of culture favoured by Cultural Materialism is not in itself oppositional. Culture needs to be redefined not just in the *conjunction* of high and low but through the disruptive forces that betray their antagonistic divisions.

The idea of a cultural politics was developed in the 1960s through the form of the counter culture: but it is important to recall that if the momentum of the counter culture was derived from the Civil Rights movement, its strategy of a cultural politics was derived not only from Antonio Gramsci but also from the notion of cultural revolution produced by non-European socialists, such as Frantz Fanon, Mao Tse-Tung, Lázaro Cardenas, Amilcar Cabral, as a means for resisting forms of colonial and neo-colonial political power, a product of the recognition of the inadequacy of the traditional categories invoked in the European arena to effect political change.[34] Here culture served as a means of unifying the fractured societies produced by colonialism, of producing an anti-colonial counter-hegemony. At the same time, importantly, it operated within the general political framework of revolutionary black Marxism.[35] If today's counter-cultural form of challenge is called 'cultural politics', then strategically from its position as a discourse of the academic institution – as the title of a book series, for example – it no longer makes the same kind of direct intervention. In its institutional formation and formulation, cultural politics has become the conventional norm of politics for many on the Left – an academic orthodoxy that can be safely contained within the system, despite the production of antithetical 'dominant' versus 'subversive' structures.

Its adoption in Europe has tended to be limited to an identification of cultural phenomena with established political positions. An indication of this is the way in which although, like the ill-fated attempt to turn all politics into questions of discourse, it represents an assault on the tendency to conceive of the political in terms of inside and outside, at times it has been found to repeat that very same inside–outside structure of nationalism and racism.[36] Cultural politics hegemonizes a range of different practices, discursive or otherwise, but without itself specifying their mode of political intervention, and often relying on an untheorized assumption of dissidence as subversive, or implicitly referring back to an unexamined orthodox structure of Left politics which cultural politics simultaneously disavows. At worst, there is a danger that cultural politics can become a substitute for all other forms of politics (the contemplative point of exteriority) rather than a part of them or a challenge to them: culture rather than politics. As politics and poetics become intermingled, the degree to which politics has been aestheticized becomes apparent.

If much of the cachet of cultural politics stems from its political popularity after the wars of liberation of the 1950s and 1960s (even the now despised term 'Women's Liberation' was modelled on the Liberation Fronts of anti-colonial wars), it is worth recalling that many of those struggles were – paradoxically in terms of today's critiques – framed in nationalist terms. For many on the Left today, Literature has been rejected because of the way, as has been so tirelessly shown, it was co-opted by the State for the purposes of nationalism. This hostility passes over the historical role which, as Eric Hobsbawm and others have argued, Literature, as well as philology and history, indeed the universities generally, played long before the advent of official nationalism, propagated through national institutions: they were often the most conscious and outspoken champions of nationalism (as well as racism) in the nineteenth century, and performed a significant historical role throughout Europe in its development and success.[37] In other words, with the critique of Literature's relationship to nationalism of the past ten years, we have also witnessed the critique of what must have been, politically speaking, one of the most significant and successful form of cultural politics ever: nationalism itself. The extraordinary historical success of nationalism for twentieth-century anti-colonial struggles, and its continuing power that has been demonstrated in the dismemberment of the Soviet Empire and Yugoslav Republic, highlights the extent to which, unlike many an authored 'ism', nationalism has very often also been a popular, if often vicious and genocidal, movement. Its costly victories put assumptions about the possibilities of cultural politics in perspective: how different in scale is the success of the idea of nationalism (however negatively we may consider its consequences) compared with the limited scope of today's academic micropolitics of subversion and resistance.

(1988)

Notes

1 Eagleton, *Walter Benjamin*, 140.
2 See Rawson, 'The Crisis, and How Not to Solve It', and subsequent correspondence in the *TLS* and *LRB* during the summer of 1982, and the discussion in Chapter 1.
3 de Man, 'The Resistance to Theory', 12.
4 See, for example, Jameson, *The Political Unconscious*, 86.
5 Cain, *The Crisis in Criticism*, 251.
6 'From the Editors', *Profession* (1984), iii.
7 The *locus classicus* of this position is undoubtedly Bate's 'The Crisis in English Studies'.
8 See Culler's 'Criticism and Institutions: the American University' in Attridge, Bennington and Young, *Post-Structuralism and the Question of History*, 82–98, for a comparison between British and American universities; for an analysis of the structure of the British literary institution in the 1980s see Young, 'Une tradition en crise'. Since this chapter was written, the Committee for University English (CUE) has emerged as an effective pressure group for English as an academic subject.
9 Derrida, 'Mochlos ou le conflit des facultés'.
10 'It might be maintained that a case of hysteria is a caricature of a work of art, that an obsessional neurosis is a caricature of a religion and that a paranoic delusion is a caricature of a philosophical system': Freud, *Totem and Taboo*, 130.
11 Jameson, *The Political Unconscious*, 10.
12 Examples of such attempts would include Ryan's *Marxism and Deconstruction*; Vogel, *Marxism and the Oppression of Women*; or, on the side of incompatibility, Barrett, *Women's Oppression Today*; Weir and Wilson, 'The British Women's Movement'.
13 Lyotard, *The Differend*.
14 Eagleton, 'Marxism, Structuralism, and Poststructuralism', 8.
15 Laclau and Mouffe, *Hegemony and Socialist Strategy*, 86.
16 Hirst and Woolley, *Social Attributes and Human Relations*, 160.
17 Weber, *The Legend of Freud*, 33. Cf. also the argument of his *Institution and Interpretation*.
18 Jameson, 'The Politics of Theory', 63.
19 This question has been raised in different ways by Derrida, Eagleton, Gasché, and Macherey; it was also the topic that the Johns Hopkins Symposium of 1966, eventually published as *The Structuralist Controversy*, intended to, but in fact did not, address.
20 Jardine, '"Girl Talk" (for Boys on the Left)', in Young, *Sexual Difference*, 208–17.
21 Palmer, *The Rise of English Studies*; Baldick, *The Social Mission of English Criticism*.
22 Press, *The Teaching of English Overseas*; Viswanathan, *Masks of Conquest*.
23 See Foulkes, *Literature as Propaganda*.
24 Eagleton, *Exiles and Emigrés*, 9.
25 Zabel, *Literary Opinions in America*, 889.

26 See in particular Hartman, *Criticism in the Wilderness*.

27 Dollimore and Sinfield, 'Foreword: Cultural Materialism', in Cairns and Richards, *Writing Ireland*, vii.

28 Jay, *Marxism and Totality*, 69.

29 Clifford, *The Predicament of Culture*, 273.

30 Clifford, *The Predicament of Culture*, 274. Cf. Abu-Lughod, 'Writing Against Culture', in Fox, *Recapturing Anthropology*, 137–62.

31 Lévi-Strauss, *Structural Anthropology*, vol. 2. 54–5.

32 Jameson, *Postmodernism*, 48.

33 Harris, *Cultural Materialism*.

34 See Dirlik, 'Culturalism as Hegemonic Ideology and Liberating Practice'; as Colin Prescod puts it, 'interest in culture is almost certainly derived from twentieth-century Asian, Central and South American, and African, class-based socialist movements which threw up the idea of cultural revolution', review of Gilroy, '*There Ain't No Black in the Union Jack*', 98. Cultural politics was first developed for the anti-colonial struggle in Ireland; predictably, the extent of its role has recently been questioned by Foster, *Paddy and Mr Punch*, 262–80.

35 Robinson, *Black Marxism*.

36 Gilroy, '*There Ain't No Black in the Union Jack*', 50–1.

37 Anderson, *Imagined Communities*, 69. See also Bhabha, *Nation and Narration*; Hobsbawm, *Nations and Nationalism*.

Badlands.....................................

Psychoanalysis on the brink

....

5 ....

The dangerous liaisons of psychoanalysis

> In psychoanalysis nothing is true except the
> exaggerations.
>
> Theodor Adorno

Psychoanalysis: a theory of the practice of torn halves – not only in society at large but also within the cultures of institutions. Like literature and criticism, to which it is so uneasily affiliated, the danger for psychoanalysis comes from the fact that it refuses to respect its own limits, and continually threatens to overflow its boundaries, to migrate and to mix, to metamorphosize itself into different disciplines, to move from sameness into difference. Literary theory, Marxism, and feminism are particularly vulnerable to its vampiric proclivities; the consequence is always that the transferential method, the introduction of psychoanalysis into other forms of thought as other, transforms them. The effect of the use of psychoanalysis in these disciplines has been to produce a certain theoretical and political radicalization which contrasts markedly to the more pessimistic or repressive nature of the account psychoanalysis gives of literature, culture, gender, and race. Psychoanalysis therefore provides an example within contemporary theory of the New Historicist argument about 'subversion' and 'containment': what it shows is that the two currents do not necessarily occur within the same historical practice, as well as the lack of fixity of political identity. Unlike history, which inclines towards a narrative with an ending, psychoanalysis acts out its tensions in a state of permanent, hybridized dislocation. Society's relation to psychoanalysis remains fundamentally uneasy, and this is never likely to change because psychoanalysis, as Karl Krauss pointed out, is itself the disease for which it purports to be the cure.

If the culture of institutions is determined by conflict, if it lives out the incompatibility between subversion and containment, its inside and its outside, then this goes some way to accounting for

the current influence of psychoanalysis – not as a body of knowledge but as a theoretical method. Psychoanalysis is the discipline
whose method can apparently always be transferred to others and
used by them. This is because it has itself no content – notoriously,
no empirical substance that can be proved from outside itself; it is
rather a theory of the necessity but incompatibility of the inside
and outside, of mind and world. To this extent, psychoanalysis enacts
a theory of the institution: the polar division on which cultural
theory, like psychoanalysis, is based and on whose tension it thrives
reproduces the institution's own inside–outside structure. At the
same time, the preoccupation of psychoanalysis with narcissism
and speculation impersonates the way in which institutional theory,
like psychoanalysis, works as a mirror of itself. In doing so it enables a re-assessment of the political claims that are made for the
antithetical forces and power structures articulated in contemporary cultural analysis, which amount less to subversion than to dislocation. The point about subversion and containment is that it
operates via a dissonance – it never simultaneously functions as
the one and the other within the same cultural practice. Psychoanalysis offers a method in which the analysis seems to repeat the
object of analysis, but progresses via a certain disjunction within
that specularity and thus transforms itself into a heuristic device,
through a structure of supplementation and hence, transformation.

Oedipal trouble

Psychoanalysis, which could be described as a theory of unhappy
relationships, has itself a long history of unhappy relationships. In
the first place there is the history of the tense relations between
psychoanalysts themselves, the psychoanalytic politics that have
been charted by Paul Roazen, Sherry Turkle, and others.[1] In the
second place, psychoanalysis has a history of relationships with
other disciplines; but while it has always exercised a fascination for
other forms of thought in the human sciences, liaisons have tended
to be short and not always sweet. You could say that psychoanalysis, though now at a grand old age, still finds it hard to settle down.
I want to look at three of the alliances of psychoanalysis: those with
literary criticism, with feminism, and with Marxism. For even if it
hasn't yet settled down, psychoanalysis has since 1970 undergone
a sort of sea-change and entered into a new kind of affiliation that
has almost reversed its former identity: that is, with politics.

Until relatively recently, psychoanalysis was generally regarded as the very antithesis to the political, and both Marxism and feminism, with a few notable exceptions, were generally hostile towards it. Marx's pronouncement about the relation of materiality to consciousness has always weighed heavily against any association between psychoanalysis and Marxism, or indeed sociology generally. An instance of this attitude can be found in Emile Durkheim's famous remark: 'Whenever a social phenomenon is directly explained by a psychological phenomenon, we may be sure that the explanation is false'.[2] In literary criticism, by contrast, it was the very lack of politics, the concentration on the cosy pleasures of subjectivity without having to be bothered by all those social and historical factors that provided the main attraction of psychoanalysis as a way of reading literature.

But in the 1970s and 1980s, although the psychoanalytic establishment in Britain at least remained much the same as ever, the use of psychoanalysis as a theory changed dramatically. It was employed in a whole range of specifically political literary and cultural theories, particularly feminism, Marxism, and even postcolonialism. Indeed the politicization of psychoanalysis, in direct contradiction with its former identity, meant that you were no longer able to discuss it at all without, say, raising questions of gender and sexuality. This meant that a 'pure' psychoanalytic literary criticism was no longer possible.

But what's the status of psychoanalysis in these theories? How did this change come about and why? In what ways did psychoanalysis get politicized? Perhaps it's easier to begin by asking when it came about, and here looking at the history of psychoanalytic criticism, of feminism, and of Marxism, it is obvious that the shift came with Lacan. Lacan's rereading of Freud effectively changed the whole terrain of the use of psychoanalysis in contemporary cultural theory.

Lacan changed psychoanalysis because he shifted it from a seemingly self-referential body of technical knowledge into a metaphorics of language. Less charitably, you could say that Lacan produced the most effective repression of sex of all, by turning it into a sign system and denying its ontological status in favour of that of language.[3] The transformation of sex into language, and therefore by implication of language into sex, was an exciting prospect for academia. Translating the configurations of sexuality into linguistic ones, Lacan showed how the structures of sexuality could be remapped on to a conceptual rather than familial narrative: thus the Oedipus complex, for instance, is transliterated into the story of the subject's accession into language and law. The metamorphosis of psychoanalysis into linguistics meant that it was in effect translated into a metalanguage, and became a form of semiotics. That then allowed psychoanalysis to be correlated with, or plotted on to, any other form of social knowledge or behaviour through the analytic method known as structuralism. Since structuralism was a method of investigation that used the model of language for the analysis of a whole range of cultural forms and disciplines in the human sciences, the use of the linguistic model within psychoanalytic theory meant that for the first time psychoanalysis could be grafted on to other kinds of analysis, and even become a model for them. Anywhere that structuralism had gone, psychoanalysis could follow, and generally did.

At the same time, such a translation also opened up psychoanalysis itself, no longer protected within its own discrete discourse, and made it possible to bring other forms of knowledge to bear upon it. It exposed psychoanalysis in a new way to the pressures of the social and the political. Lacan's structuralism enabled the articulation of psychoanalysis, a theory of subjectivity, with theories of culture and the social, such as Marxism or feminism. They met in language and ideology, and in Coward and Ellis.[4] Psychoanalysis appeared as the marriage broker between them. It was indeed a marriage of convenience, so seductive because suddenly it seemed as if Marxism and feminism could acquire a theory of the subject, and psychoanalysis a theory of the social.

Although the opening up of psychoanalysis to the pressure of the social and the political was all to the good, the problem was that psychoanalysis was already a theory of the articulation of the individual and society, and already offered an account of their relations. If desire, for instance, is the desire of the other, it means that desire is a social phenomenon. When forms of social analysis try to link themselves with psychoanalysis, they tend to forget the fact that psychoanalysis is already a theory of the relations of the psyche to the social, and the theory is that they are unable to link up. That is the reason for the existence of desire. The result is that those marriages between forms of social explanation and psychoanalysis, far from being able to exploit psychoanalytic theory, end up repeating the narrative that it theorizes.

Let me illustrate this by returning to the story of Oedipus – which I want to suggest already comprises an allegory of the rise and fall of structuralism, and of the problem of the articulation of the individual subject and society, and thus, of the articulation of psychoanalysis with politics.

During the course of the play, Oedipus goes through a double process of interpretation. He begins by considering that the truth of things corresponds to the way in which he sees the world. His own interpretation of the experience of his life shows him to be entirely innocent – he has done nothing wrong and has avoided fulfilling the dreadful prophecies. But then Tiresias accuses him, as René Girard puts it, of being 'a man who, at all times, is what he thinks he is not, and is not what he thinks he is'.[5]

All the play then consists of, in a way, is a divorce: a process of massive reinterpretation by Oedipus of his own life in which he has to separate his own experience from what emerges as the real social truth about it – that is, that he has killed his father and married his mother. The play shows that far from constituting his own meaning he has been caught as a bearer of a larger impersonal process utterly indifferent to, and unrelated to, his own initial suppositions and account of his experience. Oedipus undergoes the rather painful discovery that, in Lévi-Strauss's words, 'to reach reality we must first repudiate experience' – or that there is a gap between being and meaning, between what the life-text says and what it means.[6] What has happened to Oedipus is that his subjective view of his story has been replaced by an objective, or social one. He has to learn to live in the discourse or locus of the other. From being the subject of his interpretation, and of his curse, he discovers that he is their object.

When Oedipus finally abandons his own account of things in favour of that of others, he is effectively decentred from the usual position of the human subject as a single, determinate being, as an agent who is the source of his or her own actions, responsibilities, experience, and self-identity. 'My words', Oedipus comments, 'are uttered as a stranger to the act.' The paradox of his story is that he becomes a stranger to his own tale, and to himself.

This reversal illustrates the polarity within the possibilities for any form of interpretation which means that the result of your interpretation will depend on the position from which you started. There are basically two positions from which you can start any interpretation, or indeed any philosophy in general, and that is, as Coleridge puts it, the I AM or the IT IS – in effect, Kant or Spinoza. It all depends on the position from which you are doing the interpreting. Now interpretation, especially literary interpretation, has tended to emphasize the I AM, that is the perspective of the individual on

society and the world, rather than the IT IS, that is that of the individual from the perspective of the social, and certainly psychoanalysis has seemed to do the same.

But if there is one shift that is common to many recent but
different forms of theory it is that this has been reversed, that is,
that the individual is considered from the perspective of the social
rather than the social from the perspective of the individual. Structuralism, for instance, constitutes a method of analysis which regards the meaning or significance of any individual element not in
terms of any intrinsic identity that it may possess in isolation but
in terms of its relation to the system of which it forms a part. It
represents a shift from seeing experience from the perspective of
the first person to that of the third, or, a shift from the philosophical starting point of the I AM to the IT IS.

Oedipus Rex, then, could be said to constitute an allegory of the
shift from the I AM to the IT IS, or the story of what happens with
structuralism – or indeed any form of thought that characterizes
individual entities in terms of external or collective identities (such
as class), singularities in terms of universals, immanence in terms
of transcendence. The play is an attempt to think experience in
other terms than those centred on the consciousness of the individual subject – to think of experience in the manner of the late as
well as the early Oedipus. This suggests that in addition to the
spontaneous account of the individual human subject and her or
his view of things, there is another account of that individual from
the perspective of the society of which he or she forms a part. In
the traditional literary critical terms that Freud uses, the play is,
as he puts it 'a tragedy of destiny' in which the individual learns to
submit to divine will.[7]

Experience can thus be interpreted from the perspectives both
of the first and the third persons, and, as Oedipus discovered, these
two accounts often exist in an incompatible tension with each other.
The play, in Freud's words, shows that 'the attempt to harmonize
divine omnipotence with human responsibility must naturally fail'.[8]
The living through of this incompatibility is the subject of psychoanalysis. In Freud's account, everyone has to learn to live in the third
person; we manage this affront by repressing it so that it becomes
unconscious, an act of secretion most memorably suggested by the
constant motif of archaeology, the ruins of a city that the forces of
repression bury, like Pompeii, in the psyche. Psychoanalysis is not
the narrative of this subjugation; the story it tells is rather the
continuing effects of the tension that its structure produces, of the

incompatibility of the individual and the social. What Lacan did was to show that psychoanalysis is about nothing other than the story of Oedipus – which was always what Freud had said in the first place. But Lacan said it again in a different way, emphasizing that it is about the conflict of the fact that we experience in the first and third persons simultaneously: to use his terminology, our psyche is made up of an incommensurable antagonism between the Imaginary and the Symbolic, neither of which can claim a total fit with the Real.

Both Marxism and feminism, in incorporating psychoanalysis, have tried to use it as a way of incorporating the individual with the social, or subjectivity with society. When Marxism and feminism attempt to marry the two together, it inevitably exacerbates conjugal strife. In appropriating a theory of subjectivity they then find themselves acting out the incompatibility between the psychic and the social. The lesson of psychoanalysis is rather that these have to be lived as two incompatible entities, that both are misfits for the real, and that is why we have an unconscious. We are all, in our different ways, the scarred children of interminable proceedings for divorce.

Psychoanalysis does not just offer a theory: it also makes therapeutic claims that it can help us deal with this divorce trauma. In this respect its difference from deconstruction becomes clear, in so far as the latter, like Adorno's cultural criticism, never tries to reconcile the torn halves. It is only in emphasizing this incommensurability that psychoanalysis has the capacity to become a critical instrument. At the same time, psychoanalysis is a theory and (institutional) practice of dissension which acts out the conflicts produced as an effect of the torn halves. This means that it is not just descriptive or analytical but is itself performative, an acting out of dislocation that can never be comfortably put together with any other body of theoretical knowledge.

Psychoanalytic criticism

If Marxism and feminism have both a history of unsuccessful relationships with psychoanalysis, the same could be said for literary criticism. Psychoanalytic literary criticism itself has not generally been considered as a political literary theory. Indeed, it seems to encapsulate everything that Marxists and feminists object to: a dwelling on subjectivity (whether of author, reader, or character), with no reference to social or historical determination. Psychoanalytic criticism began with Freud himself, but in spite of continued attempts to develop it as an autonomous critical form, it has always remained, as Peter Brooks has remarked, something of an embarrassment to the academic literary establishment.[9] But those awkward days for academia are over, because psychoanalytic criticism, as an autonomous critical method, no longer exists. You just can't be 'a psychoanalytic critic' any more.[10]

This was the inadvertent effect of the 'return to Freud'. In 1977 Shoshana Felman announced the arrival of a new, Lacanianized form of psychoanalytic criticism in her introduction to the influential Yale French Studies *Literature and Psychoanalysis: The Question of Reading: Otherwise* (1977).[11] Declaring that the relation between literature and psychoanalysis had to be 'reinvented', Felman called attention to a problem in the very concept of a 'psychoanalytic criticism': it implies bringing a body of knowledge, psychoanalysis, to bear on a body of unselfconscious experience, literature, the first of which can then be invoked in order to interpret and understand the second. Effectively, this means that one discourse is being read in terms of another, a work of translation. This is essentially the structure of a whole range of criticisms, such as Marxist criticism, which bring in an external body of knowledge in order to interpret or understand a text. Felman questioned the usefulness of this enterprise; for one thing it does not produce anything that the body of knowledge did not know in the first place, and secondly, it consigns to oblivion the specificity of the object being examined, namely that it is constituted in language. 'The psychoanalytical reading of literary texts', she commented, 'precisely misrecognizes (overlooks, leaves out) their literary specificity' (6). The renewed emphasis that Lacan placed upon the function of language in psychoanalysis led to the realization that literature contained more of the knowledge of psychoanalysis than had been allowed for. After all, psychoanalysis must have a special interest for the literary critic because of all the disciplines, only psychoanalysis appeals to the evidence of literature for its verification. Moreover, psychoanalysis uses literature not only to test its hypotheses but also in order to construct its conceptual framework and even to name itself – the Oedipus complex, narcissism, masochism, sadism etc. (Perhaps it would be unwise to speculate too much on what this list suggests about literature.) If psychoanalytic knowledge is grounded *in* literature, then it cannot provide a grounding *for* literature.

Felman therefore spoke of there no longer being an *application* of psychoanalysis to literature, but of it being a question of mutual *implication*, or interimplication. Literature and psychoanalysis are enfolded within each other, traversed by each other, simultaneously both outside and inside each other. This seemed to auger well, and the volume brought a real sense of a new phase in which psycho-analytic criticism would no longer be concerned with self-affirming, reductive readings of literary texts as symptoms or case histories of their authors. But today, some years later, it is clear that what was not realized at that juncture was that Felman's redefinition implied the end of a psychoanalytic criticism as such.

The problem was that, as the title of the volume – *Literature and Psychoanalysis* suggests – as soon as you reject the notion of psy-choanalysis as a masterful body of knowledge being applied to lit-erature, then the notion of a 'psychoanalytic criticism' as such must be rejected also, for it precisely indicates the use of psychoanalysis as a perspective that is being brought to bear upon literature, in the same way as with Marxist or structuralist criticism. Ironically, then, Felman's re-invention of the relationship between literature and psychoanalysis had the effect of ending it.

Or rather, reversing it. If the Lacanian reading of Freud was to read Freud with an awareness of the patterns of repetition and repression at work in the text, it was not long before critics realized that Freud's writings offered an exceptionally rich text for literary analysis. For many, it was far more interesting to read the texts of Freud in this way than to read literary texts via Freud; this coin-cided with the appearance of a new way of reading, itself heavily influenced by Lacanian psychoanalysis and deconstruction, which no longer sought to discover or impose a meaning on a text but to tease out its repressions, self-contradictions, logical and non-logical arguments, figurative contaminations, and the like. Instead of a new psychoanalytic criticism, what developed was a 'literary' reading of psychoanalysis.

So, the 'new psychoanalytic criticism' never really materialized but became something else. There was one last reason for this, and that was because subjectivity itself became a matter for intense political debate, and therefore any use of psychoanalysis could not but raise political concerns. In particular the Lacanian rereading of Freud emphasized the question of sexuality and of gender, and was itself increasingly challenged on these grounds. The idea of writing a psychoanalytic criticism without engaging with these issues be-came unthinkable. The function of psychoanalysis in criticism and cultural theory therefore changed radically. Instead of being au-tonomous and apolitical, it was used instrumentally for specific political ends. For feminism and even Marxism, the analysis of the forms of subjectivity was no longer a refuge, but a way of understanding, and changing, dominant ideological formations.

Paradoxically, when literary criticism decided that it could not be grounded on psychoanalysis because in some sense psychoanalysis was itself based on literature, when it stopped considering psychoanalysis as a science and realized that Freud's texts were a form of literature, that was the moment when feminism and Marxism began to relent in their hostility towards it. At the very time when psychoanalytic criticism became untenable, versions of psychoanalytic feminism and Marxism appeared. But if it is no longer a ground for criticism, can psychoanalysis be a ground for anything else?

Marxism

The basis of Marxism's traditional objections to psychoanalysis are summed up in Max Horkheimer's story about the beggar who one night dreamt that he was a millionaire. As he awoke, he had the good fortune to meet a psychoanalyst and so he told him his dream. The psychoanalyst explained that the millionaire was a symbol for his father. 'Curious', remarked the beggar, not entirely convinced.[12]

This story illustrates quite neatly the way in which the real problem in the relations between Marxism and psychoanalysis is that they both provide mutually exclusive causal explanations, that is, economics and class versus sexuality and the unconscious. And in spite of what might seem like a possible rapprochement when Marx begins *Capital* with a section on fetishism, or Freud writes an essay with the suggestive title of 'The Economic Problem of Masochism', the explanations of economics and sexuality tend to stay resolutely separate. Marxism, as a global explanation, is duty-bound to subsume another competing global explanation: its relations with psychoanalysis therefore resemble a contest between two imperial powers that alternates between uneasy alliance and the outbreak of actual hostilities and war.

The common, and plausible, Marxist accusation has always been that psychoanalysis is a refuge of bourgeois individualism and its philosophy of consciousness. This is certainly the position that can be found in the thirties in a writer like Christopher St John Sprigg – better known by his less aristocratic nom-de-plume, Christopher Caudwell – who states categorically in *Illusion and Reality* that:

Psycho-analysts are idealist in their approach to the practical problems of living, and in no way take up an attitude different from that of
the great class religions. For if man's subjective feelings of misery,
unease and unhappiness, are not due to outer material causes but to
Sin (as the religions put it) or Complexes (as the analyst puts it), then
man's misery, unhappiness and unease can be cured by casting out
sin, by self-control, by salvation, by abreaction.[13]

The surroundings and obstacles in social relations are the real causes
of human misery, Caudwell contends, and only material change can
eliminate it. For Lukács, psychoanalysis was itself a symptom of the
ideology of capitalism: in his essay 'The Ideology of Modernism'
Lukács berated modernism for its morbid subjectivism, for portray-
ing 'man as a solitary being, incapable of meaningful relationships',
a comment which might apply equally well to psychoanalysis itself.[14] The pathological, according to Lukács, is the surest refuge of
modernist writers, and 'it is the ideological complement of their
historical position'. He continues:

> This obsession with the pathological is not only to be found in litera-
> ture. Freudian psychoanalysis is its most obvious expression. The treat-
> ment of the subject is only superficially different from that in modern
> literature. As everybody knows, Freud's starting point was 'everyday
> life'. In order to explain 'slips' and day-dreams, however, he had to
> have recourse to psychopathology. . . . Freud believed he had found
> the key to the understanding of the normal personality in the psychol-
> ogy of the abnormal. . . . It is only when we compare Freud's psychol-
> ogy with that of Pavlov, who takes the Hippocratic view that mental
> abnormality is a deviation from a norm, that we see it in its true light.[15]

Lukács's claim that 'as everybody knows, Freud's starting point was
"everyday life", slips of the tongue and daydreams', suggests that
his own reading of Freud was somewhat limited, though it has to
be said that a similar idea seems to form the basis of Sebastiano
Timpanaro's critique.[16] But such detailed knowledge was not in itself necessary, since he was at this point simply following party
doctrine in rejecting Freud in favour of Pavlov. Curiously enough, in
spite of the general hostility to psychoanalysis that one encounters
so frequently in Marxist criticism of the older variety, it is quite
difficult to find sustained Marxist critiques of psychoanalysis, presumably because writers such as Lukács felt that it was appropriate
to leave such work to 'proper' psychiatrists.

But there is another reason, I would suggest, and that is that in
spite of a general hostility it is quite obvious that psychoanalysis
has exercised a continual fascination for Marxism: its relation to it

has taken the form of an interminable oscillation between attraction and repulsion. In the early days in the Soviet Union psychoanalysis seems to have been perfectly acceptable, or was at least the subject of intense debate. One of the few sustained Marxist critiques, Voloshinov's *Freudianism: A Critical Essay*, published in 1927, the same year as Pavlov's *Conditioned Reflexes*, contained a long chapter 'devoted to a refutation of arguments by four Soviet scientists in favour of incorporating at least certain aspects of psychoanalysis into Marxism' – a chapter which is, symptomatically, omitted in the English translation.[17] Ironically, it was the visit to the Soviet Union two years later by the Marxist psychoanalyst Wilhelm Reich that was partly responsible for the clampdown on psychoanalysis, after Reich claimed that unless there was a sexual revolution too Communism would degenerate into a bureaucratic state.[18] Perhaps he was right.

Reich is only one of what Jameson has called 'the experience of a whole series of abortive Freudo-Marxisms'.[19] Marxism's continual fascination with psychoanalysis is sometimes explained because it offers the theory of subjectivity which Marxism lacks. This is the way in which the fusion of existentialism with Marxism has been justified.[20] The philosophy of Jean-Paul Sartre, particularly his concept of mediation, did offer a way of integrating a theory of subjectivity or consciousness with a theory of the social; however, this was effectively achieved at the expense of psychoanalysis, specifically the theory of the unconscious. It was only at the moment that his commitment to Marxism began to wane that Sartre turned to psychoanalysis.

The basic problem with the project of trying to combine psychoanalysis with Marxism is that, as Laclau has pointed out, the whole idea of adding a theory of subjectivity to Marxism is misconceived since Marxism is constituted in the first place by a negation of subjectivity.[21] If psychoanalysis offers a theory of the (mis)integration of the psychic with the social from the perspective of subjectivity, the problem with classical Marxism is that in its desire to be a science, it rejects all forms of subjectivity, including its own, and does not question the stability of the interpretive position. As Althusser put it: 'The author, insofar as he writes the lines of a discourse which claims to be scientific, is completely absent as a "subject" from "his" scientific discourse.'[22] The way in which this could be modified would not be by appropriating a theory of subjectivity, but by displacing and reinscribing the subjectivity of the interpreter, the desire of the subject, within the analysis – in psychoanalytic terms, through the transference. At this point the method of such a Marxism might indeed begin to resemble that of psychoanalysis; after all, as Kristeva has pointed out, the two already have a certain affinity in so far as their hermeneutics are both designed to produce forms of action, namely revolution and cure.

It was, however, through the anti-humanist description of subjectivity that the most recent major rapprochement of Marxism and psychoanalysis took place in the work of Althusser and Lacan. For the first time since Herbert Marcuse, Althusser brought psychoanalysis into the mainstream of Marxist theory. He declared not only that psychoanalysis was a science, comparable to Marxism itself, but went on to claim that psychoanalytic theory was implicitly based on historical materialism because it took the form of an analysis of 'the familial ideology'.[23] This is striking considering that it is the apparent dependence of psychoanalysis on 'the familial ideology' that often constitutes the grounds for Marxism's rejection of psychoanalysis.

Althusser's integration of the two was somewhat precariously achieved through his reformulation of the concept of ideology. One long-standing ground of dispute between Marxism and psychoanalysis had been the conflict over their conceptions of histories. Althusser's description of ideology as being eternal in the same way as the Freudian unconscious – that is, that they have no history – provided a new basis for the pact between them. Althusser's definition of ideology through Lacan's concept of the imaginary, his stress on the representational structure of ideology, and his description of the interpellated subject in terms of Freud's account of the stages of sexuality, meant that psychoanalysis effectively became the mode through which to understand the place of the subject in ideology. This was in spite of the fact that the theory of ideology was supposed to provide an account of the reproduction of class relations.

But it is rather the question of gender that becomes increasingly more overdetermined in Althusser's account. Take his example of being hailed through a closed door:

> We all have friends who, when they knock on our door and we ask, through the door, the question 'Who's there?', answer (since 'it's obvious') 'It's me'. And we recognize that 'it is him', or 'her'. We open the door, and 'it's true, it really was she who was there'.[24]

It's difficult not to believe that Althusser is here reversing Lacan's famous example of the girl and boy in the train drawing up alongside

the two doors labelled 'Ladies' and 'Gentlemen'. Althusser insists
on the question of gender difference in the construction of individuals as subjects, and returns to it several times. But after his most
extended discussion, in relation to the unborn child, the Father's
name, and Freud's stages of sexuality, he ends, as so often when he
gets to a more adventurous idea, by saying 'But let us leave this
point . . . on one side' (165). It is a question to which he does not
return. Nevertheless, although Althusser leaves us in no doubt that
the formation of subjects in ideology is a process to be discussed
in relation to the class struggle, it remains the case that he can't
stop himself from bringing in the question of gender too.

The place of the subject was left so empty in Althusser's account that it needed further definition. The problem for Althusser,
or rather Althusserianism, however, was that if it borrowed a theory
of subjectivity from Freud for its account of ideology, that account
placed a primacy on gender rather than on class. And that, indeed,
was what did happen to his account of ideology when it was subsequently developed. What went wrong for the theory of the subject was that although Althusser's theory of interpellation seemed
to offer a place for sexuality, the old difficulty of the primacy of
class or gender refused to go away. The predicament, as always,
was that as long as Marxism held on the primacy of class it always
had to subsume other categories such as those of gender, race etc.
– a position graphically evident in Jameson's now notorious remark
in *The Political Unconscious* when he spoke of: 'The reaffirmation of
the existence of marginalized or oppositional cultures in our own
time, and the reaudition of the oppositional voices of black or ethnic cultures, women's and gay literature, "naive" or marginalized
folk art, and the like . . .'. And then added: 'Only an ultimate rewrit-
ing of these utterances in terms of their essentially polemic and
subversive strategies restores them to their proper place in the
dialogical system of the social classes'.[25] The problem for Marxism
in its engagement with any contemporary form of politics of
marginalized groups is that in classical Marxist theory a politics
based on identification with a group of any sort, that is 'local' alle-
giances such as cultural community, gender, or race, must be tran-
scended as a necessary prelude to the higher realm of class
consciousness. Except in Gramsci, identification with any community, gender, or race, actually inhibits the development of class
consciousness. Here Marxism differs markedly from feminism which
can offer an account of a general theory of marginality. At the same
time it is striking that when Marxism does use psychoanalysis, it

always sticks to the patriarchal versions. The question is whether Marxism can continue such neglect or whether the force of other forms of politics, notably feminism, will make this impossible.

Althusser's theory of ideology did produce some extremely important work, notably in the area of visual representation, particularly film and related forms of cultural analysis. In literary criticism, the story is not quite as happy, largely because psychoanalysis was used with a good deal less precision. Althusser's disciple, Pierre Macherey, attempted to produce an Althusserian theory of literary criticism, but failed to develop a theory of the interpellation of the subject by a literary text, beyond his important analysis of the function of literature within the educational Ideological State Apparatus.[26] In as much as Macherey did attempt an examination of the representational form of ideology, he proposed an analogy between the literary text and that of a dream, and in *Criticism and Ideology* Eagleton demonstrated how far this could be extended.[27] But the literary text as dream was already the oldest trick in the psychoanalytic critical book. Macherey's version remained nothing more than an updated analogy, still dependent on a theory of reflection, and merely provoked a seemingly endless hunt for gaps in literary texts which could be arbitrarily identified as their unconscious moment of ideological conflict. But this hardly needed the weight of Althusser and Freud: after all, it is not surprising if the bourgeois novel leaves out any fundamental analysis of the exploitative economic relations from which its own social class is derived.

The only other concerted effort to use Althusser's theory of ideology in Marxist literary criticism has been that of Jameson, first in an article in *Yale French Studies*, and then in his book *The Political Unconscious*. This latter is an extremely interesting work the complexity of which I have analysed elsewhere. There is, however, one basic problem in its use of psychoanalysis that is of relevance. Jameson, correctly in my view, criticizes certain Marxist theorists in terms of their continued reliance on categories of the individual subject: even 'the notion of "class consciousness", as it is central in a certain Marxist tradition, rests on an unrigorous and figurative assimilation of the consciousness of the individual subject to the dynamic of groups' (294). Althusser's influential description of history as a 'process without a subject' is precisely designed to counter this tendency to be found not only in Lukács, but in the Frankfurt School.

Nevertheless, Jameson himself tends to slide towards the use of Lacan's account of the psyche as an analogical model for the

State as a whole. For instance, he defines Althusser's ideology as 'a representational structure which allows the individual subject to conceive or imagine his or her lived relationship to transpersonal realities such as the social structure or the collective logic of History' (30). Here, implicitly in Althusser's version, the Imaginary ideological representations of the individual become the psyche, the social structure becomes the Symbolic, and the collective logic of History, the Real. This schema then becomes a descriptive model for society itself. Similarly, though he criticizes what he considers to be the perfunctory introduction of a Freudian scheme into a discussion of cultural or political history in the work of Adorno and Horkheimer, and the use of psychological categories for the description of social categories in Christopher Lasch's *The Culture of Narcissism*, Jameson's own use of Lacan's account of schizophrenia to describe the fragmented subject of the 'new cultural norm' of postmodernism quickly becomes a description of the 'randomly heterogeneous', the 'fragmentary and the aleatory' structure of society itself.[28]

In spite of the problems, Althusser's intervention has meant that psychoanalysis has been allowed a more credible place within Marxist theory. But in effect this has meant a tendency to revert to an older Marxist–psychoanalytic tradition, that of the State-as-psyche repression theories of mass society of the Frankfurt School. Here it becomes apparent that Adorno's torn halves that don't add up come close to the incompatible realms of the conscious and the unconscious. The use of the model of the psyche for the State can be a problematic if it is used as an untheorized transference.

The use of the psyche for the social is simply a contemporary version of the time-worn metaphor of the State as a body, familiar from Thomas Hobbes, Menenius's speech in *Coriolanus*, repeated throughout the sixteenth and seventeenth centuries, and represented most notably by Burke in his long reflections on the constitution of the body politic. To the degree that the mutual solidarity of the parts of the body, generally presented as an organism, was useful for Burke's vision of one nation, the image of the body was not an appropriate metaphor for Marxism in so far as Marx's argument was always that capitalism is less of a community (a homogeneous body) than a system of mutual antagonisms (the body at war, in 'crisis'). Freud's account of the psyche as a system of conflictual forces seems to offer itself as a perfect metaphor for the class antagonisms of the social. From a Marxist perspective, these psychic torn halves will themselves be the effect of their social *dopplegängen*: the danger of describing the social as if it were the psyche is that the social becomes the double of the psyche, not vice versa.[29] The psychoanalytic model, it must be recalled, is precisely about the incommensurability of the psyche's relation to the social: it therefore makes little sense to apply that model to society as such. If psychoanalysis is about the tension between psyche and social, and if society is like a psyche, then what's 'the social' for the society?

The missing paternal realm of the social when the psychoanalytic model of the psyche is translated into a model of the State is doubtless why the latter tends towards paranoid descriptions of global capitalism, the culture industry etc., which offer no possibilities of resistance, and in which nothing seems possible to be done beyond a nostalgia for the unfragmented totality of the lost bourgeois subject. This adaptation seems to inherit something of the pessimism of the late Freud evident in its use by the Frankfurt School. The general conservative tendency of images of the State as a body makes it clearer why the image of the State as a psyche tends to take on the same political colour.

Althusser's work, then, facilitated the (re)introduction of psychoanalysis, but since Althusser there has been no fundamental reassessment of Marxism's relation to psychoanalysis. Marxism has always tended to restrict its use of psychoanalysis to the occasional importation of one or two concepts in order to construct a model; it has never allowed it to affect the substance of its own theory, and there have doubtless been good reasons why it hasn't, for in its own terms it is duty-bound to subsume it. Psychoanalysis always remains marginal to it, and Marxism has rarely attempted to rethink the Cartesian inside/outside dichotomy on which this division is based and which psychoanalysis is concerned to bridge. The question that follows, however, is whether psychoanalysis does indeed seek to overcome the division between inside and outside, or whether it seeks to heal the effects of the outside on the psyche, by interpreting and accounting for the effects of the social and the political according to the operation of psychological economies. In Marxist terms, what psychoanalysis is doing here is attempting to heal the wounds of capitalism itself, the effects of its irrevocable splitting between the public and private realms, between the economico-political domain and that of the unconscious, between civilization and libidinal sexuality. But if so, it must equally be the case that Marxism, in denying the subjective realm, also finds itself determined by capitalism's division between public and private. As

Jameson has argued, theories of 'desire' such as those of Kristeva or Deleuze, and one should add Marcuse here, which regard the force of desire as strong enough to fracture the ideological hold of capitalist society, can be powerfully countered by the argument – which can also be found in Deleuze, and no doubt accounts for the magnitude of the theoretical shift between the two volumes of the *Anti-Oedipus* – that desire itself constitutes the dynamic that empowers and drives the economy of consumer capitalism.[30] Meanwhile few forms of Marxism, apart again from Deleuze and Guattari's *Anti-Oedipus*, have attempted to project any monistic alternative to the experience of the division between public and private. Deleuze and Guattari's reworking of that dualism shows that such a move must also include a rethinking of the exclusive claims of the forms of rational logic on which orthodox Marxism is predicated. The corollary of this is that when Marxism reworks its relation to psychoanalysis, as in the work of Deleuze and Guattari, Laclau and Mouffe or Slavoj Zizek, it seems to have little alternative to finding that it has ended up in the ignominious position of being 'post-Marxist' – or as Adorno put it, that it has thrown the baby out with the bathwater.

Feminism

Feminism, in its modern phase, began in an aggressively anti-psychoanalytic mode, with Freud regarded as one of the worst of patriarchs by de Beauvoir (1949), Betty Friedan (1963), Eva Figes (1970), Kate Millett (1970), and Germaine Greer (1971). As late as 1975, Miriam Kramnick, the editor of the Penguin edition of Mary Wollstonecraft's *A Vindication of the Rights of Woman*, wrote in her Introduction that:

> The twentieth century has also seen the popularization of a formidable anti-feminist ideology – Freudianism. Once again women are put back into the home, their natural sphere; this time, however, not because of innate mental inferiority, but because of another kind of biological necessity. Freud's dictum that 'anatomy is destiny' has encouraged his popularisers to preach that women find satisfactory fulfilment only in motherhood. More worldly ambitions signal a woman's failure to be reconciled with her own body.[31]

As corroboration of her argument, Kramnick cites a book published in 1947 by two (male) psychoanalysts, Lundberg and Farnham, called *Modern Woman: The Lost Sex*, in which they suggest that 'feminism is a deep illness' and trace its symptoms back to 'a single fateful book' – the *Vindication of the Rights of Woman*. Marxist feminism, too, has often taken up the same position with regard to psycho-analysis, adding complicity in the oppression of women to the more habitual objections of Marxism. So Lilian S. Robinson, in a refine-ment of Lukács's comment, argues in *Sex, Class and Culture* that Freud's 'ideas are simultaneously a product or symptom of a cul-tural evil and a force to justify and perpetuate it'.[32]

But then came French Freud, Lacan, anti-biologism, and anti-essentialism, which changed the politics of psychoanalysis. The rehabilitation of Freud succeeded by shifting the emphasis towards psychoanalysis as an analytic rather than a therapeutic activity: in Britain, for example, Juliet Mitchell in *Psychoanalysis and Feminism* suggested that psychoanalysis was not 'a recommendation for a patriarchal society but an analysis of one' (xv), and could therefore be of central importance both in the analysis of the construction of gender under patriarchal ideology and in ending that ideology and the oppression of women.[33] In particular she stressed, as she was to do again in her introduction to *Feminine Sexuality*, that Freud had opposed the Jones/Horney position of an essential femininity, and that his position was being reformulated, restressed and re-worked in the writings of Lacan.[34] The disputes between Lacan and feminist analysts such as Irigarary were, initially, played down.

Marxism is a constant point of reference in Mitchell's book (she was herself at that time on the editorial board of *New Left Review*) and in introducing the name of Lacan she allied the enterprise of feminism with that of the contemporary Marxism of Althusser. Althusser's theory of ideology which used Lacanian psychoanalysis in its account of the interpellation of the subject in ideology, was obviously open to the reinscription of a gendered subjectivity. Mitchell pointedly ends her book by setting feminism alongside Marxism: 'as the end of "eternal" class conflict is visible within the contradictions of capitalism, so too, it would seem, is the swan-song of the "immortal" nature of patriarchal culture to be heard'.[35] This happy coupling of Marxism's eye with psychoanalytic femi-nism's ear was not to last.

Psychoanalysis did not turn out to be an effective marriage broker between Marxism and feminism. Alliances between the two have tended to be predicated upon the exclusion of psychoanaly-sis. In *Women's Oppression Today* (1980), for example, Michèle Barrett admits the problem of Marxism's neglect of feminism, and adds that 'it is certainly true that many aspects of sexual relations are simply irreducible to questions of class'.[36] But Barrett remains 'unconvinced'

by Mitchell's attempt to recover Freud for 'a materialist feminist
theory of gender and sexuality', arguing that she 'offers an unduly
charitable reading of his position' and that her interpretation 'involves some stretching of what Freud actually said' (56–8). She then
adds two further reservations about the compatibility of psychoanalysis with a Marxist feminism: the first is its universalism, the
second is its implication that women's oppression is exclusively
ideological in character rather than an effect of the material structures of women's oppression under capitalism (production, family,
the State).

There are three objections to psychoanalysis here. The problem with the first two is that they apply equally well to Marxism
itself. If Freud has to be 'stretched' to draw out a critique of patriarchy from his work, Marx has to be distorted out of all recognition.
With the notable exception of Engels, Marxism has a long history of
marginalizing and occluding women. If a Marxist feminism such as
Barrett proposes can modify that historical form of Marxism, it is
hard to see why the same should not be allowed of psychoanalysis.

In the second place, the universalism of psychoanalysis, emphasizing 'the mythic, "law"-like agencies at work in psychosexual
development' and adaptable in this form to any cultural variation,
may be universal, but is hardly more universal than Marxism's reading of all history according to the ubiquitous operation of the dialectic, with all human history, as Jameson tells us, sharing 'the
unity of a single great collective story . . . a single vast unfinished
plot'.[37] The advantage of the universalism of psychoanalysis could
be that, as Jacqueline Rose argues, it may be able to offer an account of the historical unspecificity of the oppression of women
which may indeed take different specific historical forms but which
is by no means exclusive to capitalism.[38] However, detaching the
oppression of women from the material contexts in which that oppression takes place seems an unpromising project.

Barrett's third objection is perfectly valid in its own terms, and
represents the essential argument between Marxism and psychoanalysis: thus her emphasis on an autonomy of the ideological form
of oppression at the expense of specific material structures in effect
reproduces the founding opposition between psychic and social
structures that represents the competing claims of psychoanalysis
and Marxism with which we began.

The relation of psychoanalysis to Marxist feminism remains a
problem. The difficulty always comes with balancing the competing
antithetical claims of the two: on the one hand, psychoanalysis

involves a theory of the construction of gendered subjectivity, offering analysis that can expose this process working in a whole range
of cultural and social forms, in short the sphere of ideology, that
space in which material effects are given representations and worked
on at the level of fantasy. But on the other hand, such understanding does not in itself include analyses of historical and institutional
factors or offer prescriptions for material change. In this sense,
psychoanalytic feminism could be said to have settled down into
the same polarities as Marxist criticism, that is ideology critique
versus prescriptions and material accounts of how to effect change.

Even if the feminist emphasis on the psychic as a social construction begins to break up this distinction, presenting gendered
subjectivity as one effect simultaneous with other forms of social
and cultural subject positioning, the argument still continues to be
governed by the unresolved tension between the psychic and the
social. As Cora Kaplan puts it:

> While socialist feminists have been deeply concerned with the social
> construction of femininity and sexual difference, they have been un-
> easy about integrating social and political determinations with an analy-
> sis of the psychic ordering of gender ... semiotic or psychoanalytic
> perspectives have yet to be integrated with social, economic and po-
> litical analysis.[39]

The problem seems to be that the polarization of psychic and social explanations is still seen as an antithetical subjective and objective dualism that needs to be synthesized. But the reason that
they have not yet been synthesized may well be because they are
incompatible: here I would return to my argument that psychoanalysis is itself a theory of the incompatibility of the psychic and
the social. This suggests that a different kind of thinking and different kind of logic would be necessary to think them both together at
the same time. The problem would then be to what extent such
thinking would still be Marxist, or even feminist.

Some feminists have made the claim that 'because psychoanalysis has assured the link between psychosexuality and the sociohistorical realm, psychoanalysis is now linked to major political
and cultural questions'.[40] Marxist feminists, however, such as Angela
Weir and Elizabeth Wilson point to the continuing 'absence of a
theory of the relationship between them' and suggest that psychoanalysis itself needs to be grounded in a materialist theory of ideology.[41] It is not quite so easy for feminism to reject psychoanalysis
on the classic Marxist grounds of preoccupation with subjectivity,

and the personal – although Weir and Wilson still manage to do this, even to the extent of repeating Lukács's argument about psychoanalysis and modernism. But subjectivity is less easily dismissed because the political intervention of feminism has been precisely to redefine or reclaim this ground as a valid political space. If some Marxism has tried to turn the State into a psyche, then feminism has much more effectively shown that the psyche and the body are a form of the State.

One of the forms of the oppression of women is that the personal, the domestic, sexuality, the family, are denied political, or even 'serious' status of any kind. So what feminism has done is to politicize psychoanalysis, not by adding the 'real' world of the social to it, but by showing the extent to which its own 'domestic' space is already political. Thus politics enters a new realm which was always highly political but the political nature of which had previously had been repressed. But to what extent has sexual politics been registered in Marxist theory, as they say, 'proper'?

Has the rejection of psychoanalysis helped Marxist feminism to shift Marxism itself? Here the answer varies. While cultural theorists such as Eagleton have modified their work considerably in response to feminism, many historians and political scientists have refused to do so. Take as an example Perry Anderson, one of the most influential of British Marxists: in his overview of contemporary theory, *In the Tracks of Historical Materialism*, he confidently rejects Lacanian psychoanalysis in the space of a couple of pages. Does this lead him to consider women's oppression from a more materialist perspective? Anderson comes to a consideration of feminism only in a postscript at the end of his book. While acknowledging the challenge of feminism to the traditional scope of the discourse of Marxism, and even the extent to which 'precarious recourse to less scientific bodies of thought like psychoanalysis' have 'in part' (88) made good that omission, he ends by commenting on what he calls

> the paradoxes of the relationship between socialism and feminism. For if the structures of sexual domination stretch back longer, and go deeper, culturally than those of class exploitation, they also typically generate less collective resistance, politically. The division between the sexes is a fact of nature: it cannot be abolished, as can the division between classes, a fact of history.[42]

So much for the impact of feminism on what Cora Kaplan calls 'macho mustachioed Marxism' (147).

Unlike Marxism, there is no problem for feminism in what Anderson calls the 'precarious recourse' to a psychoanalysis that is as much grounded on literature as it is 'scientific'. Literature is not as peripheral to feminism as it is to Marxism, for it is literature in particular that has been the place for feminism's self-construction of its own identity. Literature, particularly fiction, has been the historically permitted locus for women, constructed by them and written for them, as Virginia Woolf suggests when Orlando becomes a woman in the eighteenth century. Its 'marginalized' place, has constituted, for the past two hundred years especially, one of the few social spaces available to women. In the same way, while for Marxism psychoanalysis has always been a worry at the margins, for feminism psychoanalysis has always been crucial – and the different forms of feminism divide up according to their attitudes towards it. Psychoanalysis has been central to its redefinitions and its own explorations and self-identity.

Psychoanalysis has also been at the forefront of debates about the problems for feminism in the use of theory at all, and here the pressure of the political on psychoanalysis has had important effects. While for a long time psychoanalysis was brought to bear upon cultural phenomena as a form of explanation, with feminism this relation has been reversed: in France the pressure of feminism has led to a series of powerful rewritings of psychoanalysis outside the patriarchal mode – it is not just a question of the influence of psychoanalysis on feminism. In Britain and the United States, where there has been something of a tendency to defend Freud and Lacan at all cost, this process has begun only relatively recently. The reworking of psychoanalytic theory has not yet gone far enough: the Oedipal story offers only a restricted number of contained places and positions of subjectivity. The future of psychoanalysis must lie in the demonstration of the ways in which, as Jeffrey Weeks has argued, 'there are class sexualities (and different gender sexualities) not a single uniform sexuality'.[43]

This is rather different from French feminism, in which, as Jane Gallop has pointed out, in writers such as Irigaray, Hélène Cixous, and Kristeva, 'we have seen a way of thinking that appears to be at once feminist and psychoanalytic, and also highly literary'.[44] Here the literary has been one of the main ways through which Freud has been rewritten. Conversely, one of the problems with thinking about feminist literary theory is that the psychoanalytic forms of it have succeeded in breaking out of such academic categories altogether. This could be compared to Derrida's work, and indeed one of the problems of writing about feminism and psychoanalysis, particularly in France, is that its relation to deconstruction makes matters complex. Derrida was amongst those producing the earliest critiques of Lacan's phallocentrism, and he has made one of the most sustained and influential attempts to write against patriarchal discourse. The problem for Derridean feminism, however, is that as soon as it moves thus far into deconstruction, it becomes merely one part of a more general project, and falls into the same problem as with Marxist feminism of its being subsumed in a 'larger' cause.

Much French feminism has often been misread in terms of the following argument: the problem with the use of psychoanalysis for feminism is that it either leads to essentialism, which many women reject, or if it doesn't, and the feminine is proposed as a purely relational category, then it means that 'woman' has no absolute identity as such and risks being subsumed by other related forms of politics. The choice is thus portrayed as one of essentialism versus postfeminism. It is only more recently been acknowledged that the point about the deconstructive feminism of Cixous, Irigaray, *et al.*, is that it avoids this by holding essentialism and relationalism together simultaneously – in other words, preserving the theory of psychoanalysis of the unresolvable relation of the psychic to the social.

By contrast, for Kristeva, as for Lacan, to define woman is to essentialize her: 'woman' as such does not exist. So, in Toril Moi's words, Kristeva characterizes the feminine as: 'marginality, subversion, and dissidence. In so far as women are defined as marginal by patriarchy, their struggle can be theorized in the same way as any other struggle against a centralized power structure'. In her account of Kristeva, Moi emphasizes that Kristeva does not so much have a theory of femininity as one of positionality, concluding that 'if "femininity" has any definition at all in Kristevan terms, it is simply . . . as "that which is marginalized by the patriarchal symbolic order"'.[45] This means that, whether it likes it or not, this form of feminism becomes a theory of the marginal, and its theory can be appropriated for use by any other marginalized group. Feminist criticism is already distinguished by the way in which it has marked out a space for its own, marginalized groups, particularly lesbian and black women. But if feminism has become a theory of the marginal itself, this means that its theory becomes available for appropriation by any other marginalized group – not just, say, by gay men or any other minority, but even, for Kristeva, by a category such as the avant-garde. The question, therefore, is whether feminism wants to provide a theory that goes beyond itself, and overflow its borders only to lose itself.

Although this may explain some of the male interest in feminist theory, it has to be said the threatened appropriation of feminist theory by marginalized men never really occurred. Take colonial discourse analysis, for example, where the use of individual psychoanalytic concepts has concentrated on the fetishistic: metonyms that can easily be substituted for others from somewhere else within psychoanalytic theory or even from elsewhere. While certain structures of sexuality are provocatively mapped on to those of race, critics have pointed out how gender itself can be often eliminated in favour of an undifferentiated 'colonial subject'. And once again, the psychoanalysis that is used is generally the patriarchal version, never that of, say, Irigaray. A larger problem is the question, first raised by Fanon, of whether the use of psychoanalysis in the colonial context, as for example in the work of Octave Mannoni, is not simply another version of colonial discourse and less of a therapeutic practice than an oppressive colonial exercise of power. There is still much work to be done on the question of the relation of psychoanalysis to colonialism. However, as Fanon recognized, psychoanalysis, for all its drawbacks, can offer a way of theorizing and charting – but not for 'curing' – the antagonistic, pathological effects of the colonizer's social reality that has been imposed on the psyche of the colonized. With colonialism, after all, the incompatibility of psychic and social takes on the status of material fact. The question remains, as Ania Loomba has emphasized, of how psychoanalytic theory can accommodate cultural difference.[46]

Identity and the politics of difference

I want to end by returning once more to the story of Oedipus. There is a more directly political dimension to the story of Oedipus, and this is the story of the continuing rejection of psychoanalysis by some forms of Marxism and feminism. Oedipus, after all, is the King. In his first identity, in which he has avoided the curse, and solved the riddle of the Sphinx, he produces effective political power. The story, from one perspective, is about his loss of this power, about the moment when, having been a king, he wanders out into the wilderness in total abjection. So much for the decentred subject. If Oedipus's process of self-discovery is analogous to the unfoldings of psychoanalysis as Freud claimed, then it also suggests that that procedure will produce a loss of political and personal authority.

This problem has been lived out in the uses that Marxism and feminism have made of psychoanalysis: the long century of the bourgeois individual subject, from 1789 to 1917, does after all have several strikingly successful revolutionary actions to its credit; its theory of the subject also forms the basis of Marxist theory in which the working class assumes class-consciousness to become the subject of history. Deconstruct that identity, it is said, and you deconstruct the agent of history and of politics. Some have therefore responded with calls to bring back the subject on the grounds of political necessity. So Weir and Wilson, for instance, write that: 'The concept of the "fractured self" . . . questions the very possibility of a coherent identity, and this process of the deconstruction of the self could also be seen to question the very possibility of women uniting politically around their existence as "women"'.[47] And the same problem is articulated even in those more sympathetic to psychoanalysis, such as Toril Moi. Who can afford, politically, to go through Oedipus's process of self-understanding – and self-blinding? Hence vocal cries to bring back the bourgeois individualist subject. It seems odd that it should be within Marxism above all that there has been the most cogent movement to retrieve the bourgeois subject: not so much in its early neo-classical guise of the fractured self divided between the morality of the home and the market-place and only centred by being anchored to property, but rather the subject in its identity as an individual will, the defining characteristic originally foregrounded in liberal thought in order to compensate for the loss of self-determination brought about by the mechanical and impersonal processes of industrial capitalism.

This question of identity seems to remain one of the main problems in the relation of psychoanalysis to the political. But it raises as many difficulties as it offers to solve. In the first place, it requires a kind of imperialism of identity which means that we are only allowed one, and that our politics has to have a single meaning. The result of this is illustrated by Weir and Wilson's assertion that black women must dissolve the question of race into the more important question of class: 'We believe that a theoretical basis, if not for unity at least for a much needed political co-operation among different groups of women, can be most accurately and concretely developed in the context of class analysis'.[48] But this demand for a single identity 'beyond race' does assume that we can choose to have a single coherent, unproblematized identity as a matter of will. The argument for the necessity of the unified subject for politics also relies on a fairly crude theory of intentionality, whereby you need a totally unified subject to be able to have any form of will or agency; and that in turn must assume a univocal theory of language. It also assumes that politics is an entirely intentional activity, free from the ruses of history. The point about psychoanalysis is that it questions all that.

This has not been the only way in which identity has been formulated in recent years. The rise of critical positions based on minoritarian politics sets up more complex parameters. Postcolonial and black identities are frequently defined in terms of the effect of the experience of living simultaneously among different cultures through shifting subject positions. In this respect, contemporary forms of cultural identity instead of aspiring to a single class identity have rather emphasized what Stuart Hall has called 'living identity through difference . . . recognizing that all of us are composed of multiple social identities'.[49] Hall has argued that the representative postmodern experience occurs when the marginal identity has become the centre, which itself emphasizes how all identities are historically constructed and potentially unstable.[50] He describes these in terms of what he calls 'the dialogue of identities between subjectivity and culture', and here we can see that what is distinctive about such forms of displaced, nomadic identity is that they are able to articulate in a positive way the hybridized realms and incommensurable torn halves which are conventionally negotiated in psychoanalysis. Such identities are not entirely unstable either: certain moments of (no doubt, in the final analysis, fictional) closure take place – whether at the level of the self, the community, or forms of political action. Politics here speaks not only the powerless language of dispersal, but also the positive language of 'contingent closures of articulation'. Through this means, it is still possible to act, even if such action is not based on the stable identifications of classic Marxist theory. And identity through differences still allows the possibility of articulation, and of hegemonic alliance.

A clear example of such unity-in-difference can be found in certain strategic coalitions in gay and lesbian politics. While gay and lesbian theorists have increasingly defined their own political identities in terms of their sexuality, sexuality itself has been more and more understood in terms of a circulation through different, mobile and reversible subject positions. It has been argued that today's identity politics are simply a reassertion of bourgeois identity as the experience of subjectivity, going directly against Marxism's crucial move towards objective class identifications, a shift back from the IT IS to the I AM. But one of the strengths of today's identity politics, on the other hand, is that it succeeds in defining the I AM in terms of the IT IS: reorienting criticism towards a subjective perspective, but a subjective perspective that has been socially defined and which provides a point of access to a wide social structure. In that sense, today's identity politics is focused explicitly on the same sexual, social, and political incompatibilities that were once considered to require the therapies of psychoanalysis. The torn halves of the psyche will never add up any more than those of capitalism itself – but they can provide the basis for new forms of politics, and new articulations of hybridized identity.

(1990)

Notes

1 Roazen, *Freud and His Followers*; Turkle, *Psychoanalytic Politics*; Roustang, *Dire Mastery*.

2 Cited by Jameson, 'Imaginary and Symbolic in Lacan: Marxism, Psychoanalytic Criticism and the Problem of the Subject', in Felman, *Literature and Psychoanalysis*, 339.

3 Cf. Gallop, *Reading Lacan*, 141; Anderson, *In the Tracks of Historical Materialism*, 45. Jameson (*Postmodernism*, 239) questions the assumption that because all language is about language, then language itself has an ontological primacy.

4 Coward and Ellis, *Language and Materialism*.

5 Girard, 'Tiresias and the Critic', in *The Structuralist Controversy*, eds Macksey and Donato, 17.

6 Lévi-Strauss, *Tristes Tropiques*.

7 Freud, *The Interpretation of Dreams*, 364–5.

8 *Ibid.*, 366.

9 Brooks, 'The Idea of a Psychoanalytic Criticism', 334.

10 For a fuller version of this argument, see my 'Psychoanalytic Criticism: Has It Got Beyond a Joke?'

11 Felman, 'To Open the Question', in Felman, *Literature and Psychoanalysis*, 5–10. Further references will be cited in the text.

12 Cited in Jacoby, *Social Amnesia*, 73.

13 Caudwell, *Illusion and Reality*, 188–9; see also *Studies in a Dying Culture*. The forms of psychoanalytical literary criticism available at that date seem to encapsulate everything that Caudwell suggests. Either psychoanalytic criticism pursued the question of the relation of a text to authorial neurosis (or something even nastier) with a single-minded obsession with the mind of the creating subject, at the expense of all other factors, or it reduced a literary text to a crude interpretive schema which transformed all representations into phallic or other monsters.

14 Lukács, 'The Ideology of Modernism', in *The Meaning of Contemporary Realism*, 24.

15 Lukács, 'The Ideology of Modernism', 30. Pavlov's psychology went on to produce some interestingly incompatible intellectual soul mates: on the

one hand it was accepted by Brecht, who was always scathing about psycho-analysis and compared it to astrology (*Letter to an American*) as does Derrida. On the other hand, it also provided the basis for the aesthetic theories of I. A. Richards – and thus for Anglo-American New Criticism, a kind of criti-cism that Marxist criticism has always considered to be anathema.

16 Timpanaro, *The Freudian Slip*. For Lukács psychoanalysis was itself a symp-tom of the ideology of capitalism, although he seemed to give it a more general relevance when, late in life, he confessed that 'I must say that I am perhaps not a very contemporary man. I can say that I have never felt frustration or any kind of complex in my life. I know what they mean, of course, from the literature of the twentieth century, and from having read Freud. But I have not experienced them myself'.

17 Voloshinov, *Freudianism: A Marxist Critique*, 4.

18 Roazen, *Freud and His Followers*, 493.

19 Jameson, 'Imaginary and Symbolic in Lacan', 385. Wolfenstein's *Psychoanalytic-Marxism*, which represents the most comprehensive attempt to date to synthesize psychoanalysis and Marxism, was published after this chapter was written.

20 Poster, *Existential Marxism in Postwar France*.

21 Laclau, 'Psychoanalysis and Marxism', 330.

22 Althusser, *Lenin and Philosophy*, 160.

23 *Ibid.*, 177.

24 *Ibid.*, 161.

25 Jameson, *The Political Unconscious*, 86. Further references will be cited in the text.

26 Macherey, *A Theory of Literary Production*.

27 Eagleton, *Criticism and Ideology*, 90–2.

28 Jameson, *Postmodernism*, 25.

29 Cf. Jameson's discussion of homology in *The Political Unconscious*, 43.

30 Jameson, *Postmodernism*, 202.

31 'Introduction', in Wollstonecraft, *A Vindication of the Rights of Woman*, 70.

32 Robinson, *Sex, Class and Culture*, 115.

33 Mitchell, *Psychoanalysis and Feminism*, xv. Further references will be cited in the text.

34 Mitchell, Introduction to Lacan, *Feminine Sexuality*.

35 Mitchell, *Psychoanalysis and Feminism*, 416. Even here, as Michèle Barrett has pointed out (*Women's Oppression Today*, 61), Mitchell offered a dualism rather than a synthesis.

36 Barrett, *Women's Oppression Today*, 46. Further references will be cited in the text.

37 Jameson, *The Political Unconscious*, 19–20.

38 Rose, *Sexuality in the Field of Vision*, 90.

39 Kaplan, *Sea Changes*, 152–3.

40 Gallop, 'Reading the Mother Tongue', 315. Gallop makes the remark in a discussion of Garner, Kahane, and Sprengnether's *The (M)other Tongue*, the first anthology of psychoanalytic feminist criticism.

41 Weir and Wilson, 'The British Women's Movement', 97.

42 Anderson, *In the Tracks of Historical Materialism*, 88, 91.

43 Weeks, *Sex, Politics, and Society*, 10.
44 Gallop, 'Reading the Mother Tongue', 316.
45 Moi, *Sexual/Textual Politics*, 164, 166.
46 Loomba, 'Overworlding the Third World', 190 n.11.
47 Weir and Wilson, 'The British Women's Movement', 97.
48 Weir and Wilson, 'The British Women's Movement', 81.
49 Hall, 'Old and New Identities', 57.
50 Hall, 'Minimal Selves'.

6.

History, racism, nation – and psychoanalysis

If direct amalgamations between psychoanalysis and other disciplines tend to be problematic, what can psychoanalysis offer as a conceptual, heuristic device for the understanding of contemporary political and cultural questions? Can it help with the formulation of other kinds of history, or with understanding the historical problematics of nationalism and racism?

History

Does psychoanalysis challenge linear and progressive narratives of history? It was Althusser who found in psychoanalysis the insight that repetition is not necessarily the recurrence of the past as such but rather the effect of the persistence of a structure. Psychoanalysis argues that the narrative of the life history of the patient is not a triumphal development but a form of repetition which freezes the individual into a cycle in which he or she helplessly and repeatedly acts out a fantasmatic past. Yet if it is true that psychoanalysis teaches that we get ill from repetition, then, as Deleuze points out, it also teaches that we are healed through repetition, the repetitions of 'working-through' and sublimation.[1] This has two consequences: in the first place, it means that psychoanalysis covertly places the repetition of trauma within a linear or progressive model which is superimposed when psychoanalysis itself intervenes: the healing process enables the patient to break out of repetition. So the story that psychoanalysis really wants to tell is the saving of history from repetition and its transformation into the narrative of a successful case history.

In the second place, if repetition makes you ill but can also heal you, it means that there are two forms of repetition, a good and a bad one. If today history seems to have shifted from the progressive narrative of the Enlightenment to an uncanny form of repetition, of postmodern recycling, then the question that needs to be asked is whether this is a good or a bad form of repetition. Is it a repetition that will heal us or make us ill?

This actually comes quite close to Marx's account of history, despite the common tendency (in Lyotard for example) to assume that Marxism involves a straightforward Enlightenment narrative. Take Marx's famous comment in *The Eighteenth Brumaire*: 'Hegel remarks somewhere that all great events and characters of world history occur, so to speak, twice. He forgot to add: the first time as tragedy, the second as farce'.[2] This, evidently, is a bad form of repetition: history making a joke of itself, repeating itself as its own pastiche. Marx's emphasis on the limits of repetition, twice only, suggests that there a distinction to be made here between repetition as infinite, unending, the inevitable eternal return of the same, and repetition as a form of doubling, inverting, dis-orientating, or re-empowering. Marx himself saw these as the bad and the good forms of repetition: the dialectic of history, which itself progresses through reversals, means that history is enacted through repetition but a repetition which changes for the good. History, in psychoanalytic terms, is in a constant process of working itself through.

History was thought of as cyclical long before it was radicalized into a progressive narrative. Even revolution meant a cyclical repetition before it meant transformation: the revolution of the spheres, the planets, the Glorious Revolution of 1688, or, the not-so glorious revolution of capitalism's boom–slump cycles. Even Marx's radical idea of revolution as an overturning was modelled on the prototype of the French Revolution, which the Bolsheviks imitated and self-consciously repeated in 1917. This suggests that it is not necessary to have to accept a simple opposition between linear and repetitive forms of history. The question becomes what forms the narratives of history take, and what kind of repetitions are involved. Making history in the present often involves not only a retrieval of the past but an attempt to make that past repeat the priorities of the present.

In many ways, our current sense that history is repeating itself is something of a luxury: after all, you have to have had a history, or rather have been allowed a history, for any repetition to occur in the first place. In the nineteenth century, as is well known, a primary criterion for distinguishing between civilized and savage societies was whether they were regarded as having a history: the savage was thought of as timeless, living in an eternal present, like a child – or the unconscious. Meanwhile Europe looked to extend its own history through a narrative which combined its own dynamic progress with repetition: of Imperial Rome, and, in the more distant past, of the spread of Aryan civilization. The grand narrative produced by historical philology told of the linguistic diffusion which lay behind the remorseless conquests of the Indo-European tribes, which therefore anticipated and authenticated the perceived contemporary supremacy of the Aryan race. This was the history of diaspora for the English and Germans in the nineteenth century, which they saw themselves as triumphally repeating.

But the twentieth century has shown that this was a history that can be retrieved, turned round and narrated in other terms. Today, the diaspora is thought of very differently: it has become the history of the very peoples uprooted and dispersed by European colonial and imperial powers. In a similar way, we have transformed the bad category of race into the good category of ethnicity; while, most striking because apparently least examined in its metamorphosis, the bad category of the hybridity produced by interracial sex has been recast as the good category of the hybridity of postmodern culture.[3] The academic equivalent of this is doubtless the shift from the nineteenth century's preoccupation with taxonomy and disciplinary divisions into the twentieth's penchant for interdisciplinary, creative, generative work. If history repeats itself, therefore, it might seem that what we are experiencing today is a good form of repetition, in which the negative differentiating categories of the past have been recycled, and transcoded into positives.

But the ghastly appearance of the notion of 'ethnic cleansing' warns us that these transformations are still vulnerable and ambivalent. It cannot be assumed that the currently validated cultural categories have altogether reversed those of the past. Indeed, as the use of the term hybridity suggests, the sublimation may have been too successful, transmuted into the process of forgetting. For however much the past may have been repeated and worked-through, its recurrence will always include bad forms of repetition, which, like the uncanny, will erupt unexpectedly and repeat on us traumatically where it is least expected. But as long as there are good and bad forms of repetition, then history can still be coerced and transformed: we do not have to resign ourselves to inevitability, to the assumption that any particular bad repetition will always go on repeating. We need to recognize that, as psychoanalysis intimates, history works in a complex dialectic of linear movements and repetition.

Nation

So psychoanalysis suggests that if history can be thought through as a form as repetition, then there are good and bad forms of repetition that are repeated by us or which repeat on us. But it is not only history, or the history of individual patients, that work in this way. The same structures will be acted out by social and political phenomena which achieve their identity through history. Nationness, for example, is a repetition effect of this kind, an historical repetition both in the sense of the nation being a repetition (or retrieval) of history and as something which constantly repeats.

Nationness might be thought of as a form of sickness, of madness, or at the very least of neurosis.[4] And since nations must always invoke a Romantic little narrative (as opposed to the Enlightenment grand narrative of internationalism), perhaps it was this that Goethe was thinking of when he said 'Romanticism is sickness, classicism health'. The nation, too, is often imaged as if it existed in a dialectic of sickness and health, but almost any dialectic will do. No nation ever makes the mistake of defining itself permanently, in essentialist terms.

Nationalism after all is a historical, political ideology developed in the eighteenth century in order to provide a new form of legitimation for a country that could no longer find it in its heart to justify the basis of its government by the claims of a ruling monarchical dynasty. A new monarch, this time conveniently spectral and immortal – the nation – had to be invented so that the king's subjects could remain subjects, and as has been pointed out, the new dynasty of the nation was instantly given an appropriately respectable lineage or history, that of ethnicity, culture and language, which it was required to repeat in the present. Obviously, the forms and conditions of nationalism have continued to change and develop since then, particularly in the postcolonial era, to the extent that nationalism in general can hardly be discussed as such. Yet despite the argument that the question that nationalism poses is one specific to different moments of the nineteenth and twentieth centuries, ever since Renan's famous essay 'What is a Nation?', it has also been assumed that whatever the diversity of particularities, the nation at least is a category that can be analysed as such.

This is the challenge that has been taken up by Benedict Anderson, Ernest Gellner, Hobsbawm and others. What their work shows is the variety of factors that must be brought together to make the successful equation that binds the nation into a State. It also demonstrates that its 'natural' units exist in an unending tension with heterogeneity. The connections that were generally made between race, language, and religion in the nineteenth century often assumed as a norm the possibility of some kind of unitary, homogeneous form in which they could all be united: the nation. But according to the norm/deviance model that was endemic to nineteenth-century forms of thinking, from racial theory to sexology and criminology, the norm itself became best defined by those things which deviated from it, which meant in practice an obsession with the occurrence of the deviant: not only so-called sexual perversions, but also racial and linguistic hybridity. The 'nation' is constituted through a constant dialectic between these centrifugal and centripetal forces, between homogenization and heterogeneity, sameness and diversity: though it is often claimed that one part of the polarity is a recent phenomenon (for example, heterogeneity from immigration), an antithetical pressure has always been central to nationness. The problem for the nation has always been that it wants to suggest that its political formation, at the level of the State, coincides with a 'natural' cultural identity. Since cultures are always multiple and always involve a great variety of identities, the State therefore has to produce an 'imagined community', which has only been brought into being by virtue of the existence of the State itself.[5] This accounts both for the diversity of conditions of specific nations, and also for the necessarily conflictual state of the nation as such. The sickness of the nation is that it will always have too many cultures for its well-being as a State.

The nation works through a structure of polarities: images of the nation oscillate between different gender models, of masculinity, femininity, and androgyny.[6] They also shift strategically between what are seen, at different moments, as essential drives towards homogeneity and heterogeneity: whereas Englishness in the past was fabricated on a principle of sameness, in Britain today the nation is being carefully reconstructed on a principle of difference: through an increasing cultural layering and hybridization. This works even for the minority groups themselves: Paul Gilroy, for example, has noted the modern pluralization in Britain of black identity, and the development of new diverse forms of cultural identities and identifications.[7] This suggests that the complex stratifying and hybridization of cultures in Britain is moving it towards an increasing heterogeneity. At the same time the State somewhat ambivalently moves towards enforcing the larger political and cultural identity of the European Union. As European borders are removed, other borders have been developed internally, borders within, outsides on the insides, and insides on the outsides.

What this points to is the realization that 'nationness' is a state of constant tension or oscillation between heterogeneity and homogeneity, between difference and sameness, the past and the future, between processes of mixing, miscegenation, hybridization and those of separation, purity, cleansing. The nation operates in a constant transformative flow or economy between these polarities, which explains the mechanism whereby in a single historical moment the direction and priorities of one nation can seem to be so out of sync with that of another.

This double movement is doubtless the constitutive effect of the torn halves of the society which the nation seeks to bind together; but it is the psychoanalytic category of ambivalence that catches the structural economy of its oscillations, even if it removes the antagonism involved. The word nation also tends to mask over this constitutive ambivalence. The 'nation state' is more of a give-away. From a psychoanalytic perspective it might seem that the various other meanings of the word state are not at all fortuitous: alongside a sovereign body of people occupying a particular territory, state also designates a particular kind of existence at a given moment, and a condition of unresolved tension. It is psychoanalysis that helps us to recognize that *the nation will always be in a state*. Perhaps that is why nationalism also offers such a compelling form of cultural identification.

Racism

> *Alm*: I wonder what religion hee's of!
> *Fit*: No certain species sure. A kind of mule! That's halfe an Ethnicke, halfe a Christian!
> Jonson, *Staple of Newes* (1631)

Race is often one of the things which the nation gets itself into a state about. Nationalism can, but does not have to, involve racism. Semantically, and paradoxically in terms of its modern usage, the nation is much more intimately connected to ethnicity than to race. Since ἔθνος in Greek means nation, the relation of nation to ethnicity amounts to a tautology. Interestingly, this tautology also points to a reversal of sorts. 'Ethnocentric' according to its semantic origins ought to mean other-nation-centric rather than centred in one's own nation: for in Greek, τὰ ἔθνη means the non-Israelite nations, that is, the Gentiles. The word 'ethnic' was introduced into English in the fifteenth century, and at that time meant relating to nations not Christian or Jewish, namely heathens or pagans. Ethnic, therefore, already means the religion and the nation of the other: which means that ethnocentric by semantic rights should mean the very reverse of its modern usage. The development of ethnic in the words ethnography and ethnology in the 1830s and 1840s shows it losing the meaning of nationhood – no doubt because the connection between nations and other peoples was itself diminishing at that time in the history of imperialism; so while ethnography means 'the scientific description of nations or races of men' (1834), ethnology is established as the nationless 'science which treats of races or peoples' (1842). As it moves into a scientific theory, therefore, ethnos shifts from nation to race. In our current passion for ethnicity it should be remembered how closely it is affiliated to them both. Today nation, race, culture, and ethnicity are still used interchangeably. Despite the fact that you can write it without putting scare quotes round it, ethnicity is little less than our contemporary word (introduced in 1953) for the disgraced term 'race': you are born into your culture and your ethnic group, which are both already in existence; you can, by an act of free will, change your culture (for example through education or by moving to another country) but for the most part you cannot change your ethnicity any more than in the past you could change your race.[8] Those of mixed race are the major exceptions to this rule, in so far as many societies even now do not allow mixed race as a specific ethnicity. In Britain for example, the Commission for Racial Equality asks individuals to identify their ethnic origin as one of the following:

    White
    Black-Caribbean/African/Other
    Asian-Indian/Pakistani/Bangladeshi/Chinese/Other
    Other (please specify)

So too in society at large, if you are, for example, of mixed race between white and any other group, then you are generally identified as belonging to the non-white group: you are different, ethnic.[9]

The frequently cited connection between nationalism and racism can pass too quickly over the problem that racism is by no means exclusive to nationalism.[10] Here we need to distinguish two related but distinctive kinds of racism. The first is a racial prejudice that appears, like patriarchy, to be relatively transhistorical, and which amounts to a form of hostility prompted by the cultural transmission of certain stereotypical views, and can be characterized in psychoanalytical terms as a pathological fear of the other. The second would be scientific racism, sometimes called racialism, the theory of race which was specifically developed in the nineteenth century in the West as part of a political theory justifying slavery, colonialism, and imperialism. Scientific racialism consisted essentially of a scientific corroboration of the stereotyped prejudices of popular racism. Apart from racial theory proper, such scientific thinking was also developed through the disciplines (amongst others) of linguistics, anthropology, phrenology, eugenics, and social Darwinism in which the typological notion of race was adapted to a theory in which race became a form of distinct *species*. Such racial theory could consequently be justified by the iron law of nature, and culminated, as is well known, in the racial theories of Rosenberg and others that were central to the ideology of Fascism.[11] But in many European countries, including Britain, scientific racism was the basis for the process of the institutionalization of racism – a process that in many ways still continues today. The point of this thumb-nail sketch is to emphasize that, as with nationalism, racism and racialism are historical phenomena, which raises once more the whole problem of the relation of psychoanalysis to history.

The historical specificity of racism in the West means that before addressing the question of what psychoanalysis can offer to its investigation, it must be emphasized once again that the racism of our society is for the most part the continuing effect of nineteenth-century racism and its integration at all levels of the State through the discourses of colonialism and the ideology of imperialism. Although the political, geographical, and economic rationale for a theory of the innate inferiority of non-white races has now passed, it lingers on in a kind of time-lag that accompanies the continued expansion of the world economy; one that can be wheeled out at appropriate moments if politically convenient, particularly at moments of economic crisis in the life of nations.

The question of racism broaches the social and historical limits of psychoanalytic explanation, which cannot itself escape the historical specificity of the ideology of racism. Here psychoanalysis cannot evade a confrontation with history because it must itself be historicized in this context: not only Jung's apparent willingness to corroborate Nazi racial ideology, not only the willing complicity of certain psychoanalysts such as Mannoni or Ortigues with colonial government, but even with respect to Freud himself.[12] The general problem here starts with the ethnocentricity of the assumptions implicit in the universal claims of psychoanalysis. More specifically, psychoanalysis is itself deeply implicated in the norm/deviance model on which racialized thinking was constructed. Sander Gilman's arresting and valuable work nevertheless illustrates very clearly the problems that this leads to: on the one hand he shows how deeply psychoanalysis is implicated in nineteenth-century deviancy theory, and yet on the other hand he continues to use it as the basis of explanation and understanding.[13] With Freud the problems do not only manifest themselves with respect to his ideas about sexuality. The 'recapitulation' theory is also very much in evidence, probably derived from the social Darwinism of Herbert Spencer (to be found, for example, in his essay 'The Comparative Psychology of Man'), and particularly evident in Freud's *Civilization and its Discontents*, but permeating his work throughout. This involves the uncritical survivalist assumption (the origins of which go back at least to the eighteenth century) that in some way so-called primitive peoples constitute a childhood of mankind and can be analysed on that basis or the other way round, where childhood can be analysed by recourse to notions of primitivism. The complicity of certain psychoanalytical assumptions, therefore, in the history of theories of racism suggests that psychoanalysis is hardly likely to prove an effective instrument for an understanding of that which it unthinkingly or unconsciously perpetuates.[14] This is all too evident when some proffered forms of psychoanalytic explanation, such as the claim that racist revulsion is prompted by an association between black people and excrement, seem themselves to become indistinguishable from racist ideology as such. But rather than suggesting that racism pushes psychoanalysis to its limit, I want to suggest rather that it constitutes its very edge.

You might think that of all social phenomena, racism would be something that psychoanalysis would have a lot to tell us about. But there is surprisingly little psychoanalytic material that deals with racism. No doubt this was because psychoanalysis itself was deeply imbricated within the same nexus of ideas as scientific racism itself. Yet one might have expected more given the topicality of racism at the time Freud was writing many of his major texts. As one might expect, such brief discussions as we do get focus exclusively on anti-Semitism. Freud's most sustained account occurs in *Moses and Monotheism* (1937) where he stresses that it arises from a complexity of causes, many of which, he suggests, are relatively straightforward, such as envy of Jewish commercial success: the problem of racism thus starts with the fact that is not *just* irrational, it can't just be approached at the level of the symptom. Freud then goes on to give three 'deeper motives': jealousy of the special election of the Jews, that the Jewish practice of circumcision recalls what he calls 'the dreaded castration', finally positing a displaced anger among Christians for being coerced to become Christians in the first place.[15] Psychoanalytic explanation here thus comprises the same story that it repeats incessantly: rivalry and displacement, circulating around the 'bedrock' of castration. It seems that whenever psychoanalysis is brought in as an oracular master discourse in order to explain things that have resisted understanding according to the terms of their own logic, it always provides the same explanation.

In his other substantive discussions of racism, in the form of anti-Semitism, Freud describes it in terms of 'the narcissism of minor differences', adding that he is at a loss to explain why such details of differentiation prompt such readiness for hatred and aggression in groups, which can hardly have helped him much in coming to terms with his own expulsion from Vienna in 1938.[16] The problem with such psychoanalytic accounts of racism as do exist is that they bring us back to the habitual story that psychoanalysis tells every time, in which racism inevitably loses any specificity. The question for psychoanalysis is whether it can tell us anything about a fantasy that is *social* rather than individual, particularly one that, as with the Fascism to which in many respects it is clearly related, now seems to us a pathological perversion.

Reich

The primary text outside Freud in the context of psychoanalysis and racism must be Fanon's *Black Skin, White Masks*, which includes a trenchant critique of the complicity of certain psychoanalysis in racism and colonialism, and attempts a phenomenology of the psychic effects of racism as a preliminary to a call to black people to exchange the pathological compulsion of a desire for whiteness with an assertion of a new black identity. The one thing the book doesn't do, however, is to use psychoanalysis as an instrument for understanding the construction of racism's enduring social and historical affect. For this reason I want to consider briefly an earlier, rather different work, Reich's *The Mass Psychology of Fascism* which was published in 1933, the year before he broke with Freud. To the extent that he de-idealized and historicized Freud, Reich in many ways undermines the claim for the necessity of a psychoanalytical explanation. Fascism, he argues, was to a large extent what Hitler himself said it was, a political *doppelgänger*, a reaction to Marxism that imitated the forms through which it had achieved success.[17] Despite this duplicitous doubling, Reich contends that Marxism for its part needs no psychological interpretation because its appeal at the level of political philosophy is entirely rational; Fascism, by contrast, does require an explanation because its ideology is fundamentally irrational. This forms the basis for the argument about the irreducible *irrationality* of Fascism and racism that was to be developed by Adorno and others of the Frankfurt School.

Reich argues that Fascism was specifically the ideology of the lower middle class, and that its key ideological mechanism lay in the family, suggesting that the authoritarian family structure of that class provided the main psychological structure, namely identification, which led its members to endorse the authoritarian precepts of Fascism. According to Reich, the sexual repression of the lower-middle-class family allows the sublimation of desire into the various ideals of duty, honour, and fatherland, while the unquestioning allegiance to the *Führer* derives from an identification with the authoritarian patriarchal father.

Reich's account of Nazi racial theory demonstrates its clear historical links to the Darwinian accounts of differences between species that, as I have suggested, were assimilated into a theory of racial difference. In *Staying Power*, Peter Fryer shows how many nineteenth-century British versions of this assimilation state quite openly that the elimination of the weaker races, inevitably black, are simply part of the law of nature which has ensured the progress of civilization; anyone taking an active part in such extermination is, therefore, merely helping nature along its way.[18] For Nazi ideologues, the problem with this account rests in its assumption of necessity: rather as Marxist theory can be taken to describe an inevitable process leading to the fall of capitalism which therefore need involve no human agency, so there is no need in such a theory of racial development by natural selection for the active destruction and coercion of non-Aryans.

Nazi racial theory therefore articulated racial evolutionary theory with a theory of history and of the State, which, like that of Arthur comte de Gobineau, was predicated upon the rise and fall of civilizations. This posited the existence of three races: the Aryans who were the builders of civilization, the non-Aryans who were destined to serve it, and the Jews who were those who had always brought about the destruction of any great civilization. This gave the Nazi machine the basis for the justification for the appropriation of property, expulsion, and ultimately coercive operations designed to exterminate Jews altogether. Reich is concerned to show the degree to which the Nazi argument appeals psychologically and works symbolically in relation to a repressed sexuality. He ascribes the threat of poisoning, syphilis, and miscegenation to the body, and therefore ultimately the soul, of the German race from Jews always associated with dirt, decadence, and decay, to a fear of sexuality – and, being Reich, of orgasm – as such, and shows how it operates according to what today, after Said, would be called an Orientalist structure according to which the 'Nordic is equated to bright, majestic, heavenly, asexual, pure, whereas "Near Eastern" is equated to instinctual, demonic, sexual, ecstatic, orgastic' (121). He points to the complex mixture of sexual fantasies and guilt that lies at the basis of the unconscious emotional impact of Nazi propaganda, such as the following statement by Goebbels, written in answer to the question whether a Jew is a man:

> If someone cracks a whip across your mother's face, would you say to him, Thank you! Is he a man too!? One who does such a thing is not a man – he is a brute! How many worse things has the Jew inflicted upon our mother Germany and still inflicts upon her! He [The Jew] has debauched our race, sapped our energy, undermined our customs and broken our strength. (93)

Perhaps this proves that Goebbels really did have 'ner balls' after all.

It is in the context of analyses of this kind of propaganda that Reich criticizes Marxist accounts that remain narrowly economic in favour of a broader 'cultural politics' that demonstrates the effectivity and significance of ideological factors. His study of the complex mode of operation of 'seemingly irrelevant everyday habits' (103) is impressive, as is his insistent emphasis on the patriarchal, authoritarian family at what he calls the 'sex-economic core of cultural revolution' (120). But unlike Freud, the difficulty of his analysis comes from its very historical specificity: the force of his inquiry suggests that racism is specifically the product of lower-middle-class sexuality: whether this was true for Germany in the 1920s and 1930s or not, it is obviously little help in a discussion of, for example, contemporary working-class racism – particularly given that Reich claims that the working class maintains a far less fettered attitude to sexuality than any other (though interestingly he suggests that the proletariat themselves suffered the contradiction of a split psychic structure that anticipates Adorno and Althusser). The paradox of Reich's work, therefore, seems to be that when psychoanalysis (of a sort) is brought to bear in a more specific historical register, then its explanatory power becomes equally restricted.

For psychoanalysis as a system of understanding to have something to say about racism it must assume that racism is derived
from a fundamental psychic structure or constitutes a specific form
of social neurosis. Reich's analysis shows the difficulties that arise
when psychoanalysis is obliged by its own model to offer a theory
of racism as a perversion from the norm; when the norm itself is
perverted as in Nazi Germany, South Africa or the American South
into a pervasive ideological fantasy, then things become more difficult, for it necessitates a form of mass psychology that quickly
becomes a theory of Weberian types (itself closely related to the
typology of nineteenth-century racism). At this point, psychoanalysis is itself in danger of reverting to type, that is to the first use of
psychology in relation to race, 'ethnopsychology' (1886) which involved the 'study of the psychology of races and peoples': 'The
negro is lazy, crafty' etc.

To turn it the other way round, the problem is that there are
so few specific examples of case histories involving questions of
racism – presumably because in general a racist doesn't regard her
or his racism as a neurosis needing a cure: it's hard to imagine the
scenario of a Nazi worried about his anti-Semitic tendencies con-
sulting Dr Freud. For a racist, psychoanalysis, given its strong Jewish identity, would itself be regarded, à la Karl Krauss, as a symptom
of the illness that the racist wants to rid society of. The one specific
example of a case history I've come across outside of Fanon is not
a happy one. In his book *White Racism*, Joel Kovel recounts the case
of a patient analysed by Terry Rodgers; the patient was an American white Southerner, who 'under the emotional pressure of the
self-realization of psychoanalysis, moved from a stance of nonracist,
liberal support for the Negro cause to membership in the local
White Citizens Council'.[19] As always, the problem for psychoanalysis seems to emerge with the notion of cure.

For all that, however, Reich's work in this area is important
because he was the first to isolate what he called the characteristic
ambivalence of Fascist ideology, and, crude as his analysis may in
certain respects sound today, to stress the link between sexuality
and racism, a link that is constantly repressed or subject to social
amnesia. What is important about Reich's work is his demonstration that racism can't be separated from sexuality: positive or negative racist feelings share a structure of obsession with the loved or
hated object. This suggests that if it were asked where psychoanalysis itself comes closest to a symptomatic discussion of racism,
then it must be in the only concept that it takes from the racial

arena, and that is fetishism, a term first used by travellers with
reference to the religious icons of Africa – the Africa that Freud also
identifies as the dark continent of female sexuality.[20] The structure
of fetishism, of simultaneous fixity and mobility, operating together
at once in a dialectic of attraction and repulsion, seems at least to
get at the constitutive ambivalence of racism, derived from what is
in effect a surplus of signification in the other – which explains why
its other constant feature is paranoia, the disease of overinter-
pretation. This recalls Freud's idea of the narcissism of minor differences. If the constitutive factor of racism is that it finds a constant
surplus of signification in the other, it can, interestingly, work both
by there being a difference, too much of a difference (in relation to
black people) but equally well through there being a danger of their
being *no* difference (as in anti-Semitism, anti-Irish racism). There's
no pleasing the racist: the bastards are either too different or too
similar. Such a logic is a kind of perverted mirroring of the liberal
position on cultural difference, that is, ethnic minorities are the
same but different. This reversibility may suggest that either liberalism is simply the other side of racism, or that the structure of
racism doesn't have to be dismantled but can rather be turned
round. Either way, only psychoanalysis is placed to deal with this
perverse kind of paradoxical double logic – because this is the logic
of psychoanalysis. Psychoanalysis is uniquely suited to understand
the operation of such structures: psychoanalysis itself operates as
a kind of illegitimate, unlegitimated form of thought that infiltrates
the home territory of different disciplines, the other that has been
brought in to the same but which far from being assimilated remains inalienable and other to it: here psychoanalysis itself reproduces the very structure that is the object of racism – so that it
appears as the apparently foreign body within that disturbs, producing the uncanny effect of disquiet which, characteristically,
purists within the discipline seek to expel. Compare the insistent
desire of psychologists and analytical philosophers to prove psychoanalysis wrong, to delegitimate yet again something that after
all already has no legitimacy, with the insistently repeated attempts
to refute racism and racialism on logical or scientific grounds. Psychoanalysis can locate, and even dislocate, the logics of racism
precisely because, like racism, it is a discourse whose object is its
own ravelled fantasy.

If racism involves a structure of sameness and difference, it
also suggests a realignment of any simple model of 'the other'.

There is an immediate problem about using the term 'the other' dualistically in relation to racism in a psychoanalytic context in so far as for psychoanalysis the other is already a part of the psyche, the unconscious that remains unacceptable and uncanny because it is other to the ego and is not centred in a determinate self, amounting rather to the disturbing effect of the self dislocated, as it were, into the third person. Now if the symbolic structure of the social is that of the other, then the social is already the other – whereas those who are the objects of racist antipathy are precisely those who remain other to the social, in psychoanalytic terms, therefore, other to the other. At this point the trauma becomes the inkling that the other's other could in fact be the same, the double of yourself.

Forcing an uncanny recognition of what should have remained hidden, racism articulates desire and disavowal. Neither subject nor object, the structure of racism takes the form not of simple negation, but of 'denegation' (*Verneinung*), that is negation simultaneously accompanied by disavowal. This is the paradoxical form of what Kristeva calls the 'abject', a state of simultaneous revulsion and desire:

> There looms, within abjection, one of those violent, dark revolts of being, directed against a threat that seems to emanate from an exorbitant outside or inside, ejected beyond the scope of the possible, the tolerable, the thinkable. It lies there, quite close, but it cannot be assimilated. It beseeches, worries, and fascinates desire, which, nevertheless, does not let itself be seduced. Apprehensive, desire turns aside; sickened, it rejects. A certainty protects it from the shameful – a certainty of which it is proud holds on to it. But simultaneously, just the same, that impetus, that spasm, that leap is drawn toward an elsewhere as tempting as it is condemned.[21]

These two incompatible but inescapable poles of attraction and repulsion enforce a blockage that produces its own narrative logic of repetition: the point about the racial stereotype is indeed that it *is* always a stereotype, the other is thus paradoxically always the same. The threatening heterogeneity is always reduced, while the desire that the other conjures up is displaced into the (dis)pleasure of repetition, a repetition that energizes and ensures the perpetuation and continuity of the cultural and ideological forms of racism through the ages – a parasite that lives on the exercise of power.

(1993)

Notes

1 Deleuze, *The Logic of Sense*, 287.

2 Marx, *The Eighteenth Brumaire of Louis Bonaparte*, in *Surveys from Exile*, 146.

3 See my *Colonial Desire*.

4 Cf. Bhabha, 'A Question of Survival'.

5 Anderson, *Imagined Communities*.

6 See Parker, *Nationalisms and Sexualities*.

7 Gilroy, 'Ethnic Absolutism', in Grossberg, Nelson, and Treichler, *Cultural Studies*, 187–98.

8 Certain societies have had more fluid, 'Lamarckian' notions of ethnicity. See Linnekin, 'Cultural Invention and the Dilemma of Authenticity', 446–8.

9 Glazer and Moynihan, *Ethnicity*.

10 Nairn, *The Break-Up of Britain*. See also Balibar, 'Racism and Nationalism', in Balibar and Wallerstein, *Race, Nation, Class*, 37–67.

11 See Burleigh and Wipperman, *The Racial State*.

12 See Dalal, 'The Racism of Jung'.

13 Gilman, *Difference and Pathology*.

14 Freud is particularly vulnerable in his social psychology, which draws on the work of Le Bon and others.

15 Freud, *Moses and Monotheism*, 334–6.

16 In 'Group Psychology and the Analysis of the Ego' [1921], *Civilization and its Discontents*, 12:131. In a footnote Freud links it to life/death instincts.

17 Reich, *The Mass Psychology of Fascism*, 73. Further references will be cited in the text.

18 Fryer, *Staying Power*.

19 Kovel, *White Racism*, 53.

20 Apter and Pietz, *Fetishism as Cultural Discourse*. cf. Lyotard in Benjamin, *The Lyotard Reader*, 67–8.

21 Kristeva, *Powers of Horror*, 1. Kristeva has more recently elaborated her analysis of racism in *Strangers to Ourselves*.

Boundaries...............................

The institution of culture

....

7

New Historicism and the counter culture

Some time ago I was sent a poster for a Higher Education Teachers of English conference, the topic for which was boldly proclaimed as *The End of the Grand Narratives*. I put the poster up outside my office door, and after a few days noticed that someone, no doubt a postmodern pedant, had scored out the final 's' of the title, correcting it to *The End of the Grand Narrative*. The graffiti-writer's point was presumably that for the Grand Narrative to be plural is by definition a contradiction in terms. I assumed at first that correcting the typo concluded the matter. But on reading more closely I realized that that extra 's' was a symptomatic slip. For the blurb for the conference read as follows: 'The shift of "English" to "Literature" and/or "Cultural Studies" signals just one "grand narrative", one totalizing discourse, which has been fragmented in the course of the last two decades.' If the grand narrative of English has shifted to Literature and/or Cultural Studies, then all that has happened is that there are now simply two narratives instead of one, each if anything even grander than the last – except that if it is indeed a question of *'just one* "grand narrative", one totalizing discourse, which has been fragmented' then, if it was merely one of them, it can't have been that grand or that totalizing in the first place. This contradiction, which had seeped into the title of the conference, is not just a question of semantics: rather it touches upon a characteristic difficulty in the contemporary theorization of culture whereby totalization or fragmentation apparently cannot be thought, celebrated or denounced, without the admission that their opposite also simultaneously holds true. The poster presented a perfect example of the synchronous oscillation of subversion and containment within the institution, whereby subversive texts simultaneously generate (or repeat) the orthodox positions that they are supposed to disrupt but which continue to contain them safely – a structure which in turn calls into question the usefulness of the distinction between subversive and orthodox texts.

The cultural–institutional motif of subversion and containment is most often identified with New Historicism, already yesterday's vogue literary theory. Why should this be the particular narrative that it tells? New Historicism proclaims a return to history, and with it, therefore, comes the end of the long imagined antithesis between history and theory. As if history had not always been theoretical, or theory was not always historical: but their opposition has been a necessary critical fiction of our times. Institutionally, at least, New Historicism has shown that theory need not be antihistorical: indeed its great attraction lies in the fact that it seems to have avoided the problems of historicity altogether, achieving an apparently effortless movement from the writing subject to the historical domain outside. As a form of historical criticism, its focus has been upon the articulation of history and culture, a new kind of cultural politics that resituates canonical literary works in relation to other, non-literary, writings of their historical period and also to the practices of contemporary social and political institutions. Rather than assuming history to be a somehow self-evident 'background' for literature, New Historicists consider literary texts to be embedded within the cultural system. The question remains, however, of New Historicism's relation to history. For some, it seems, any mention of 'history' is enough to count someone as a New Historicist – but as Gayatri Chakravorty Spivak notes, 'when people talk about history, that proper name is generally not opened up'.[1]

The problem begins with the name, 'New Historicism'. Historicism as a term has a complex range of meanings and historical references; the diversity of definitions of the New Historicism obviously arises from different assumptions as to what historicism signifies. Sometimes it is used simply as a way of emphasizing the importance of history in the understanding of events or texts, with the implicit presupposition that such events or texts must therefore be to some extent historically determined. But more usually, 'historicism' implies a theory in which history itself is considered to be governed by general laws, and involves a philosophical scheme imposed as an underlying form upon events. Condorcet, Herder, Hegel, and Marx, for example, are some of the more notable philosophers of history who saw history as a teleological narrative of a progressive emergence of civilization, nation, reason or socialism. The term 'New Historicist' might then seem to set up a return to a historicist legacy in this second sense of the term, comparable to its current limited versions in the Frankfurt School and Cultural Materialism. The latter, although often associated and sometimes even identified with New Historicism, is concerned to trace examples of the conflict between hegemonic and subversive forces in historical texts, identifiable as parallel to the forms of political struggle in our own day. It can therefore represent a new version of the long tradition of Marxist reflection theory, although at its most radical Cultural Materialists would see history as, in Ernst Bloch's phrase, 'the persistently indicated', inciting and inspiring the political objectives of the present.

Given the sustained theoretical critique of historicism since the end of the nineteenth century, and the low standing of the historicism of twentieth-century historians such as Oswald Spengler or Arnold Toynbee, its apparent reaffirmation by the latest mode of criticism might seem surprising. In this respect, the term 'New Historicist' may be misleading, for in many ways the critical movement continues the anti-historicist tradition, eschewing grand causal or narrative schemas in favour of the tracing of synchronic links between different cultural practices, showing the processes of circulation and exchange between them, and emphasizing in particular the intricate, though not simply causal, relation between capitalism and aesthetic production. In the background here is the Foucault of *The Order of Things*, who argues that knowledge is constructed according to certain historical limits, and that rather than progressing and evolving it is simply transformed from *episteme* to *episteme*. This brings us to the third meaning of historicism, in which it amounts to a claim for historical enquiry as an understanding of events in their unique particularity, as in the radical historicism of Leopold von Ranke and J. G. Droyson. The German historicists, often linked to nineteenth-century positivism, combined a new cultural relativism with an identification of history with freedom. It has been argued that by eschewing any totalizing theory of history, they remained passive before its incomprehensibility, and thus sustained a certain conservatism.[2] Foucault himself is sometimes described as a radical positivist, so it is inevitable that the passivity often alleged in his accounts of both *epistemes* and power should be compared to the inertia of historicism in this third sense. Critics such as David Norbrook have asked to what extent New Historicism, in which history is presented as a plurality of moments, with no theory of change or of transitions, endorses the same resignation.[3] It is certainly the case that New Historicism frequently espouses history as a series of punctual incidents, a 'succession of modernities', and tends to see culture and history in synchronic terms, setting aside its relation to any linear processual schemas, and eschewing meaning except in so far as it is made in each instant – or in the analogies drawn by the New Historicist's own analyses.

The dissonance in the term 'historicism' operates in the different positions taken by the New Historicists themselves, in which some return to Stephen Greenblatt's more Foucauldian or anthropological account of the historical relation of literature to other cultural practices and others to the historicism of Cultural Materialism.[4] In practice, therefore, New Historicism hovers uncertainly, if productively, between being a return to history in its positivistic singularity and particularity, and a return to the long tradition in which history is formulated as an overall narrative with its own meaning and necessary development.

The complex theoretical and political problems involved in historicism have not, however, for the most part been addressed by New Historicists, which is not to say that the achievements of individual analyses have not been remarkable. What is unusual is that with New Historicism the theory has followed rather than preceded the examples – itself a good indication of the kind of thinking that distinguishes it from certain precepts of structuralism and many a tedious theory-and-practice textbook. As H. Aram Veeser remarks, while New Historicists show a characteristic tendency to critical self-scrutiny, there has been little systematic discussion of their methodology. Veeser's anthology, entitled *The New Historicism*, might therefore have been expected to provide a substantial theorization of the new historical method, but in fact it does not, despite its promise to do so. A number of contributors voice various forms of anxiety with respect to its complex and productive relationship to Marxism and poststructuralism; of these, the account by Greenblatt, who can justly be said to be the founder of New Historicism, is the outstanding example. Greenblatt makes much of the disinclination of New Historicists to establish a theoretical position before proceeding with their analyses. New Historicists don't theorize history, so the saying goes, they prefer to do it – a position which silently (and tellingly) repeats the anti-propositional theories of New Criticism such as 'poetry isn't about experience, it is experience', or 'a poem should not mean, but be'. This substantiates Jameson's claim that New Historicism is a form of immanent criticism.[5] But as Hayden White observes, 'to embrace a historical approach to the study of anything entails or implies a distinctive philosophy of history'.[6] If the implicit politics of New Criticism are anything to go by, these silent presuppositions of New Historicism about history ought to be articulated so that they can be examined critically. What is it, therefore, that the New Historicists do? And what is new about it?

Greenblatt characterizes New Historicism's difference from positivist historical scholarship by its 'openness to theory', while admitting at the same time that its relation to Marxism and poststructuralism (though not, apparently, to anthropology) is 'unresolved and disingenuous'. He seeks to situate New Historicism's theoretical position by specifying its critical relation to these two dominant theoretical camps, which he analyses through the metonymic device of an analysis of Jameson ('Marxism') and Lyotard ('poststructuralism'). The positing of the two theorists in this antithetical way allows Greenblatt to assume a separation between them which he then proceeds to undo. He begins by citing Jameson's argument that 'privatization' constitutes one of capitalism's most enervating effects: 'the convenient working distinction between cultural texts that are social and political and those that are not becomes something worse than an error: namely, a symptom and a reinforcement of the reification and privatization of contemporary life'.[7] A typical instance of this sort of process would be Kant's account of the aesthetic in which art is defined as everything that the market is not. Such a demarcation, Greenblatt argues, is not specific to capitalism as such: the separation of cultural from social and political discourses can be found in European society before the seventeenth century, and in many other societies besides. For Jameson, however, the enforcement of this division represents the specific maiming force of capitalism, an argument which Greenblatt suggests

> has the resonance of an allegory of the fall of man: once we were whole, agile, integrated . . . politics and poetry were one. Then capitalism arose and shattered this luminous, benign totality. The myth echoes throughout Jameson's book, though by the close it has been eschatologically reoriented so that the totality lies not in a past revealed to have always already fallen but in the classless future. A philosophical claim then appeals to an absent empirical event. (3)

As Greenblatt observes, this biblical vision, so fundamental to a Marxist teleology, has been a prime focus of questioning by poststructuralism which has shown how such an argument must work by a supplementary, always deferring structure which posits the absent plenitude of both an origin and end in order to provide the basis for its own dialectical 'materialist' schema. But if this has been the basis of the poststructuralist challenge to Marxism, Greenblatt argues that, in his example of Lyotard, disagreement simply takes the form of an exact reversal.

Once again, as in Jameson, the question focuses on the differences between the discursive realms of the aesthetic and the political. For Lyotard the problem rather amounts to the way in which capitalism has broken down the distinctions between them, creating a homogeneous totality which no longer allows differentiation and disparity. Greenblatt cites Lyotard's claim that 'Capital is that which wants a single language and a single network, and it never stops trying to present them'.[8] Yet this, Greenblatt argues, now apparently more sympathetic to Jameson's argument, is a 'monologic' description of capitalism – for it is also capitalism that so insistently inscribes individual identities, and demarcates the boundaries that separate them; it is capitalism that undoes the collective identities and values of the community. Both Jameson and Lyotard, he concludes, present monologic descriptions of capitalism, which, in their different ways, amount to equally totalizing arguments – of absolute detotalization and totalization:

> Jameson . . . finds capitalism at the root of the false differentiation; Lyotard . . . finds capitalism at the root of the false integration. History functions in both cases as a convenient anecdotal ornament upon a theoretical structure, and capitalism appears not as a complex social and economic development in the West but as a malign philosophical principle. (5)

Both theorists, therefore, are necessarily oversimplifying, and the question that they ask, which amounts to 'what is the historical relation between art and society?', cannot be answered by a single theoretical formula of the kind that they provide. The clear inference is that empirical history is more complex than theory. It cannot be collapsed into a moral philosophical imperative.

And yet Greenblatt's response is not to attempt himself a mapping of that historical complexity, but rather to provide a dialectical resolution of such Marxism and poststructuralism in strictly theoretical terms. For Greenblatt the problem is not so much the incompatibility of the two theories as their inability 'to come to terms with the contradictions of capitalism'. Although he concedes that in principle both theories define themselves by their focus on such contradictions, he argues that in practice they nevertheless efface it through their production of monological principles, themselves the result of 'theory's search for the obstacle that blocks the realization of its eschatological vision' (5). A New Historicist enquiry into the relation of art and society, free of both Marxist nostalgia and poststructuralist paranoia, would, Greenblatt suggests, be able to address the terms of both the contradictory paradigms, of totalization and detotalization, through which capitalism operates. So capitalism's 'complex social and economic development' has been characterized not through empirical history but through a more complicated model.

There is a further disingenuousness at work here in so far as Greenblatt implies that the individual monolithic stance of two particular arguments of Jameson and Lyotard accurately describes the positions of Marxism and poststructuralism – when both are in their different ways dialectical forms of thought. The combined movements of totalization and detotalization that he delineates as New Historicist can easily be found in both Marxism and poststructuralism, and the theorization of their relation to each other is certainly not exclusive to New Historicism as such. Indeed all philosophies of history have been riven by such tensions since at least the end of the eighteenth century, vacillating between a Rousseauesque pessimism in which history constitutes the force of fragmentation and alienation, and a Hegelian–Marxist optimism in which it comprises an emancipatory force for progress. It is worth noting the salutary fact in this regard that while philosophers of freedom produce pessimistic accounts of history, determinists are also generally optimists. In the terms of the opposition he sets up, Greenblatt claims that New Historicism is distinguished from all its predecessors by its ability to see that the two processes operate synchronously. He comments:

> For capitalism has characteristically generated neither regimes in which all discourses seem coordinated, nor regimes in which they seem radically isolated or discontinuous, but regimes in which the drive towards differentiation and the drive towards monological organization operate simultaneously, or at least oscillate so rapidly as to create the impression of simultaneity. (6)

This antithetical whirling, he suggests, provides a better foundation for an analysis of the 'relation between art and surrounding discourses in contemporary capitalist culture' which plays upon a 'complex dialectic of differentiation and identity' (7). For Greenblatt this cashes out in a demonstration of the ways in which aesthetic and capitalistic discourses intermingle and flow from one to the other, a circulation that takes the form of a continual movement of flows and blockage, an unending and unresolved struggle between subversion and containment. So the alleged totalizations of Marxism and poststructuralism are set against a Nietzschean schema of an irresolvable oscillation between immanent and transcendent forces.

Greenblatt himself in effect produces a third model here, a whirl of contraries which invokes Bakhtin's paradigm of a continuous warring between centripetal and centrifugal forces. It omits, however, the destabilizing energy of differentiation that is to be found in the dialectical doubleness of Bakhtin's dialogic principle. Although, as he demonstrates, Greenblatt avoids the trap of identifying exclusively with one of the torn halves that are the product of capitalist society, his move is restricted to that: he stands above contemplating and comprehending the two antithetical processes without reversing and reinscribing them as Adorno does to enable the development of a new form of cultural criticism of society. To the extent that they are presented as antithetical, the crucial difference is that for Greenblatt the two are complementary: they *add up*. For Greenblatt, capitalist society is ultimately one, at peace with itself.

In Greenblatt's historical criticism, it might have been expected that any critical move would involve time. What distinguishes Greenblatt's 'melodramatic polarities of absolute autonomy or absolute dissolution' from other binaries with which they might be compared – Arnold's Hebraic and Hellenic forces, Freud's clash between Eros and Thanatos, or even Derrida's account of history as a form of supplementary excess, is indicated by his description of how the processes work 'simultaneously'.[9] There is only a homogeneous empty time here, with no dislocating delay between the drives towards differentiation and identity, or between subversion and containment.[10] There is difference, but not deferral. Such simultaneity means that the forces of centralization and decentralization must necessarily be complementary; as perfectly matching ambivalent halves, there can only be an endless oscillation of subversion and containment. The problem with Greenblatt's account therefore is that he follows the Nietzschean assumption that these agonistic forces work in a relation of binary opposition of attraction and repulsion to each other, or, as in Bakhtin's primary schema, an unceasing antithesis of monoglossia and heteroglossia. In short, Greenblatt's account of history has written out the disjunction of time. Its dialectic is simultaneous, at a standstill in an eternal return. This suggests the possibility that a certain dislocating time interval needs to be allowed into the New Historicist account of the subversion–containment process which would then open up – by not adding up – its assumption of a static (if dynamic) totality and at that point paradoxically reintroduce history, temporality, and therefore change.

Yet however much temporality may be missing, Greenblatt still proposes a historicism of sorts after all, in the sense of a philosophical schema imposed as an underlying form upon events, even if the model for history is that of the oscillating dynamics of the market-place rather than one of progressive evolutionary struggle.

History as an egg

Let us leave Greenblatt with his simultaneous, perfectly matched antithetical forces whirling on the spot for the moment, to turn to the other essay in *The New Historicism* which discusses New Historicism's theoretical basis – that by Joel Fineman.[11] Fineman's essay is distinguished by the fact that he makes a genuine effort to address the theoretical paradox implied in New Historicism's own name. In the course of a somewhat laboured opening, he describes how he wishes to establish a more philosophical placing of the theoretical position of New Historicism through an enquiry into what might appear to be its most trivial aspect, its fondness for anecdote. Fineman's investigation is to be

> concerned both with the formal operation of the anecdote, understood as a specific literary genre, with peculiar literary properties, and also with a practical literary history of the anecdote in so far as the formal operation of the anecdote bears on the history of historiography, i.e. on the history of the writing of history. (50)

Here at last the question of New Historicism's formal relation to historicism is broached, albeit anecdotally.

Fineman argues that it is possible to relate the apparently disordered and amorphous practice of New Historicism to 'an historical tradition of historicity or historicizing within which . . . the New Historicism can be understood to occupy a coherent time and place' (52). He specifies its intervention in terms of what amounts to the major conceptual problem for any theorization of history, a version of the more general question of how to produce a concept that can conceptualize the non-conceptual, to include the non-conceptual 'within' the concept (Adorno), or the outside in the inside without its losing its identity as outside: for history this becomes the question of the relation between the historical particularity, the singular event, and the overall framework of a concept of history as a 'metahistory', in Hayden White's term. If it is through its affiliation to the latter that the particular takes on meaning and historical significance, the same process also necessarily has the effect of usurping and undoing its singularity. Fineman characterizes the troubled interrelation of event to history in terms of the opposition of the 'this' to the 'meta'.[12] He argues that the anecdote can play a special part in the continuing philosophical labour that has ensued in the face of the dominance of Hegel's philosophy of history. For Hegel, because the purposeful unfolding of the Spirit can let nothing happen by chance, because history is, in a sense, already written, then paradoxically history cannot be historical. Fineman suggests that the question ever since has been how 'to find some way to introduce into the ahistorical historicality of Hegelian philosophy of history some break or interruption of the fullness and repletion of the Spirit's self-reflection, so as thereby to introduce to history the temporality of time' (57). He charts the history of such attempts, from Wilhelm Dilthey to Husserl, from Heidegger to Derrida, as a labour in which the 'self-completing self-reflecting of Hegelian historicity' has been turned around, prised open, shifted out of the precepts of identity thinking, so as to reintroduce into it the punctual moment of the temporality of time. The history of philosophy thus becomes the history of endeavours to insert an opening into the totality of the self-enclosed circle of Hegelian history. [13]

It is in the context of this scenario that, according to Fineman, New Historicism makes its theoretical intervention:

> The oxymoron, if that is the right word for it, embedded in the rubric – the cheery enthusiasm with which the New Historicism, as a catchy term or phrase, proposes to introduce a novelty or an innovation, something 'New', into the closed and closing historiography of successive innovation, 'Historicism' ... this oxymoron is witness to or earnest of an impulse to discover or to disclose some wrinkling and historicizing interruption, a breaking and a *realizing* interjection, within the encyclopedically enclosed circle of Hegelian historical self-reflection. ... As a title, the New Historicism strives to perform and thereby to enable the project it effectively entitles, and thus to earn thereby its access to the real through the excess of its name.[14]

For Fineman, it is the anecdote that can open up history in so far as it amounts to the narration of a singular event which uniquely exceeds its literary status and any narrative schema, and so achieves a referential access to the real. The anecdote introduces an aperture into the schema of history, 'by establishing an event as an event within and yet without the framing context of historical successivity, i.e. it does so only in so far as its narration both comprises and refracts the narration it reports' (61). Fineman's anecdote thus succeeds in breaking down the inside/outside duality of concept and event, and opens up the potential for a form of history that is able to do justice to both. As long, that is, as it maintains its somewhat precarious status as anecdote – which lasts only so long as it avoids sliding into the metonymic status of the example (as in Greenblatt's use of Jameson and Lyotard, or indeed my use of Greenblatt and Fineman), in which the relation of the part is to illustrate and comprise the whole. For Fineman the anecdote must work in a non-metonymic excessive relation to a history formulated as a historicist totality. New Historicism's use of anecdote, he argues, bespeaks not methodological and theoretical indifference but is itself a means by which to open history's self-enclosed immediacy. Fineman's antithesis of anecdotal event to metahistory therefore assumes without question that the Hegelian self-enclosed history is indeed self-enclosed: he concludes that his task is to puncture the totality of history, to make an opening with the can-opener of time. In doing so, however, he has shifted from a problem of the relation of event to concept to the model of an outside to a totality. Although he could be said to be seeking to reintroduce time into Greenblatt's self-enclosed dialectical immobilization, he has, like Greenblatt, produced a spatial model where in this case all that is required is that the egg-like history be punctured by an outside agent in the name of retrieving the singularity of the event.

And yet, again like Greenblatt, despite the attempted cracking of the egg, there is a failure to relate this move to any critical, as opposed to philosophical, intervention. Here Fineman's argument contrasts to Walter Benjamin's account of history, where all developmental schemas, including that of Marxism itself, are associated with totalization and domination. Benjamin's emphasis on moments that break and blast open history's continuity is designed not to reintroduce time as such but rather to open up history so as to effect the work of cultural and political transformation.[15]

Immanence and transcendence

Given that they both offer theoretical descriptions of New Historicism, what is the relation between Greenblatt's subsumption of Marxism and poststructuralism into a dialectical irresolution of centripetal and centrifugal forces and Fineman's anecdote which chisels into the global totality of history so as to prise it open? The difference between the two would be that for Fineman the totality is closed and it is a question of the anecdotal event levering it open; whereas for Greenblatt the point is that the antithetical totalizations of Marxism and poststructuralism are never actually achieved – what he offers instead is an irresolvable oscillation of the two which New Historicism is somehow uniquely able to comprehend in a new totality.

Are these models reconcilable? They involve two modes of thinking incommensurability dynamically. Fineman's prising open the totality involves an injection of time and chance into theory, and is thus anti-totalizing and anti-historicizing. With respect to historicism, he is, therefore, 'subversive'. By contrast, Greenblatt projects a new totalizing model, albeit of a non-totalizing process, in a strategy of 'containment'. The two thus reproduce exactly the dialectic of subversion and containment, the dissolving forces of Thanatos and the binding forces of Eros, that they find operating within and between historical texts.[16] These two positions complement each other, indeed require each other to function in their bizarre economy of life and death. Greenblatt's argument, that New Historicism contains both Marxism and poststructuralism and therefore constitutes a higher form, itself declares a totalization which goes counter to the whole New Historicist emphasis on the discrete fragmented moments of history and which according to his own logic should be impossible – for, in the terms of his own argument, how can New Historicism comprehend and definitively encompass the other two through another single schema? Greenblatt asserts such a totalizing claim via the classic speculative formula of transcendence whereby an outside is posited from which the observer can comprehend the totality of the phenomenon under discussion – for Hegel the position of the philosopher, or, as also for Arnold, of the State; for orthodox Marxism the dialectic as the law of nature; for Lukács the collective subject of history; for Gramsci, the party, etc. Fineman, despite the differences of his model, also positions himself in this way when he posits New Historicism as standing outside history in order to break into the totality of historicism. Despite the emphasis on temporality, this remains an essentially static, spatial model. Paradoxically, as with Greenblatt's argument, it also reproduces the totalizing gesture itself, for Fineman totalizes history in order to supplement it with the one thing that he has left out – by chance, himself. As Sartre discovered, in theory and in history, there can be no totalization without a totalizer. In both cases here the New Historicist's own enunciative position contradicts his anti-totalizing stance by producing totalization. To put it another way, despite the apparent immanence of the New Historical method, both New Historicists theorize their own position in terms of models of transcendence.

New Historicism itself has always been distinguished by its awareness of the difficulty of the writer's role in the writing of history. Whereas historicist analysis tended to gravitate towards the most grandiose of objective sounding schemas, New Historicists are almost painfully alert to their own relative limitations and introduce such qualifications explicitly into their writing. This self-consciousness, often amounting to a self-deprecatory advertisement of one kind or another, an excuse for a certain self-indulgent subjectivism, does touch upon a substantial theoretical difficulty, namely, the position of the writing subject. This is not, however, theorized as a technical difficulty as it is in Hegel or Sartre. The problem of New Historicism is that although it recognizes the need to consider the position of the writing subject, its hesitance towards theorization in general means that it does not theorize its own position of enunciation – and therefore finds itself repeating the totalizing gestures it seeks to undo.

Both Greenblatt and Fineman produce a position of exteriority, an outside to an inside, which rather than taking subjectivity into account in the manner of Sartre totalizes the very history that they seek to detotalize. At this point it becomes clear that the apparent irresolvability of the totalization/detotalization structure exactly repeats the paradigm of subversion and containment which is proposed as the interpretive political insight of New Historicism. The questions of subversion and containment, of agency and domination, that New Historicism likes to raise as a historical and textual problem re-enact the theoretical problematic determined by its own model.

The historicist schema of New Historicism therefore has specific consequences. Both Greenblatt and Fineman when theorizing New Historicism move into an inside–outside structure, and this in turn implies a duality of disempowerment and empowerment. In these terms, if the subject is outside the totality then it seems empowered, but if it's inside, then it seems disempowered. This inside–outside structure also stages the position of those subjects inside the institution, and, in Stallybrass and White's terms, reproduces the institutional position of the academic subject, asserting an identity by looking out at the world beyond. Given that it is the production of the point of exteriority which conventionally empowers the transcendent critique, it might be expected that New Historicism posits the possibility of effective intervention in the processes which it analyses. Why then do New Historicist texts characteristically imply disempowerment? For it is only if the subject cannot control and intervene, that the processes of culture and of history themselves assume an autonomous form – Max Weber's iron cage, or the alien forces of domination described in the cultural critique of Georg Simmel, the Adorno of the culture industry, or Foucault. Greenblatt refuses this 'monological' view by positing the antimony of totalization and detotalization. But it is only the historian who is empowered by being on the outside, while the historical subject is disempowered by being caught inside, her or his actions always containable by the historical schema into which he or she is placed by the historian.

At the same time, such a schema repeats the dissonance within historicism as such, another improper name set against itself. So in its first meaning, it implies the existence of immanent laws through which history progresses and according to which its future can be predicted. Here both history, and the historian as knowing subject, can assume the position of exteriority. In the second, historicism becomes the very degree to which knowledge is itself entrenched in historical frameworks, culturally limited and, necessarily, relative. Here knowledge and the historical subject are constituted within a framework that has no outside. There is no point of objectivity. There are thus two modes in operation: one of history containing everything and making it meaningful, the other of history constantly threatening non-meaning, or subverting any meaning that had been made – the two modes, in other words, of transcendence and immanence.

Subversion and containment

Let us take a closer look at the notion of 'subversion' and 'containment'. The New Historicists are concerned to track the circulating relations between aesthetic and other cultural forms of discursive production, assuming, it seems, that it is possible to take a kind of 'essential section' across society's discursive productions at any particular historical moment in what Laclau calls 'pure relations of interiority'.[17] They thus challenge directly the Cultural Materialist's practice of looking at an historical text for today's political meanings. Greenblatt, in particular, argues that this is a self-confirming rather than in any way radical activity:

'subversive' is for us a term used to designate those elements in Renaissance culture that contemporary authorities tried to contain or, when
containment seemed impossible, to destroy and that now conform to
our own sense of truth and reality. That is, we locate as 'subversive'
in the past precisely those things that are *not* subversive to ourselves.

By contrast, those elements which we identify with Renaissance
principles of order would, if we took them seriously, undermine our
own contemporary assumptions (absolutism, hierarchies of class
and gender, religious intolerance, etc.). They are not threatening,
however, because our own values are strong enough for us not to
regard them as real alternatives. Greenblatt suggests that exactly
the same holds for the subversive elements of Renaissance texts –
which could be articulated only because they could be effortlessly
contained: 'the subversiveness that is genuine and radical . . . is at
the same time contained by the power it would appear to threaten'
(30). This troubles, as will be obvious, the possibility of any radical
reading; as Greenblatt puts it, adapting Kafka, 'there is subversion,
no end of subversion, only not for us'.

Subversion's radical Gramscian origins have thus themselves
been subverted by New Historicism. Greenblatt's argument sets up
a significant general characterization of the function of literature
and of culture within our society: at a textual level the radicalism
of a text, whether literary, critical, or whatever, can only institute
a form of subversion to the extent that it can already be accommodated – because it is not subversive. It is for this reason that
Greenblatt emphasizes the ease with which the institution absorbs
and contains whatever subversion radicalism can throw at it. Such
as New Historicism itself, perhaps, for Greenblatt and Fineman's
theorizations of their own activity, as historians gazing upon the
whirligig or egg of history, have placed themselves in the position
of producing the containing gestures of totalization. Greenblatt and
Fineman thus reproduce the antithesis which we have been charting in this book of immanent and transcendent critiques. But whereas
Adorno showed how it was possible to use this antithesis as a
critical instrument, the New Historicists separate it into the singularity of history set against the containing move of the historical
analyst, and thus claim transcendence over all other forms of history and cultural criticism. Similarly, the way in which the New
Historicists use the paradigm of subversion and containment dis-
counts the possibility of a dialectical criticism which can, in Bakhtin's
terms, posit an organic and an intentional hybridization that work
against each other.

An objection to the conservatism of the New Historicist position has been made by Edward Said, Gerald Graff and Jerome McGann, among others, who complain that 'since every form of culture is destined to be co-opted, the very notion of oppositional criticism is nonsense'.[18] I want to suggest that this position is because New Historicism is itself an example of what it describes. The New Historicism represents not only a theoretical but also an institutional repetition – posing as a form of cultural analysis – of the very failure that it portrays as inevitable.

Counter culture

On 21 October 1967 a collection of anti-war protesters, students, hippies, pacifists, intellectuals, Norman Mailers, as well as, according to a report in *The East Village Other*, contingents of 'witches, warlocks, holy men, seers, prophets, mystics, saints, sorcerers, shamans, troubadours, minstrels, bards, roadmen, and madmen', besieged the Pentagon.[19] After the march, the speeches, and the protests, the shamans performed an exorcism, 'casting mighty words of white light against the demon-controlled structure', which, they hoped, would effect a levitation, and lift the whole of the Pentagon right off the ground into the air.

It didn't budge. But no single incident of protest of this time better illustrates the style and inherent presuppositions of the politics of the late sixties. Ostensibly, at least, we have moved a long way today from trusting in magic and psychedelia for our political futures. But despite the reliance on shamanism, what is in retrospect remarkable about this event is its focus not on the conventional mode of political intervention, Congress or the House of Representatives, but on the institution of war. What was most characteristic of the politics of this time was its insistence that the political front line operated at the level of the institution as much as, if not more than, the technical seat of democratic control. Although certain aspects of the style may have changed, I want to pause to consider the concept that was used to describe the mode of unrest of this period: counter culture.

Despite its laughable unfashionableness, many of the tenets of the counter culture survive today. The distrust of technocracy could be said to have become the global paranoia of postmodernism; the ecological sympathy has developed into the Green movement; the relativism and accompanying interest in other cultures has become our contemporary espousal of the validity of 'cultural difference';

and, as I shall be arguing, the distrust of all institutional forms of organization, the attempt to 'deschool society', has been mediated into forms of theory and practice of how to subvert the institution, founded on the work of institutional analysis produced by Althusser and, particularly, Foucault. R. D. Laing's advocacy of the truth of experience over theory, the inside over the outside, has re-emerged in the form of identity politics. Only the mysticism, the shameless espousal of shamanism, has gone, its traces surviving solely with the New Age travellers.

The roots of the counter culture could be, and indeed were, traced back to Romanticism. A dislike of the global and controlling networks of technocracy, a sympathy with nature and hostility to those human forces which degraded it, a religious emphasis on changing the world through a visionary imagination such as to be found in the poetry of Blake that takes radical issue with the scientific world view, an interest in the religion and cultures of non-Western societies, an anarchist (in its technical sense) distrust of all institutions – even those proclaiming a radical politics – and a belief in the justice of minimal, local forms of social organization. What interests me in the present context, however, is the sense that despite the great diversity both of style and substance, it was widely accepted that there was a hegemonic unit, the singular 'counter culture', which was opposed to the dominant forms of orthodoxy and institutional power.

This antithetical structure is very different from the circulating self-undermining structures of power traced in the work of Greenblatt. The accompanying suggestion that subversion can never be strong enough to effect substantial change, that it can always be recuperated, can be traced to the keen awareness at this time of the possibility of what Marcuse called 'repressive desublimation' – that, as Theodor Rozsak put it, 'the technocracy does indeed seem capable of anabolizing every form of discontent into its system' (14). The constant Marcusian cry at that time was the warning that 'everything can be co-opted' (70–2). This fear of assimilation was doubtless the result of the fact that the counter culture itself co-opted the methods and oppositional stance of the Civil Rights movement which started on 1 December 1955, when Mrs Rosa Parks was arrested in Montgomery, Alabama, for refusing to give up her seat on a bus for a white man. The campaign of peaceful civil disobedience developed with the demand for integrated classes in schools at Little Rock, Arkansas, and the first 'sit-in' movement which sought to achieve integrated lunch-counters in Woolworth stores (thereby creating an undivided counter culture).[20] The last great campaign, the War on Poverty of 1968, during which Martin Luther King was assassinated, was structured round the march on Washington (starting symbolically from the poorest town in America, the appropriately named Marks, Mississippi). King had now moved the agenda from racial injustice to include the social injustice of poverty and inequality of wealth. The counter culture in many respects consisted of the appropriation by middle-class students of one aspect of this political campaign, the protest against the Vietnam War; its extension of the campaign of the Civil Rights movement into a more general civil disobedience no doubt contributed to the narrow Democratic defeat in 1968, and the end of the Civil Rights movement itself. Despite its widespread achievements, immediately apparent in the integration within the educational system, much of the social injustice to which that movement drew attention remains. Today the political emphasis has moved away from King's ideal of social integration, it often being claimed that it always had to take place on the terms of the dominant white culture. The drive now is for equal rights, social justice, and justice before the law, combined with the recognition and continuance of social and ethnic difference. The heterogeneity emphasized by modern theory is a reflection of that social ideal. In this context it is important to recall that other contemporary political movement, the rise of black nationalism associated with the Nation of Islam and the Black Panther movement, was specifically excluded from the counter culture on account of its 'orthodox' revolutionary politics. Today the Muslim Malcolm X has become a more central cultural figure than the Christian Martin Luther King. The idolization of Malcolm X, the Frantz Fanon of black America, suggests that a new revolutionary militancy may be on the horizon, already reflected in the return to popularity of the Nation of Islam. Unless, that is, that idolization of Malcolm X has really been a process of aestheticization – and assimilation.

The current academic assimilation of the counter culture marks the very structure of incorporation that the counter culture decried but itself acted out and which today the New Historicists warn of (or perhaps celebrate) – without acknowledging that they themselves could also be the very agents of such institutional recuperation. David Norbrook has pointed out how the context for New Historicism is that of a period of disillusion after one of political turmoil, a phase of political conservatism combined with economic liberalism, a combination which repeats that which followed the alleged failures of the counter culture as a revolutionary movement (if indeed it did fail), and of May 1968.

Those who were, say, eighteen in 1968 are today in the 1990s in their forties. The students of that era participated in what must have been one of the most serious attacks on the university system in the whole of its history: the Campus War.[21] Where are those students now? We have colour supplement articles telling us what has happened to Daniel Cohn-Bendit; we can see Tariq Ali on Channel 4 virtually any day of the week. But a certain number of those students became academics, carrying on from the heady days of 'student power' to become lecturers and professors. It was this generation of academics who were to lead the inquiry into 'the institution', and who were to proclaim a general shift towards 'Cultural Studies' and 'cultural politics'. They achieved nothing more, and nothing less, than the institutionalization of the counter culture. At the same time, the paranoia that seems to accompany the preoccupation with postmodernism is nothing more than a reflexive anxiety that the counter culture has indeed been incorporated into the processes of the technocracy and its institutions.[22] 'Pushed back and repressed, incarcerated within and finally able to discharge and vent itself only on itself':[23] in a gesture of *ressentiment*, New Historicism relates its own hidden story of the co-option of the 'Great Refusal' of the 1960s and its 'culture of disaffiliation'.

That process goes on: if deconstruction and poststructuralism have been associated with the Reagan and Thatcher years by commentators, is it significant that with the dismantling of Marxism in the Soviet Union, the decolonization of Eastern Europe, and the consequent removal of the Communist threat, that Marxism is increasing its influence in the American academy? Here we might recall Greenblatt's argument that subversion is only admissible when the culture feels that it is not under threat. At the same time, it is worth recalling that however absurd the political project of levitating the Pentagon may appear to us now, it did form one of the decisive series of protest – the Campus War constituted another, the development of feminism another – which helped to bring about the end of the Vietnam War. So the counter culture did achieve political successes before its subsequent assimilation, just as there were many political and institutional changes initiated in Western Europe as a response to May 1968.

In any case the levitation of the Pentagon is a perfect example of Greenblatt's category of something that current ideology can contain so effortlessly that it doesn't appear to us today to be subversive at all. What has become equally unthinkable, in our contemporary world of sub-cultures, of the marginal, the subaltern, and the deviant, in our affirmation of the incommensurability of cultural difference, is the very concept of a general counter culture – the most sustained, but already devalued and almost forgotten, recent example of the production of a politically effective counter-hegemony in Western society. It's noticeable that the counter culture achieved its political effects to a large extent by challenging the conventional forms and modes of political intervention. If the political argument of New Historicism is that the radically subversive can be exactly what we no longer recognize as subversive, then what has been institutionally assimilated is less the effectiveness of the counter culture's political intervention than the lesson of its effectiveness.

(1990)

Notes

1 Gayatri Chakravorty Spivak, 'The New Historicism: Political Commitment and the Postmodern Critic', in Veeser, *The New Historicism*, 281.

2 Grumley, *History and Totality*.

3 Norbrook, 'Life and Death of Renaissance Man', 89–93.

4 See the various contributions to Veeser, *The New Historicism*.

5 Graff, *Poetic Statement and Critical Dogma*; Jameson, *Postmodernism*, 188.

6 White, in Veeser, *The New Historicism*, 302.

7 Jameson, *The Political Unconscious*, 20, cited by Greenblatt, 'Towards a Poetics of Culture', in Veeser, *The New Historicism*, 2. Further references to this essay will be cited in the text.

8 Lyotard, cited by Greenblatt, 'Towards a Poetics of Culture', 4.

9 Norbrook, 'Life and Death of Renaissance Man', 108. On history as excess, see my *White Mythologies*, 19, 66.

10 Benjamin, *Illuminations*, 263.

11 Fineman, 'The History of the Anecdote: Fiction and Fiction', in Veeser, *The New Historicism*, 49–76 (reprinted in Fineman, *The Subjectivity Effect in Western Literary Tradition*, 59–87). Further references will be cited in the text.

12 Here I pass over the problem that ensues when Fineman redescribes this as the relation of event to context – which is altogether a different matter.

13 Cf. D'Amico, *Historicism and Knowledge*; Grumley, *History and Totality*.

14 60. Fineman continues: 'In this sense, if only in name only, the New Historicism amounts to a gesture which is the very opposite of Fredric Jameson's essentially ahistorical injunction in *The Political Unconscious* to "always historicize"'.

15 Cf. Arato, *Frankfurt School Reader*, 205–6.

16 We may make a comparison with Bakhtin here according to which these processes remain undialogized until they enter the novel, i.e. they need a further totalization to be detotalizing.

17 Laclau and Mouffe, *Hegemony and Socialist Strategy*, 16.

18 Graff, 'Co-optation', in *The New Historicism*, 169–81.

19 Cited by Roszak, *The Making of a Counter Culture*, 124. This book is based on articles that originally appeared in the spring of 1968. Further references will be cited in the text. For analyses of the alleged failure of the counter culture in the United States and Britain, see Bell, *The Cultural Contradictions of Capitalism*, and Martin, *A Sociology of Contemporary Cultural Change*.

20 Segal, *The Race War*, 246–9.

21 See Roszak, *The Dissenting Academy*; Searle, *The Campus War*.

22 Of course you could argue that the counter culture always was part of the culture to which it was nominally opposed. It's significant, for example, that Roszak, of all contemporary radical phenomena, excepts the Black Panther movement from the counter culture.

23 Deleuze and Guattari, *Anti-Oedipus*, 214.

8.

The idea of a chrestomathic university

> When an University has been doing useless things for
> a long time, it appears at first degrading to them to be
> useful.
>
> Sydney Smith

Should education have any use? Put like that the question seems hardly worth asking, let alone answering. Yet this apparently absurd topic constitutes the major issue that has dominated debates about higher education in Britain for the past two hundred years. What is most remarkable is that such a controversy should have managed to sustain itself into such extreme old age; a suppurating scission within British culture, through which British culture repeats its irreconcilable antagonisms.

It is true that not even Oscar Wilde dared to assert publicly, at least, that universities should be like art – that is, perfectly useless. But to suggest that universities should be useful, that they should teach practical forms of knowledge, has been, for many, to go too far. And that has not been because like Foucault, they have suspiciously characterized the university as an 'institutional apparatus through which society ensures its uneventful reproduction, at least cost to itself':[1] on the contrary, they have considered that society is best served and sustained by the universities teaching knowledge that is useless. The wisdom of the university, in this account, should not have a use value: it should be outside the circuit of exchange, its very exteriority assuring its special value as a signifier, no doubt transcendental, that guarantees the stability of society itself.

This by no means implies, however, that the university's particular function is to embody the principle of reason, as the Germans were to argue.[2] No English university (English because the systems elsewhere in Britain are separate and would require altogether different analyses) is founded on reason.[3] If the principle of reason is itself situated on an abyss, the first and most famous universities of Britain, Oxford and Cambridge, by contrast, were founded quite literally on a void, a dissemination, that is as a result of an academic diaspora.[4] If we pose the question of the basis, principles, and function of the English university, we find that, suitably enough for a country with an unwritten constitution, there is no founding document or even prospective philosophical account of the function and system of the university such as those which formed part of the national reconstruction in Germany after the Napoleonic invasion. All that can be found is a charter by which the State granted the university certain privileges. In this sense, no English university can claim that it thinks that it knows what it is doing. Even the institution of the Ph.D. had no more glorious rationale than that in the 1920s, discovering that their Master of Arts degree could not compete with the Ph.D. of foreign universities in attracting overseas graduate students, British universities pragmatically introduced a doctorate of philosophy.[5]

Nor in the eighteenth or nineteenth centuries, can there be found any conflict of faculties such as Kant describes, if for no other reason than because by then the higher faculties of theology, law and medicine, had largely disappeared, leaving the faculty of arts in uncontested domination.[6] But if there was no internal conflict within the universities, the State itself constantly challenged the validity of the knowledge that was taught within them. The history of the universities in the nineteenth century is about the contestation of academic freedom in that sense: do the universities have the right to teach what they like? Does the State have the right to call into question the knowledge that the universities impart – and given that the universities are themselves by definition the highest authorities on the subject of knowledge and its validity, what are the grounds on which the State opposes them?

To contest the prerogative of the universities is no easy matter. Oxford and Cambridge – which have always most seriously defended their right to teach useless knowledge – are, as ecclesiastical corporations, founded on nothing other than the Logos itself. No lesser word than the Word has constituted the authority of the university – exclusively from the beginnings of the University of Oxford in the twelfth century to the founding of the secular University of London in 1826. For six centuries Oxford and Cambridge held a monopoly over university education in England. The charters by which they were established, which guaranteed them certain forms of freedom from the State, and allowed them to exercise a monopoly over the degrees necessary for candidates for ordination in the Church of England, together with the successive endowments which they accrued over the centuries, meant that they became wealthy – and, in the opinion of some, virtually useless.

It is generally agreed even by the official historians of the universities themselves that by the eighteenth century they had fallen into a serious decay:[7] testimony after testimony can be found of their degenerate condition in this period. One of the best known is Wordsworth's description of Cambridge in *The Prelude*, published after his death in 1850 at a very timely moment, just when the university was under investigation by a Royal Commission. Edward Gibbon recalls of his tutor at Magdalen College, Oxford:

> Dr Winchester well remembered that he had a salary to receive, and only forgot that he had a duty to perform. Instead of guiding the studies and watching over the behaviour of his disciple, I was never summoned to attend even the ceremony of a lecture; and except one voluntary visit to his rooms, during the eight months of his titular office, the tutor and pupil lived in the same college as strangers to each other.[8]

Magdalen's response to Gibbon's criticism was to institute a special section in the College Library (which exists to this day) devoted to books written by fellows of the College.[9] The state of the universities at this time is most economically summed up in Adam Smith's remark, which seems to have gone uncontested, that 'in the university of Oxford, the greater part of the publick professors have, for these many years, given up altogether even the pretence of teaching'.[10] College fellowships were regarded as a reward for achievements attained rather than implying any obligation to teach; other considerations were also important – even in Newman's day, Oriel College was the only college in Oxford that elected its fellows on the sole grounds of academic merit.[11]

This strength of Oxford against outside interference was to some extent a reaction to the events of the Civil War, when Oxford, having been Charles's most loyal royalist stronghold, was subsequently forced to reform itself and to appoint the radical supporters of Baconian new science such as Wallis and Wilkins who were nominated by parliamentary commissioners. This was not, at least, as extreme a measure as Milton, who had wanted to abolish the university altogether, had advocated. With the Restoration, the old loyalists were reinstated, and the former radicals moved to London.[12] The university's loyalist history meant that it became impervious to outside pressure, all the more strongly enforced by the dark memory of the activity of the commissioners around the Civil War period. Demands for reform began to be made again with increasing vociferousness in the eighteenth century but achieved little. The universities argued that, as ecclesiastical institutions, no contract with the State existed beyond that between Church and State; their close affiliations with the Government kept them unharmed. Until, however, the State itself changed once again: in 1854, despite strong opposition particularly from Oxford (which argued that it had already revised its academic arrangements satisfactorily, in 1636), the State reasserted its ultimate legal powers and rewrote the statutes. The subsequent history of Oxford and Cambridge during the nineteenth century is a story of reforms directly or indirectly imposed upon them. This history is not a reassuring one for any advocate of an absolute academic freedom.

Paradoxically enough, until the time of J. S. Mill it was the Liberals who attacked the principles of a 'liberal' education. The assault on Oxford and Cambridge from outside the universities focused on two related issues: the exclusion of Dissenters, that is, any one who was not a member of the Church of England, and the university curriculum – both of which were justified by the same doctrinal truth. In 1809, declaring that he had been long waiting for the opportunity, Sydney Smith attacked the whole rationale of the classical education which formed the syllabus at Oxford. (Cambridge by contrast demanded a little classics, but mostly pure mathematics.) In the place of truth Smith substituted use: 'the only proper criterion of every branch of education', he argued, is 'its utility in future life'. According to this criterion:

> there never was a more complete instance in any country of such extravagant and overacted attachment to any branch of knowledge, as that which obtains in this country with regard to classical knowledge. A young Englishman goes to school at six or seven years old; and he remains in a course of education till twenty-three or twenty-four years of age. In all that time, his sole and exclusive occupation is learning Latin and Greek: he has scarcely a notion that there is any other kind of excellence; and the great system of facts with which he is the most perfectly acquainted, are the intrigues of the Heathen Gods: with whom Pan slept? – with whom Jupiter? – whom Apollo ravished? These facts the English youth get by heart the moment they quit the nursery; and are most sedulously and industriously instructed in them till the best and most active part of life is passed away. Now, this long career of classical learning, we may, if we please, denominate a foundation; but it is a foundation so far above ground, that there is absolutely no room to put any thing upon it.[13]

Smith concluded that 'nothing would so much tend to bring classical literature within proper bounds, as a steady and invariable appeal to utility in our appretiation [sic] of human knowledge'. In this way he set up the terms of a debate that was to continue to the present day.

His attack stirred Oxford to the extent of provoking a series of ripostes. In 1810 Edward Copleston, the Professor of Poetry, published *A Reply to the Calumnies of the Edinburgh Review against Oxford*, and, then, *A Second Reply ... to the Calumnies*, and even *A Third Reply ... to the Calumnies*.[14] It was hard to defend the Oxford curriculum in terms of the idea of a liberal education, since, with its exclusive emphasis on Latin and Greek, it could hardly be described as liberal; nor could Copleston invoke the other meaning of liberal in the sense of freedom, given the severe financial, gender, and religious restrictions on attendance at the university. So instead he fought his ground on the long-established claim, so often to be repeated subsequently, that if a literary education did not prepare the student for any specific kind of employment or profession, its very lack of specificity meant that it prepared him (women were not admitted) for everything. Citing Adam Smith on the increasing partiality and narrowness of perspective that results from the division of labour among the professions, Copleston argued:

> In the cultivation of literature is found that common link, which, among the higher and middling departments of life, unites the jarring sects and subdivisions in one interest, which supplies common topics, and kindles common feelings, unmixed with those narrow prejudices with which all professions are more or less infected. The knowledge, too, which is thus acquired, expands and enlarges the mind.... And thus, without directly qualifying a man for any of the employments of life, it enriches and ennobles all. Without teaching him the peculiar business of any one office or calling, it enables him to act his part in each of them with better grace and more elevated carriage....
>
> There must be surely a cultivation of the mind, which is itself a good: a good of the highest order; without any immediate reference to bodily appetites, or wants of any kind.... And if Classical Education be regarded in this light, there is none in which it will be found more faultless.[15]

A sublime elevation versus a rational ground, a glorious truth versus vulgar utility, knowledge for its own sake versus debasing instrumentality, quality of mind versus practical needs, the universal versus the particular: such were the terms of the debate which, in spite of local variations, has remained the basis of discussions of university education from that day to this.

Copleston's argument reflects the extent to which the university's

function had by the nineteenth century come to be seen as providing young men with a version of the civility and refinement which
in former times they would have acquired from a sojourn at the
royal Court. Copleston assumes that the recipient of such a form of
education is in a position to disregard such trivialities as 'wants of
any kind'; in other words, that the student does not need education
in order to provide the wealth to support him afterwards. It seems
likely that classical literary education survived precisely because
anyone who could afford at that time to go to Oxford or Cambridge
was by definition not in need of a profession, and therefore was not
in need of anything but a gentlemanly education. This is clear from
the failure of attempts to transplant the Oxford model to the new
University of Durham in 1832, founded because in the year of the
Reform Bill the Church of England was afraid that the Government
might appropriate some of its surplus wealth; thirty years later,
however, Durham still had no more than forty-six students.[16] A similar fate befell the new Catholic University of Dublin, founded in
1852, whose rector, John Henry Newman, ironically provided in his
rectorial addresses the most eloquent defence of this idea of university education. The 'cultivated intellect' that is its object produces the true gentleman, whose magnanimous and fastidious
qualities are described by Newman with some fervour for several
pages.[17] However, the reality of such high ideals, at a university
designed solely for Irish Catholics who had been oppressed and
prevented from holding office or power for several centuries, was
rather different: as Newman himself admitted, 'the great difficulty is
that there seems to be no class to afford members of a University'.[18]
In fact, only the useful part of the university, the medical school,
survived.

If certain class interests were involved in the idea of a literary
education, the authority of the Anglican Church – in Britain consti-
tutionally part of the State – was also at stake, as well as its power
to control university education. For this reason, as Newman's lectures make abundantly clear, the dispute over useful as against
useless knowledge is also an argument about secular, or free thinking, versus religious education – and about the place of religion in
knowledge generally, which was, in the sphere of natural philosophy, being increasingly contested. This is apparent from the controversy that surrounded the founding of the University of London in
1826 – the first English university designed to teach useful knowledge. What shocked the more conservative members of the public,
including Coleridge who immediately announced that he would give

three lectures on the subject of the university, which he never gave, was that the University of London was, as it was termed, a 'godless university'. This meant that the Church of England's monopoly over university education had at long last been broken: the teachers were not required to be clergymen as they were at Oxford and Cambridge; students did not have to take a religious test by swearing allegiance to the doctrines of the Church of England in order to matriculate, and religion was not even taught.

The University of London was founded if not on reason as such, then at least upon the reasoned argument of the utilitarians that a university should teach useful knowledge. It was modelled not on Oxford and Cambridge but on the Universities of Edinburgh and Virginia, and, particularly, the new reformed universities of Germany, from which it took the professorial and lecture system. Its intellectual inspiration was derived from the ideas of the radical utilitarian, Jeremy Bentham, whose mummified body is still preserved in University College London, and which – rather less reasonably – on the instruction of his will is carried out to take its place at certain college functions each year, allegedly on the grounds that his silence will amount to more sense than the rest of what is said. Bentham, though too old to take an active part in the planning of the new university, had established an important precedent in his *Chrestomathia, Being a Collection of Papers explanatory of the Design of an Institution, proposed to be set on foot under the name of the Chrestomathic Day School, or Chrestomathia School, for the Extension of the New System of Instruction to the higher Branches of Learning. For the Use of the middling and higher Ranks in Life* of 1816.[19]

This remarkable work proposed a new system of instruction designed to produce more effective teaching, based on the latest theories of associationist psychology; it also advocated the abolition of flogging, the admission of girls on an equal basis with boys (a principle that the University of London, however, did not endorse until 1878), as well as such details as the employment of what Bentham with his love of abstruse terminology called the 'Psammographic principle', that is, the use of sand-writing instead of slates. The school itself was to be built as a panopticon, so as to allow the most economical use of the teacher's capacities, with additional instruction by pupil-monitors on the 'Madras system' (so called because the method had first been tested in Madras in India). Efficient forms of teaching, together with a detailed scheme of progressive structures through which knowledge could be taught, meant that instead of just a 'scraping together', as Milton had put it, of 'so much miserable Greek and Latin', pupils could be quickly taught an impressively wide range of knowledge. So J. S. Mill, who was himself instructed by his father on strictly Benthamite principles, reckoned that by the age of eighteen he was, in intellectual terms, twenty-five years ahead of his peers.

An influential review of the *Chrestomathia* in the *Westminster Review* of 1824 suggested pointedly that its method could be adapted to higher forms of learning, declaring, 'here then is a machine of immense power capable of producing the most extraordinary effects'.[20] Accordingly, the University of London adopted Bentham's 'chrestomathic' principle, chrestomathic, as Bentham himself explained, meaning 'conducive to useful learning'. (He might have added that the word was not, as a word, an example of itself.) This spanned the whole range of contemporary knowledge at both a theoretical and technical level, as is evident from Bentham's 'Chrestomathic Instruction Tables' and encyclopaedic 'Art and Science Table', a tabular diagram in which every branch of art and science is arranged in an 'exhaustively-bifurcate mode' that demonstrates how each is conducive to well-being or 'eudaemonics'. Notwithstanding his definitions of ethics and aesthetics as functions of *Pathoscopic pneumatology*, with aesthetics defined as *Anergastic* (no-work-producing) and *Aplopathoscopic* (mere sensation regarding), what is not clear in Bentham's account is quite what reconciles the chrestomathic with the eudaemonic, how an institution that is conducive to useful learning at the same time produces happiness. Bentham attempts to reconcile them through a tortuous definition of 'eudaemonics' as the maximization of well-being. However, it was to become evident that the double object of utilitarianism produced a bifurcating tendency that could not be permanently resolved by a neologism or the containing power of a very long sentence.

Undeterred by such difficulties, however, the 1825 *Prospectus* of the University of London announced that 'the object of the Institution is to bring the means of a complete scientific and literary education home to the inhabitants of the metropolis'.[21] The University therefore offered comprehensive instruction in all forms of knowledge – in medicine, engineering, mathematics, the sciences, political economy, law, classical and modern languages, Hindustani and Sanskrit (suggesting the extent to which the university, many of whose original shareholders were British administrators and businessmen in India, was designed to service the Orientalist needs of the East India Company, a colonial connection developed with the subsequent founding of Imperial College) as well as, for the first time in an English university, 'British Literature'.[22] The kind of professors appointed, who were mostly Scottish or German, with a few from Cambridge, ensured that the university taught the most advanced subjects and forms of knowledge of its day. Except, that is, in British Literature, where a candidate, whom Bentham supported, specializing in the new Scottish rhetorical studies, was passed over in favour of a traditional moralist, as a gesture to the evangelicals who had given the university such strong support.[23]

New forms of knowledge, as always, involved important political stakes.[24] Arguments for changes in education were quite clearly part of a power struggle: the University of London embodied, for the first time in competitive institutional form, the counter-ideology of the radical middle classes, particularly that of the Dissenters. British higher education since that time has been the product of these two different systems whose politics and effects can still be found at work today. Schematically but only provisionally we could characterize them as the ecclesiastical, conservative model and the vocational, radical model, corresponding, as the opponents themselves often specified, to the politics and religion of the upper and middle classes. The first, identifiable with Oxford and Cambridge, the Tory party and the Church of England, regarded the universities as sustaining the State by embodying its religious and cultural heritage in an elite form of education for the ruling class. Here the university's function was to be an organ for the transmission of truth, with knowledge regarded as an end and a good in itself, a form of morality, and of doctrinal veracity. Pedagogy, consequently, was the privileged activity for such an institution which remained hostile to the idea of 'research' or the 'advancement' of knowledge; its preferred subject area was not the future but the past, particularly the Bible, the Graeco-Roman tradition and the literature of the classics.

By contrast the competing radical educationalists rejected the ecclesiastical notion of truth as both partial and political: their strategy, however, was not so much to challenge it on the grounds of its class interests as to characterize it as useless, a manoeuvre later modified with great success into the long-running opposition of 'science' versus the 'arts'. These liberal utilitarians and nonconformists argued that knowledge should be up to date, useful, practical, changed according to the results of theoretical investigation and scientific research, and taught in a democratized secular form. At their most radical, the liberals regarded education as a political force, not only for their own benefit but also as a potential means

of liberation for disadvantaged groups, such as religious nonconformists, women, the poor, colonized peoples, in fact anyone suffer-
ing political oppression.[25]

Thus the possibility of social change through education, first
advocated by Helvétius, was already the radical position of the
utilitarians and liberals, such as Bentham, Mill, or Wollstonecraft, in
all of whom there can be found a deep commitment to education
and its power. These utilitarians were also radical in ways that are
once again being endorsed today – advocating rights for women, for
instance, and the rights of minorities against established groups. It
was the utilitarians who promoted the cause of education, suffrage,
women's rights, or the abolition of slavery, in the nineteenth century. Although they placed much greater emphasis on the possibilities of education rather than change in the capitalist system to
which they remained fully committed, in some respects the utilitarians were less different from Marx than he himself was prepared
to admit: Smith's *Wealth of Nations* (1776) formed the basis of all
radical, anti-Tory politics throughout the nineteenth century until
the advent of socialism; in their different ways, furthermore, both
Marx and Adam Smith were economic determinists. Bentham, a
philosopher whose legalistic mind is comparable only to Kant's,
was a vigorous advocate of a welfare state with free education,
sickness benefits, minimum wages, and guaranteed employment. It
was Bentham who declared of the German idealist philosophers
long before Marx's more famous statement in the 'Theses on
Feuerbach': 'The Germans can only inquire about things as they
are. They are interdicted from inquiring into things as they ought
to be'.[26]

The radical utilitarian ethos of science and practicality remained
sufficiently powerful for there to be comparatively little space for
intervention in the area of higher education from the socialist
movement that developed in the nineteenth century. The position
of the British Left with regard to education was one of profound
ambivalence. From Robert Owen onwards, the socialist movement
did regard access to knowledge as a means to political power and
social transformation. But following Marx's critique of Smith and
later utilitarians, socialists were hostile to an ethics of knowledge in
which education is designed to be useful, and amounts to the learning of skills necessary for efficient capitalist production; similarly
they had learnt to be wary of such progressive educational institutions as the Society for the Diffusion of Useful Knowledge which
was designed to teach the poor the virtues of political economy.

Socialists therefore tended to form an unholy alliance with more conservative outlooks which stressed the value of a general education. This also suggests a tacit acceptance of the political reality by which the possibility of social change through education was already the radical position of the utilitarians and Liberals. One effect of this was the striking absence of a politics of higher education identifiable with the aspirations of the working class. The lack of any effective socialist argument for higher education partly accounts for the extent to which the issues of 'truth' versus 'use', arts versus sciences, continue to dominate the politics of education.[27]

This lacuna can partly be explained by the fact that the political aspirations of socialists at this time were fixed on the demand for a national system of primary – let alone university – education, which was not to be made compulsory until 1880.[28] In the second place, the elitism of higher education meant that it was never regarded as a possible means of enabling the generation of a mass movement, but was rather seen as a force of opposition to it. The latter perception was not entirely mistaken. The two antithetical ideologies of higher education, ecclesiastical and vocational, were initially embodied in two different kinds of universities: Oxford and Cambridge, and the University of London. The latter acted as a spur both to the creation of the so-called civic or 'red-brick' universities during the course of the nineteenth century, which were often founded as technical colleges and funded by industrialists, and to the reform of the Universities of Oxford and Cambridge from the 1850s onwards. This meant that, to a large extent, the conflict between Tory and utilitarian Liberal interests was internalized into institutional differences within the university system. It also gave different disciplines specific class identities: even today, arts and science tend to be associated with different taste cultures, with the arts firmly middle-class, science as lower-middle or working-class.[29]

By the 1830s and 1840s, the political differences between the upper and middle classes become less marked in the face of increasing working-class agitation. The gradual rapprochement between the dissenting middle classes and landed gentry in the face of a militant working class also brought about a compromise over the role of higher education. This is best exemplified in the writings of Mill, who, while regarding the institutions of Oxford and Cambridge 'with sentiments little short of utter abhorrence', nevertheless rejected the utilitarian objectives of reform.[30] Mill advocated instead university reform that would bring about 'the regeneration of individual character among our lettered and opulent classes'. In proposing the function of the university as an 'institution of spiritual culture' for 'forming great minds', he laid the foundations for the theory of the university that would be elaborated by Newman and Arnold.[31] From this time on, the universities were mobilized as a significant form of resistance to working-class demands, not only in terms of creating and preserving an ethic of a shared national culture, but also through the strategy of what might be termed institutional imperialism. For the alternative self-help institutions of education, such as the mechanics' institutes, often set up by the working classes themselves were, as Engels complained, gradually taken over by the State and turned into technical training colleges; in the twentieth century they were eventually safely absorbed into the State education system as new universities and polytechnics.[32] And as the older working-class institutions became universities, so they gradually lost contact with their radical origins or the class for whom they were originally set up to cater.

Throughout the nineteenth century, the question of access to higher education was a topic of constant debate. Political agitation moved through a succession of excluded groups, from Dissenters, to women, to the working class. The latter two are well represented in the literary sphere by Tennyson's *Princess* (1847) and Hardy's *Jude the Obscure* (1896).[33] From 1854 onwards Oxford and Cambridge were gradually opened up to excluded minorities; in 1902 the first student grants were awarded, and other movements were initiated about this time which tried to extend the reach of education, such as the university extension movement, and the Workers' Educational Association. Important though these innovative developments were, the question of access has always tended to exclude consideration of the function of universities as such, particularly in socialist theory. The Left has never succeeded in defining a politics of higher education that can be distinguished from those already in operation: on the one hand, a distrust of the gentlemanly mode tends to lead it to emphasize more practical and vocational forms – hence the founding of the polytechnics by a Labour Government in 1966 – on the other hand, distrust of education as merely a training in those skills currently useful for capitalism, of arguments such as Chadwick's for the purely economic value of education, has led the Left to endorse the notion of education for personal self-improvement that formed the basis of the self-help institutes, but which, by emphasizing the benefits of mental development for the individual, comes intriguingly close to the conservative and later Liberal position. This explains why the radical Left in the literary sphere, such as the Left Leavisites, in many ways merely invert the older ecclesiastical position of the university as an institution of spiritual culture. It is time to look at its theoretical arguments more carefully.

Useful uselessness

It is not without significance that the most famous analysis of the university by an English writer, that of Cardinal John Henry Newman, should take the form of a defence of the idea of the university as truth itself. Newman's work could be said to define the English idea of a university, as against all contemporary alternatives which were based on foreign models, be they Scottish or German. Although at the very moment when he was proposing such an ethos, the university which inspired it was already in the process of being reformed by the State, Newman's idea of the university remains the basis of a whole educational and political ethic.

Newman's lectures, gathered together at various times under different titles but best known by the last, *The Idea of a University* (1852–73), demonstrate an ambivalence between an endeavour to reassert the religious basis of education against the advance of secular, scientific knowledge and an attempt to treat religion as separate from the general idea of a 'liberal education' whose function would be to produce quality of mind, social cohesion, and, ultimately, the religious truth from which it was initially separated. While Newman tries on the one hand, to justify the idea of a university education as one of knowledge for its own sake, on the other he attempts to establish the place of theology as the faculty that functions as the architectonic, or idea, of all the diverse knowledges in the university.

Newman bases his idea of a university – ominously enough – on what etymologists consider to be a false derivation, claiming that a university 'by its very name professes to teach universal knowledge'.[34] This allows him, according to what Freud would characterize as the logic of the broken kettle, to offer three defences of the role of theology in the university: first, if a university is a place of universal knowledge, then it must include theological knowledge; second, while all such knowledges must be understood in their connections together in an institution that claims to teach universal knowledge, only religious knowledge can complete and correct the other sciences and give each particular field an appreciation of its place from the perspective of the whole; and, third, if theology is not taught, then its place will be usurped by the sciences which will teach other, irreligious, doctrines instead. Theology is thus, like philosophy for Kant, both a part of the system of the sciences of the university and also that part which operates over and above the rest. It does not, however, have the function of judging the truth of other forms of knowledge, as it does for Kant, but of fusing such knowledge of partial truths into a higher truth, truth itself, correcting the 'false peculiar colouring of each' into the Platonic whiteness of the Idea (153). Theology is both a science in itself and the product of all other forms of knowledge, a higher knowledge of the philosophic mind which transcends all others; the perspective of the whole which it provides comprises the function of a university education, with the result that it finally becomes identified with the institution of the university itself. As Newman puts it, the student

> apprehends the great outlines of knowledge, the principles on which it rests, the scale of its parts, its lights and its shades, its great points and its little, as he otherwise cannot apprehend them. Hence it is that his education is called 'Liberal'. A habit of mind is formed which lasts through life . . . what . . . I have ventured to call a philosophical habit. . . . This is the main purpose of a University in its treatment of its students. (96)

What, however, Newman is obliged to ask, is the *use* of such an education? The answer is none. None, that is, if use is thought of only in terms of 'ulterior objects', such as training for the professions or for commerce. Knowledge, he counters, does not require a use, for it 'is capable of being its own end. Such is the constitution of the human mind that any kind of knowledge, if it be really such, is its own reward' (97). Knowledge is aestheticized to the extent that it becomes a condition of mind, of judgement and of taste; finally involving no formal learning at all, merely requiring the company of fellows, of nature, or solitude, the haunts of the scholar gypsy (132–3). In his attack on London University Newman goes so far as to suggest that he would prefer a university which did nothing at all over 'that which exacted of its members an acquaintance with every science under the sun' (129).

Such knowledge as the university teaches need have nothing useful in view: it is a good in itself. It may be useless but not valueless. Yet if the good is an end in itself, it cannot stop itself from producing an end beyond itself, a surplus which will, in turn, be useful:

> though the useful is not always good, the good is always useful. Good is not only good, but reproductive of good; this is one of its attributes;

nothing is excellent, beautiful, perfect, desirable for its own sake, but
it overflows, and spreads the likeness of itself all around it. . . . A great
good will impart great good. If then the intellect is so excellent a portion of us, and its cultivation so excellent, it is not only beautiful,
perfect, admirable, and noble in itself, but in a true and high sense it
must be useful to the possessor and to all around him; not useful in
any low, mechanical, mercantile sense, but as diffusing good, or as a
blessing, or a gift, or power, or a treasure, first to the owner, then
through him to the world. I say then if a liberal education be good, it
must necessarily be useful too. (143–4)

Knowledge, therefore is its own reward. But if it has no use value,
it brings a surplus value in its wake, the good, which is indeed
useful: the 'state or condition of mind' (105), that is the product of
a liberal education, in turn produces 'the gentleman':

Liberal Education makes not the Christian, not the Catholic, but the
gentleman. It is well to be a gentleman, it is well to have a cultivated
intellect, a delicate taste, a candid, equitable, dispassionate mind, a
noble and courteous bearing in the conduct of life; – these are the
connatural qualities of a large knowledge; they are the objects of a
University. (110)

The story of the spontaneous generation of a liberal education does
not, however, stop even there.

Although Newman claims to separate the benefits of a liberal
literary education from those of religious education, he does so
only to unite them again in the same terms, so that the second is
the product of the first. For if the object of the university is a
gentlemanly condition of mind, then this philosophic expansion
produces a spiritual reward, whereby the perfection of the intellect
becomes indistinguishable from the form of religious truth: 'Religious Truth is not only a portion, but a condition of general knowledge. To blot it out is nothing short, if I may so speak, of unravelling
the web of University Teaching' (71). Newman mixes his metaphors,
literary and religious, blots and webs, in order to appropriate that
comprehensive knowledge which, as John Barrell has argued, was
contested in the eighteenth century between the 'man of letters'
and the 'gentleman'.[35] Newman resolves this by effecting a synthesis in which the two contending parties are uplifted into a higher
universal term – the university.

A university training, according to Newman, aims at elevat-
ing the intellectual tone of society, 'at cultivating the public mind,
at purifying the national taste, at supplying true principles to popular enthusiasm, and fixed aims to popular aspiration, at giving

enlargement and sobriety to the ideas of the age, at facilitating the exercise of political power'; its function of producing health is to act as a safeguard against 'excesses and enormities of evil' and 'social disorder and lawlessness' (162–3). The product of the university, the gentleman, is 'at home in any society, . . . has common ground with every class' (155), so that he functions as a kind of metaperson who unites society as he unites knowledge. This elevated position that the gentleman occupies in society clearly corresponds with the form of knowledge that produces such a character; just as the philosophical view produced by the liberal education produces a comprehensive view of things, keeps knowledges in check, and holds them all together, so the gentleman does the same for society at large. Indeed in some of Newman's descriptions, knowledge and society become indistinguishable from each other as the function of the university expands with ever more imperial metaphors:

> We count it a great thing, and justly so, to plan and carry out a wide political organization. To bring under one yoke, after the manner of old Rome, a hundred discordant peoples; to maintain each of them in its own privileges within its legitimate range of action; to allow them severally the indulgence of national feelings, and the stimulus of rival interests; and yet withal to blend them into one great social establishment, and to pledge them to the perpetuity of the one imperial power; – this is an achievement which carries with it the unequivocal token of genius in the race which effects it.

> Tu regere imperio populos, Romane, memento [*Remember thou, Roman, to rule the nations with thy power*]. . . .

> What an empire is in political history, such is a University in the sphere of philosophy and research. It is . . . the high protecting power of all knowledge and science, of fact and principle, of inquiry and discovery, of experiment and speculation; it maps out the territory of the intellect, and sees that the boundaries of each province are religiously respected, and that there is neither encroachment nor surrender on any side. It acts as umpire between truth and truth, and, taking into account the nature and importance of each, assigns to all their due order and precedence. (370)

It is in this context of this 'philosophy of an imperial intellect' (371) that the significance emerges of Newman's stress on the stability of the institution of the university and its authority derived from 'a connected view or grasp of things' set against the 'random theories and imposing sophistries and dashing paradoxes which carry away half-formed and superficial intellects' (11, 13). 'Such parti-coloured ingenuities', Newman affirms, are one of the chief evils of the day, discoverable in the extempore productions of periodical literature and journalism that divides everything up according to the demands of the moment; it is university education that can act as a bulwark against them. For Catholics in particular it is important that people should be taught a wisdom safe from the excesses and vagaries of individuals, embodied in institutions which have stood the trial and received the sanction of ages, and administered by men who, unlike the reviewers, have no need to be anonymous, for they are supported by their consistency with their predecessors and with each other. The complicity between such a view of society and the function of knowledge in the university begins to become apparent. The role of the university as an institution is to act, strictly speaking, as a form of politics, reconciling the conflicting interests and opinions of society through an authority which can call upon a tradition more substantial than any individual.

If this account begins to sound like a description of the Catholic church, or an anticipation of T. S. Eliot's 'Tradition and the Individual Talent', its theory of institutions is essentially derived from Burke. Newman makes his argument by invoking the aid of a powerful conservative literary–political tradition. As will have become obvious to any student of Romanticism by this point, the product of Newman's literary liberal education, 'the philosophic habit', is remarkably similar to what Wordsworth and Coleridge termed 'the philosophic mind'. Newman's description of the place of theology in relation to the university, of the university in relation to knowledge, and of knowledge in relation to the State, repeats a version of Coleridge's theory of organic form, where the 'esemplastic' imagination fulfils not a critical or scientific differentiating function but a metaphysical cohesive one, holding all knowledge together as a whole by endowing it with 'life' and a spiritual centre. Philosophy, says Newman, must be the form of knowledge: 'its matter must not be admitted into the mind passively, as so much acquirement, but must be mastered and appropriated as a system consisting of parts, related one to the other, and interpretative of one another in the unity of the whole' (156). Like the Coleridgean imagination, its high truth is opposed to fancy; its special function is 'to draw many things into one' (369), and to show how they form a whole or a system: 'it would communicate the image of the whole to every separate portion, till that whole becomes in imagination like a spirit, every where pervading and penetrating its component parts, and giving them one definite meaning' (123). Naming this process 'culture', Newman identifies it with the good that will soon be shown in the Platonic form of the 'Eternal and Infinite' – the Idea of a University (185).

What often seems to be less obvious to students of Romanticism is the no less political than spiritual function of this impressive form of unification. Newman claims that

> the process of imparting knowledge to the intellect in this philosophical way is [the University's] true culture; that such culture is a good in itself; that the knowledge which is both its instrument and result is called Liberal Knowledge; that such culture, together with the knowledge which effects it, may fitly be sought for its own sake; that it is, however, in addition, of *great secular utility*, as constituting the best and highest formation of the intellect for social and political life. (183) [emphasis added]

The defence of useless knowledge can be made because such knowledge serves an important and indeed highly useful function in the service of the State. That secular utility was first spelt out by Copleston in a passage which Newman himself cites verbatim: 'In the cultivation of literature is found that common link which, among the higher and middling departments of life, unites the jarring sects and subdivisions into one interest'.[36] It only remained for this reconciling, healing function to be extended to the lower 'departments' as well for the course of literature, and the university itself, to be set. Even useless knowledge, it seems, turns out to be useful. This dialectic exactly repeats, as one might expect, the fate of the corresponding theory of the work of art defined by its purposelessness, which was developed and endorsed so enthusiastically by the academic institution in the same period. As Martin Jay puts it:

> The principle of idealistic aesthetics – purposefulness without a purpose – reverses the scheme of things to which bourgeois art conforms socially: purposelessness for the purposes declared by the market. At last, in the demand for entertainment and relaxation, purpose has absorbed the realm of purposelessness.[37]

Plebification and popularization

It is not hard to chart the relation of the secular utility of Newman's university back to Coleridge's *On The Constitution of the Church and State According to the Idea of Each* (1829) or forward to Arnold's *Culture and Anarchy* (1869), where an ecumenical 'culture', often indistinguishably literature, philosophy and religion, provides both an intellectual and social function of cohesion.[38] For his part Coleridge, in what he pointedly terms his 'concluding address to the parliamentary leaders of the Liberalists and Utilitarians', makes the connection quite explicit between his attack on 'the commercial spirit' of secular and useful knowledge and his advocacy of the necessity for a counterbalance in the institutional conservation of religion and the State:

> a permanent, nationalized, learned order, a national clerisy or church, is an essential element of a rightly constituted nation, without which it wants the best security alike for its permanence and its progression; and for which neither tract societies nor conventicles, nor Lancasterian schools, nor mechanics' institutions, nor lecture-bazaars under the absurd name of universities [i.e. the University of London], nor all these collectively, can be a substitute. For they are all marked with the same asterisk of spuriousness, shew the same distemper-spot on the front, that they are empirical specifics for morbid symptoms that help to feed and continue the disease.
>
> But you wish for general illumination: you would spur-arm the toes of society, you would enlighten the higher ranks *per ascensum ab imis* [by ascent from the lowest levels]. You begin, therefore, with the attempt to *popularize* science: but you will only effect its *plebification*. It is folly to think of making all, or the many, philosophers, or even men of science and systematic knowledge. But it is duty and wisdom to aim at making as many as possible soberly and steadily religious; – inasmuch as the morality which the state requires in its citizens for its own well-being and ideal immortality, and without reference to their spiritual interest as individuals, can only exist for the people in the form of religion. But the existence of a true philosophy, or the power and habit of contemplating particulars in the unity and fontal mirror of the idea – this in the rulers and teachers of a nation is indispensable to a sound state of religion in all classes. In fine, Religion, true or false, is and ever has been the centre of gravity in a realm, to which all other things must and will accommodate themselves. (69–70)

Coleridge could hardly have made the alliance between truth and power, between politics and knowledge clearer. The very extent of his claims indicates the scope of an argument which provides a carefully articulated basis for Newman's description of the place of the university in upholding this scheme of permanence and progression. Coleridge's text is an extremely complex one which would require a detailed separate analysis: here I would only remark the deep complicity between a literary and a political ideology in a founding text of a literary theory that in the twentieth century has been supposed to be defined by the separation of the two.

Arnold's purposes, though more secular in tone, work towards the same end. In *Culture and Anarchy* he transposes Newman's idea back to the university from which it was derived – although in its own way Arnold's Oxford remains just as much an ideal, even if already tainted by reformist government interventions:

> Oxford, the Oxford of the past, has many faults; and she has heavily paid for them in defeat, in isolation, in want of hold upon the modern world. Yet we in Oxford, brought up amidst the beauty and sweetness of that beautiful place, have not failed to seize one truth: – the truth that beauty and sweetness are essential characters of a complete human perfection. When I insist on this, I am all in the faith and tradition of Oxford. (61–2)

In evidence of this Oxford spirit, Arnold cites Newman himself and his attempt to uphold the power of the Anglican Church over the university during the Tractarian movement. Arnold, like many lapsed Christians of the nineteenth century, wished to preserve the religious perspective by presenting it in as ecumenical a form as possible. In the face of the potentially dangerous growing calls for democracy and socialism, culture could act as a force of civilization upon the people at large, particularly the anarchic Irish and the English working classes. The repository of culture, the ideal towards which the whole country should strive, Arnold posits as nothing less than the material institution of the university itself: it acts as a bastion against anarchy – specifically class division – preserving and producing a metaphysical aspiration that can counter political unrest:

> [Culture] does not try to teach down to the level of inferior classes; it does not try to win them for this or that sect of its own, with ready made judgements and watchwords. It seeks to do away with classes; to make the best that has been thought and known in the world current everywhere; to make all men live in an atmosphere of sweetness and light. (70)

Although Arnold can no longer appeal to religion for this ideal, its secular substitute, literature, can function just as effectively. If for Marx, the class struggle between the bourgeoisie and the proletariat constitutes, as he puts it, 'the great lever' – *mochlos* – 'of the modern social revolution', for Arnold literature is the power that can dissolve the division on which that lever pivots.[39]

After Arnold literature became the privileged embodiment of a culture assigned the role of truth both within the university and in society at large. Whereas for Kant the lower faculty of philosophy judged the rest by the truth of reason, in England this function, abandoned by philosophy, was appropriated by literature which gave judgement according not to rational but poetic or Platonic truth.[40] We might speculate that if religious truth was followed by poetic truth as the architectonic of knowledge, the contemporary assertion of political truth as the most comprehensive metalanguage, specifically and noticeably in the realm of literary theory, is an attempt to win back that higher function extending over society at large – Newman's 'imperial intellect' – which poetic truth has now lost.

The influential 1921 report for the British Government by Sir Henry Newbolt, *The Teaching of English in England*, gave official endorsement to Arnold's position, and, as has been argued, set up the terms of the form and function of the teaching of literature in secondary and tertiary education that have been maintained ever since. Significantly enough, Newbolt cites Wordsworth's discussions of education in *The Prelude*, Newman's *Idea of a University*, misquotes Arnold as claiming that 'culture unites classes', before concluding that an education based upon the English language and literature would dissolve the debilitating effects of class differences through an appeal to a civilizing common national 'English' culture.[41]

The discomfort felt at the discovery of the explicitly political nationalistic and racialist origins of English as an educational subject, corroborated even further by demonstrations of its role in the service of colonial subjugation in India, has resulted in a call to transform literary studies into cultural or communication studies, that is to shift its attention from an elite to a mass culture.[42] Literature and the literary as such have certainly been under attack of late, and in many quarters they now have very strongly marked negative connotations. But what suggestions about changing the object of literary studies have neglected is the place of literature in the theory and institutional practice of the university as a whole – which cannot be changed quite so simply. In other words, to convert the disciplinary object from English to Cultural Studies merely inverts the site of its truth. The attempt by Raymond Williams and his followers to reappropriate the Arnoldian cultural tradition for an oppositional position preserves intact its political and ideological function in the university and in society at large. This has led to some acute political difficulties.

Since 1979 the policies for higher education of the Conservative Government have been conducted strictly according to the terms of the debate that I have been charting. The disorienting part, however, is that they have, as it were, come from the wrong political corner, invoking not tradition and the value of a general education but rather all the utilitarian arguments against the humanities to advocate science, and more skills-oriented usefulness instead. For more traditional literary critics, this has presented no problem, for the whole literature of the nineteenth century was already to hand: Leavis even refers to the anarchy, barbarianism, or, as he likes to put it, 'Americanism', that he is fighting against as the 'technologico-Benthamite' age. Nothing illustrates so clearly Leavis's place in a tradition of argument about the function of education than this anachronistic and no doubt deliberately inelegant phrase. Dickens's *Hard Times*, to which Leavis attached special significance, is the most famous literary attack on what was represented as the utilitarian view of education, but it is easy to find many other writers of the 'great tradition' who opposed such a philosophy just as passionately.[43] As a literary critic, therefore, one is already positioned in the debate: both in terms of the arguments of the literary and critical texts themselves, and in terms of the very existence of one's own discipline within the institutions of higher education; even current Conservative education policy was partly initiated by the *Black Papers on Education* of a literary journal, the *Critical Quarterly*.[44]

The difficulty for literary theorists, when faced with a new 'technologico-Thatcherite' assault on the humanities, was that the terms by which their subject was established historically, and the only effective ones with which it could still be defended, were those of the cultural conservatism and humanist belief in literature and philosophy that 'literary theory' has, broadly speaking, been attacking since the 1970s. When theorists found themselves wanting to protect their discipline against successive government cuts during the Thatcher regime they discovered that the only view with which they could defend themselves was the very one which, in intellectual terms, they wanted to attack. You might say that the problem was that the oppositional literary or theoretical mode was not the oppositional institutional one – a situation that in itself illustrates the limitations of oppositional politics. In short, for theorists the problem was that in attacking humanism they found themselves actually in consort with Government policy. This has meant, effectively, that it has often been left to those whom they opposed to defend the study of the humanities as such: symbolized when the University of Oxford, traditionally the main object of utilitarian hostility, refused to award Mrs Thatcher the customary honorary degree given to British prime ministers. A curious historical mutation has thus occurred by which the Conservatives, as they claim, have indeed become the radical party, if not of today, then of yesterday, by returning to a middle-class radicalism which regards not

Edmund Burke as its founder, but Adam Smith. This means, however, that they, in turn, are also already positioned in terms of their
attitude towards education and the universities.

Useless usefulness

In the mid-1980s, Mrs Thatcher began telling interviewers that what
the press called 'Thatcherism' was really nothing other than the
philosophy of Adam Smith, an identification institutionalized in the
most influential and radical government 'think-tank', the Adam Smith
Institute. Legend has it that when Keith Joseph became Minister for
Education in 1979, his first act on arriving at the Ministry was to
give a copy of *The Wealth of Nations* to all his senior civil servants.
In the context of today's renewed demand that knowledge be useful, therefore, university teachers of the humanities in Britain, who
have been feeling the brunt and uncertainties of successive educational cuts, followed by a cycle of unfunded expansion, since the
Conservatives came to power, might find it worth their while to
turn to *The Wealth of Nations* to discover what theory of the university it involves.

The origins of the utilitarian arguments that we have been re-
hearsing could be traced back to Milton and Locke at the very least
– with their own attendant political contexts of protestantism and
republicanism. But in the sphere of university education, it was
Smith's account that laid the basis for the subsequent attacks on
the inefficiency of the universities, the uselessness of classical education and the counter-proposals for science and vocational training. In a letter of 1774 Smith claimed that 'I have thought a great
deal upon this subject, and have inquired very carefully into the
constitution and history of several of the principal Universities of
Europe'.[45] The results of his research are to be found in Book V of
The Wealth of Nations where he broaches the question of what is
now called public expenditure, and addresses such topics as defence and the administration of justice. Education appears in a
section entitled 'Commercial Institutions', which discusses the public institutions designed to facilitate commerce and to instruct the
people. In certain cases these pose the problem that however beneficial they may be for society as a whole they cannot be left to the
efforts of individuals because the profit obtainable from them does
not repay the expense that members of the public would need to
incur in order to maintain them. Education falls under the category
of a non-economic institution whose ultimate benefit nevertheless

makes it 'in the highest degree advantageous to a great society' (V.i.c.1). Smith then focuses on the difference between what might be called the immediate and deferred profits of education: education is an institution whose use-value cannot be measured by the immediate exchange-value of its product, or, to put it another way, whose cost is greater than the immediate exchange-value of the product that it produces, that is, the newly-graduated student.

Smith solves this difficulty by elaborating a version of an educational theory that was to become popular in the 1960s and has recently given rise to precise quantification exercises at the Department for Education: that is, the theory of human capital, developed by T. W. Schultz and Gary Becker.[46] Smith formulates this theory very succinctly when accounting for wage differentials: one of the factors he points to is that 'the wages of labour vary with the easiness and cheapness, or the difficulty and expense of learning the business':

> When any expensive machine is erected, the extraordinary work to be performed by it before it is worn out, it must be expected, will replace the capital laid out upon it, with at least the ordinary profits. A man educated at the expense of much labour and time to any of those employments which require extraordinary dexterity and skill, may be compared to one of those expensive machines. The work which he learns to perform, it must be expected, over and above the usual wages of common labour, will replace to him the whole expence of his education, with at least the ordinary profits of an equally valuable capital. It must do this too in a reasonable time, regard being had to the very uncertain duration of human life, in the same manner as to the more certain duration of the machine. (I.x.b.6)

Smith illustrates his argument in relation to apprenticeships, adding that 'education in the ingenious and in the liberal professions, is still more tedious and expensive. The pecuniary recompense, therefore, of painters and sculptors, of lawyers and physicians, ought to be much more liberal: and it is so accordingly' (I.x.b.9). For Smith, this line of reasoning suffices to excuse the State from any necessity for providing such forms of education.

On the basis of this, Smith is fiercely critical of any subsidy for higher education which he considers would only lead to an academic freedom that would be abused. The human capital theory of education allows him to consider the remuneration of teachers, as well as the contents of courses of instruction, from the perspective entirely of market forces. Smith contends that the best system occurs where teachers are directly rewarded according to the estimation of their students – a system under which Smith himself worked in part at the University of Glasgow, and which was originally proposed for the University of London.[47] Any form of endowment, salary, or organization as a corporation will, he argues, set a teacher's duty in opposition to a teacher's interest; as proof of this, he instances the state of the University of Oxford. Similarly, all forms of university discipline over students Smith merely considers to be 'contrived, not for the benefit of the students, but for the interest, or more properly speaking, for the ease of the masters' (V.i.f.15). In other words, they are an attempt to assert authority through force where it cannot be derived from intellectual respect.

Through an historical analysis Smith argues that Latin and Greek originally made up the curriculum at Oxford and Cambridge because of their ecclesiastical function: 'What was taught in the greater part of those universities was, suitable to the end of their institution, either theology, or something that was merely preparatory to theology' (V.i.f.19). The courses, as he shows in some detail, were developed for the needs of the education of ecclesiastics, not for men of the world or for the education of gentlemen. In other words, even at Oxford and Cambridge the teaching was originally organized according to a criterion of utility that has now been forgotten, with the result that the universities continue to teach these courses in a debased form: 'In some of the richest and best endowed universities, the tutors content themselves with teaching a few unconnected shreds and parcels of this corrupted course; and even these they commonly teach very negligently and superficially' (V.i.f.33).

This has occurred because the universities are now insulated from any need to respond to market forces; such protection means that any estimate of the value of knowledge becomes irrelevant. For Smith, academic freedom in effect means simply that the public institutions of education teach knowledge

> universally believed to be a mere useless and pedantick heap of sophistry and nonsense. Such systems, such sciences, can subsist no where, but in those incorporated societies for education whose prosperity and revenue are in a great measure independent of their education, and altogether independent of their industry. (V.i.f.46)

Few improvements in philosophy, he comments, have been made in universities; they have acted instead as the shelter of 'exploded systems and obsolete systems'. The poorer universities (that is, the Scottish), in which teachers depend upon their individual reputations, have been more forward-looking and receptive to 'the current opinions of the world' (V.i.f.34). At Oxford and Cambridge, by contrast, 'the diligence of publick teachers is more or less corrupted by the circumstances, which render them more or less independent of their success and reputation in their particular professions' (V.i.f.45). The universities' imperviousness to market forces becomes a powerful weapon with which Smith attacks academic freedom: the academic cannot be left to his own devices because laziness will encourage him to continue to think according to systems that in the eyes of the world are outmoded and useless. Instead, Smith proposes a form of contract, or bargain, between the imparters and receivers of knowledge, founded on a direct relation between reward and the use of such knowledge, an idea that has also today once again found favour.

The belief in market forces means, however, that Smith nowhere considers the possibility that it might be the market itself that resists new ideas or proposals for change. Can it be assumed that the market is always right? Smith's argument seems quite convincing until, in the next paragraph, he compares the academic system, where a gentleman finishes his education ignorant of everything that is of interest or use in the outside world, with the education of women: they, by contrast, are taught 'what their parents or guardians judge it necessary or useful for them to learn', that is, 'either to improve the natural attractions of their persons, or to form their mind to reserve, to modesty, to chastity, and to oeconomy: to render them both likely to become mistresses of a family, and to behave properly when they have become such' (V.i.f.47). Unlike the Benthamites and utilitarians, the Whiggish Smith was no advocate of feminism or of equal opportunities of education for women: suddenly usefulness has become a criterion that ensures the ideological control of certain groups. In other words, it enables education to fulfil a double function, facilitating useful knowledge and useful social control, both in the name of the general good. However, the latter role must necessarily conflict with Smith's overriding moral imperative, the ethos of the free market.

The logic of this aspect of the argument is brought out when Smith reverses his position according to which university education ought to operate solely on the basis of market demand, and suggests that the State ought to provide for the education of the working class – who might well neither demand it nor be able to pay for it. Smith argues that whereas people of rank and fortune will look after the education of their sons, who will then take up chiefly intellectual occupations providing variety and stimulation, the division of labour that has been accentuated under capitalism means that work for the poor has often been reduced to a few mindless activities. This situation has the effect of reducing the populace to a condition of virtual imbecility; the State ought therefore to provide education 'in order to prevent the almost entire corruption and degeneracy of the great body of the people' (V.i.f.49). Smith suggests that some basic education in reading, writing, and arithmetic, geometry and mechanics could be provided by subsidized schools, financed, on the Scottish model, by local parishes. The reason for this apparent benevolence on the part of the State is then given very clearly:

> The more they are instructed, the less liable they are to the delusions of enthusiasm and superstition, which, among ignorant nations, frequently occasion the most dreadful disorders. . . . They are more disposed to examine, and more capable of seeing through, the interested complaints of faction and sedition, and they are, upon that account, less apt to be misled into any wanton or unnecessary opposition to the measures of government. (V.i.f.61)

This theory of what Samuel calls 'nondeliberate social control' is entirely predicated upon an Enlightenment belief in the power of reason that never countenances the idea that the interests of the poor may be at variance with those of the ruling class.[48] Smith's suggestion should, however, also be seen in the context of contemporary opposition to any education for the poor whatsoever on the grounds that it might lead them to question their poverty and work less efficiently. Marx, who was scornful of Smith's prescription for education to alleviate alienation 'in prudently homeopathic doses' as he puts it in *Capital*, notes how Garnier, Smith's more conservative French translator, protests at this point.[49]

But *The Wealth of Nations* is a theory of contracts rather than conflict, in which institutions are utilized as a means of resolving through mutually beneficial bargains the different self-interests of individuals into the general interest of society as a whole – on the face of it, at least, a benevolent theory of institutions, though it has not been much appreciated by the universities when turned into a device for allocating funding. The strategy becomes clear when Smith goes on to suggest that the State should also encourage regular carnivals (V.i.g.15). It is hard to understand why it is that those who make claims for carnival as radically subversive of the social order always forget to mention that Adam Smith shared their enthusiasm. If Smith proposed education and carnival as a way of easing the ills of alienation, the opportunities a State system of education afforded for the behavioural training of the industrial classes – to be taught the benefits of the 'preventative check' – were soon recognized by Thomas Malthus and others, as William Godwin, the great critic both of Malthus and of State institutions, had predicted.[50]

This points to a significant paradox in the logic of Smith's account of the free market, where an attack on public educational institutions for the wealthy is accompanied by a prescription for public instruction for the poor. The ambivalence of the place of education merits attention, for its function points to nothing less than a problem in the theory of *The Wealth of Nations* as a whole. If Smith was the first to produce an economic interpretation of history, the progress and increase of the wealth of nations leads paradoxically, in his account, to a moral and material decline.[51] The material decline is based on a proto-Malthusian principle of economic growth that leads to a population explosion which, in turn, produces eventual economic stagnation. Smith attributes the ensuing moral decline as a condition of reduced well-being produced by the effects of industrialization, described at length in one of the best known passages of the book:

> In the progress of the division of labour, the employment of the far greater part of those who live by labour, that is, of the great body of the people, comes to be confined to a few very simple operations; frequently to one or two. But the understandings of the greater part of men are necessarily formed by their ordinary employments. The man whose whole life is spent in performing a few simple operations, of which the effects too are, perhaps, always the same, or very nearly the same, has no occasion to exert his understanding, or to exercise his invention in finding out expedients for removing difficulties which never occur. He naturally loses, therefore, the habit of such exertion, and generally becomes as stupid and as ignorant as it is possible for a human creature to become. The torpor of his mind renders him, not only incapable of relishing or bearing a part in any rational conversation, but of conceiving any generous, noble, or tender sentiment, and consequently of forming any just judgement concerning many even of the ordinary duties of private life.... His dexterity at his own particular trade seems, in this manner, to be acquired at the expense of his intellectual, social, and martial virtues. But in every improved and civilized society this is the state into which the labouring poor, that is, the great body of the people, must necessarily fall, unless government takes some pains to prevent it. (V.i.f.50)

Smith contrasts this state of alienation with the conditions of what he calls 'barbarous societies', that is societies before/without manufacturing and foreign commerce, where necessity spurs the population into a quickness of intelligence:

> In such societies the varied occupations of every man oblige every man to exert his capacity, and to invent expedients for removing difficulties which are continually occurring. Invention is kept alive, and the mind is not suffered to fall into that drowsy stupidity, which, in a civilized society, seems to benumb the understanding of almost all the inferior ranks of people. (V.i.f.51)

According to the first theorist of capitalism, then, the division of labour necessary for the economic progress of commercial societies leads to an intellectual and moral decay – an alienation that sounds strikingly similar to the argument of a later theorist. The paradox in Smith's whole account is that whereas the free market is supposed to lead to the increasing well-being of society for some it produces a material and moral deterioration. Smith's analysis of the effects of the division of labour, therefore, eventually does lead to a class division in which the different interests of society conflict. This is the point where the contract founded on Smith's assumption of a constant characteristic of 'human nature' – the mutual interest of a desire for 'self-betterment' – breaks down and antagonism begins: it is here that Marx's analysis, which substitutes the dialectical logic of historical progression for a static notion of self-interest, could be said to start.

Yet, Smith does offer one major palliative with which he attempts to sustain that contract, that is, the general education of the populace. This, he suggests, would be primarily an education in the principles of useful sciences, particularly geometry and mechanics, which would be of practical help in the trades to be followed later in life. But by itself this would be contradictory, in so far as education, which is supposed to be an anodyne for the effects of capitalism, would merely constitute a training for the trade that would go on to produce capitalism's enervating effects. Smith therefore proposes that such education would involve what he terms 'the necessary introduction to the most sublime as well as to the most useful sciences' (V.i.f.55). But what would be the use of a knowledge that is 'sublime' in a scheme according to which everything must be justified by its usefulness? E. G. West draws attention to a significant passage in the earlier description of the virtues of a barbarous society before the division of labour:

> Though in a rude society there is a good deal of variety in the occupations of every individual, there is not a great deal in those of the

whole society. . . . In a civilized state, on the contrary, though there is little variety in the occupations of the greater part of individuals, there is an almost infinite variety in those of the whole society. These varied occupations present an almost infinite variety of objects to the contemplation of those few, who, being attached to no particular occupation themselves, have leisure and inclination to examine the occupations of other people. The contemplation of so great a variety of objects necessarily exercises their minds in endless comparisons and combinations, and renders their understandings, in an extraordinary degree, both acute and comprehensive. Unless those few, however, happen to be placed in some very particular situations, their great abilities, though honourable to themselves, may contribute very little to the good government or happiness of their society. (V.i.f.51)

Capitalism, therefore, though it reduces diversity for each individual, increases the total variety at play in society as a whole. Those who can contemplate this reach a state of comprehensive understanding unavailable to anyone in a precapitalist society. Unless, however, they 'happen to be placed in some very particular situations', such philosophers can contribute little to society's happiness. 'Notwithstanding the great abilities of those few, all the nobler parts of the human character may be, in a great measure, obliterated and extinguished in the great body of the people' (V.i.f.51). West comments that

Smith seems to have been cautiously hopeful about the prospects of such 'philosophers' communicating their new knowledge and excitement to others through the medium of specially devised institutions. Provided that the intellectual delight of contemplation could be shared throughout society, order, contentment, fulfillment, and the pursuit of excellence would be ensured for all.[52]

Why should Smith have had to be cautious? Whatever place or institution he may have had in mind in his comment about 'some very particular situations', it is obvious that this special function for society's philosophers, who have access to a form of sublime knowledge which could feed into the general education system as a palliative for capitalism, cannot be justified in so far as it contradicts the very grounds for the basis of public institutions of higher education that Smith has been at pains to elaborate.[53] According to the logic of *The Wealth of Nations*, those institutions should be restricted to the utility of the knowledge that they can sell and which the student can accumulate as a form of capital for his own increased remuneration. To impart knowledge on the grounds of its sublimity for the alleviation of the population as a whole could form the basis of no such academic contract based on market criteria.

Even therefore according to the rigorous analysis of Adam Smith's economics, in which education is constituted solely according to market forces, knowledge outside the orbit of a strict criterion of utility has to be invoked in order to provide something beyond the system that can save it from its own consequences. That philosophical knowledge can only not be assigned to the university because, having in the first instance been rigorously excluded, its introduction would contradict the rest of Smith's argument so absolutely as to call his entire premises into doubt. Smith therefore leaves his suggestion hanging on the borderline of the aesthetic and the political, outside the logic of his text in the sublime aerial situation of the philosophers he describes – doubtless the very place of the idea of the university itself.[54] The conclusion we, as readers, may draw is that in *The Wealth of Nations* the university, though in the first instance made directly useful, is then called upon to fulfil a role strikingly similar to that which it would be required to play in the theories of Newman, Arnold, or Leavis – who nevertheless present themselves specifically in opposition to the utilitarian ethics of the function of education in a free-market economy. At the same time the university could be said to be in the unique position of being both an example, as Mill was to argue, of 'market failure' and, as Smith conceded in his special prescription for philosophers, the necessary palliative for the failure of the market.

As it stands in *The Wealth of Nations*, with little apparent prospect of those who possess such higher knowledge being placed in the very particular situations from which they can contribute to the happiness of society, Smith's account means that the paradox for the universities is that the more useful to the State that they are, the quicker the system to which they contribute will succeed and therefore go into decline. In other words, the most beneficial thing the State could do to ensure its own survival would be to encourage the universities to be useless. Or to put it the other way round, the most politically subversive thing you could do would be to help the universities to be useful.

The hidden hand

Useful for whom, though? Newman comments: 'Utility may be made the end of education, in two respects: either as regards the individual

educated, or the community at large' (141). This locates a fundamental dissension in utilitarian doctrine: the overriding good of
happiness assumes that that of the individual and the general good
of the State are the same. But the principle of utility, the means by
which this happiness is achieved but which quickly becomes an
end in itself, increases the polarity by which it can be measured
either from the perspective of the individual or from that of society.
According to Smith, it is the institution, economic or otherwise,
which reconciles the conflicting interests and demands of the two.
Here we get a different take on the opposition between immanence
and transcendence: the function of the academic institution is to
reconcile these two antithetical perspectives in a 'universal particular' or 'concrete universal', as was evidently the project of many
nineteenth-century philosophers and literary critics. But despite
this philosophic conformity to political need, the educational institution also seems to exacerbate the division: because of its double
function with regard to the individual and to society, it finds it hard
to face both its addressees at the same time. Education can be
measured according to its use for the individual, in which case it
may well be seen pragmatically, in terms of a qualification, but it
will also tend to lead to ideas about knowledge being a condition of
mind, and, at its extreme, require no formal knowledge at all; alter-
natively education can be measured according to its use for the
State, in which case it will end up being employed in the service of
production and social control. In the latter case, its function is not
so much to mediate as to coerce a form of reconciliation between
the individual and the State, a necessity most glaringly stated in the
classical economists' belief that children should be taught the principles of political economy, so that they could learn at an early age
the principle of mutual interest that the theory of political economy
assumes as its basis.[55]

   This division around which the theory of the university spirals,
starting from this double end of utility and well-being, recurs in an
increasing number of bifurcations that repeat through such apparently fundamental differences as those between science and arts,
or research versus teaching, or instrumental knowledge versus
knowledge for its own sake. The arguments around these divisions
are not so much about alternatives as an acting out of an internal
conflict within educational theory, itself restaging the agonistic structure of a society that does not add up. Thus the differences between
the utilitarian and the humanist are more like spectacular, dislocated
and distorted reversals of each other: for Smith, if the university

was required to operate by a criterion of immediate usefulness, it was nevertheless in the end called upon to exert a unifying synthesis over society at large. For Newman, though usefulness was initially rejected in favour of the cultivation of the individual mind, nevertheless that mind finally became so cultivated that it could exercise the useful function of ensuring the cohesion of the State. What becomes clear is that both ideas of the university, which seem to be set directly in opposition to each other as radical to conservative, are equally necessary to the State, and so is the conflict between them. To enter into that struggle by resisting one with the other is to remain oblivious to the extent to which each is implicated in the other and will only ensure the loss of any point of leverage whatsoever. The university too pivots on the torn halves of our culture; it bears the scars of capitalism, but in repeating them, it finds itself also marked with the stigmata as a sign of divine favour. The aporetic scission within culture articulated by the useful and useless university also enables a fulcrum for cultural critique.

The question today's philosophers need to ask is in what ways and with what effects can the university, useful and useless, both inside and outside the market economy, functioning for the needs of that economy but also necessary to it as a surplus outside that economy, provide a point of dislocation? The problem is more complicated than Derrida's prescription of 'working at the outer limits of the authority and power of the principle of reason' because the idea of the university is already predicated on the doubled dissonance of providing useful and non-useful knowledge.[56] The deconstruction of the institution of reason is doubtless a particularly French concern; unlike the Kantian university, the English university is not governed by the monological principle of non-contradiction: founded as an institutional incarnation of the Logos, it has also incorporated its own instrumentality, the orientation of its knowledge, within its dialectical operation of useless and useful, inside and outside. Although its function as a surplus outside the market-system might seem to offer some possibility of perspective if not of power, the fact that that surplus is not only necessary but also reabsorbed by the market in a second more complex stage of the economy casts serious doubts on the university's ability to function in any oppositional position from the 'outside' as such. The market performs according to a contradictory economy, and succeeds in making that outside integral to itself. The same assimilation of such an inside–outside structure could also be said to hold for the relation of the intellectual to the institution. Though the knowledge of the university may appear to be without a market value, and to operate beyond that circuit of exchange, its very exteriority gives it a special value that helps to ensure the internal stability of society itself. The university thus reveals itself as the body behind Smith's mysterious 'hidden hand' which, in Bernard de Mandeville's phrase, turns private vices into public benefits. This means that the university comprehends both the principle of reason and that which operates at its very limits. In other words, it already includes the excessive place of resistance to instrumentality that Derrida advocates – which is what enables it to function as an institution that harnesses the interests of the individual to the needs of society, designed to ensure that the two are not conflictual. In order to do this, however, the university must be permanently at variance with itself: the dissension produced by this dislocation is acted out interminably in educational theory and practice.

(1992)

Notes

1 Foucault, *Language, Counter-Memory, Practice*, 224. On the following page Foucault argues that the events of May 1968 were sparked off by the attempt to transform the university from a liberal to a technical institution. Cf. Bourdieu and Passeron, *Reproduction in Education, Society and Culture*.

2 The texts of the German idealists on the subject of the university are collected and translated in *Philosophies de l'université*, eds Ferry, Pesron, Renault. See also Derrida, 'The Principle of Reason'.

3 For education in Scotland, see Anderson, *Education and Opportunity in Victorian Scotland*; for Wales, see Jenkins, *The University of Wales*.

4 Historically, both universities were founded as a result of academic dissipation: the conventional method for resisting disagreeable attempts at papal control was for the university simply to disperse itself when faced with a papal edict: thus Oxford began as a result of the dissolution of the University of Paris in 1167, Cambridge as a result of that of the University of Oxford in 1209. See Rasdall, *The Universities of Europe in the Middle Ages*, 3, 11–13. No one has yet suggested such a response to the increasing Government control experienced by British universities in the 1980s and 1990s.

5 For a full account see Simpson, *How the Ph.D. came to Britain*. On the history of higher education generally see Jarausch, *The Transformation of Higher Learning, 1860–1930*, Stephens and Roderick, *Post-School Education*, and Stone, *The University in Society*.

6 Kant, *The Conflict of the Faculties*; Derrida, 'Mochlos ou le conflit des facultés'.

7 See, for example, Ward, *Georgian Oxford*.

8 Gibbon, *Memoirs of My Life*, 83. Wordsworth, *The Prelude*.

9 I owe this information to David Norbrook.

10 Smith, *The Wealth of Nations*, V.i.f.8. Further references will be given in the text. For Smith's own experiences at Balliol College, Oxford, see Campbell

and Skinner, *Adam Smith*, 23–6. Rogers (*The Eighteenth Century*, 24) notes that Thomas Gray, Professor of Modern History at Cambridge, gave no lectures whatsoever; Joseph Spence, the antiquarian, his counterpart in Oxford, did not even live there in twenty-five years.

11 Adamson, *English Education*, 177.

12 See Webster, *The Great Instauration*. For debates on the role of the university at the time of the Civil War which at that time was identified above all with the training of the clergy for the established church, see Hill, *The Intellectual Origins of the English Revolution*; and *Change and Continuity in Seventeenth-Century England*; and Kearney, *Gentlemen and Scholars*.

13 Smith, review of R. L. Edgeworth's *Professional Education* (1809), 44, 45–6.

14 Copleston, *A Reply to the Calumnies of the Edinburgh Review against Oxford; A Second Reply . . . to the Calumnies*; *A Third Reply . . . to the Calumnies*. Copleston was, until 1810, a fellow of Oriel College; he was later to become Bishop of Llandaff (see Copleston, *Memoir of Edward Copleston*).

15 Copleston, *A Reply to the Calumnies of the Edinburgh Review*, 111–12, 168–9.

16 Green, *British Institutions*, 108.

17 Newman, *The Idea of a University*, 179–81.

18 Cited in Newman, *Select Discourses from the Idea of a University*, xi.

19 Bentham, *Chrestomathia*.

20 Smith, 'Literary Education', *Westminster Review* 1 (1824), 68.

21 *Prospectus of the London University*, 1. For a history of University College, see Bellot, *University College London*; for the history of the University of London, see Harte, *The University of London 1836–1986*. Court's *Institutionalizing English Literature* appeared after this essay was written; focusing on the study of English Literature, in many ways its detailed discussion of utilitarianism and university education complements the account given here.

22 Simon, *Studies in the History of Education*, 122.

23 For a full account of the first professor, the Revd Thomas Dale, see Palmer, *The Rise of English Studies*, 18–25. Dale's moralisms were subsequently superseded by the more utilitarian factual sciences of philology, historical criticism, and Anglo-Saxon studies. Eventually Oxford began to feel the effects of the arguments that it was not abreast of modern knowledge; at this time, for instance, as Simon notes, at Oxford, which considered itself the centre of theological and classical studies, 'there was almost complete ignorance of the great advances in historical criticism and philology' (87). Oxford became a good deal more receptive to historical criticism during the course of the nineteenth century, but it is perhaps characteristic of its slow and stately pace in the advancement of knowledge that it has kept to the historical method ever since.

24 In 1824, for instance, Baden Powell, Professor of Geometry at Oxford, wrote: 'Scientific knowledge is rapidly spreading among all classes EXCEPT THE HIGHER, and the consequence must be, that that class will not long remain THE HIGHER. If its members would continue to retain their superiority, they must preserve a real pre-eminence in knowledge, and must make advances at least in proportion to the classes who have hitherto been below them. And is it not a question, whether the same consideration does not in some measure apply to the ascendancy and stability of the University itself?' (*Quarterly Journal of Education*, IV:8, October 1832, 197–8, cited by Simon, 92).

25 'Knowledge brings with it the want and necessity of political amelioration, a necessity which must be satisfied' declared the opening issue of the *Westminster Review* (1 [1824], 81).

26 Cited by Halévy, *The Growth of Philosophical Radicalism*, 436. For Marx's comments on Bentham, the 'arch-philistine', see Marx, *Capital*, vol. 1, 758–9, n.51.

27 For an account of socialist politics of education in the nineteenth century see Simon, *Studies in the History of Education; Education and the Labour Movement; The Radical Tradition in Education in Britain*; and Vaughan and Archer, *Social Conflict and Educational Change in England and France 1789–1848*.

28 Primary education was not made compulsory until ten years after Forster's 1870 Education Act (see Musgrave, *Society and Education in England*, 45). William Forster was Matthew Arnold's brother-in-law.

29 Cf. Bourdieu, *Distinction*.

30 Mill, 'Civilization' (1836), in *Dissertations and Discussions*, 1, 193.

31 *Ibid.*, 196, 195.

32 Engels, *The Condition of the Working Class in England*, 244.

33 For the history of women's struggle for university education, see Killham, *Tennyson and the Princess*; Burstyn, *Victorian Education and the Ideal of Womanhood*; Delamont and Duffin, *The Nineteenth-Century Woman*.

34 Newman, *The Idea of a University*, 19. Further references will be cited in the text. For detailed analysis of Newman's essays, see Culler, *The Imperial Intellect*.

35 Barrell, *English Literature in History 1730–80*, 207.

36 Newman, *The Idea of a University*, 147, citing Copleston, *A Reply to the Calumnies of the Edinburgh Review*, 111.

37 Jay, *Adorno*, 122.

38 Coleridge, *On the Constitution of Church and State*; Arnold, *Culture and Anarchy*. Further references to both these volumes will be given in the text. Analyses of *On the Constitution of Church and State* include Colmer, *Coleridge, Critic of Society*, Mill, *Mill on Bentham and Coleridge*; and Morrow, *Coleridge's Political Thought*. For Arnold's other writings on the university, see Arnold, *Schools and Universities on the Continent* (1865–7); see also Connell, *The Educational Thought and Influence of Matthew Arnold*, 269–70; Walcott, *The Origins of Culture and Anarchy*.

39 Marx, *Selected Writings*, 575.

40 The authoritative text, widely deployed in this context, for literature's claim to the highest form of Platonic truth is Shelley's *Defence of Poetry* (1821), first published in *Essays, Letters from Abroad, Translations and Fragments* in 1840. Baldick, in *The Social Mission of English Criticism,* cites an article from 1860 by H. G. Robinson, entitled 'English Classical Literature', which illustrates perfectly the extent to which literature takes theology's function as a metasubject, claiming its cohesive function through its access to a higher truth at the most ecumenical level: 'Large views help to develop large sympathies; and by converse with the thoughts and utterances of those who are intellectual leaders of the race, our heart comes to beat in accord with the feeling of universal humanity. We discover that no differences of class, or party, or creed, can destroy the power of genius to charm and instruct, and that above the smoke and stir, the din and turmoil of man's lower life

of care and business and debate, there is a serene and luminous region of truth where all may meet and expatiate in common' (66).

41 Newbolt, *The Teaching of English in England*.

42 The argument, for example, of Eagleton's *Literary Theory: An Introduction*. The standard account of the political strategies of the institution of English Literature as a university discipline is Baldick's *The Social Mission of English Criticism;* for its mission in India, see Viswanathan, *Masks of Conquest*.

43 Apart from those mentioned, other obvious examples would include Wordsworth, De Quincey, George Eliot, T. S. Eliot. These values are not confined to the conservative Right: similar assumptions provide the basis for E. P. Thompson's arguments in *Warwick University Ltd*.

44 Cox and Dyson, *Fight for Education: A Black Paper*, and *Black Paper, 2: The Crisis in Education*. For Leavis's writings on the function of the university (for him, more or less synonymous with that of English Literature) see *Education and the University*, and *English Literature in Our Time and the University*.

45 Letter to William Cullen of 20 Sept. 1774, in *The Correspondence of Adam Smith*, 174.

46 Schultz, 'Investment in Human Capital'; Becker, *Human Capital*. For the relation of the 'Human Capital' theory to Adam Smith see Skinner and Wilson, *Essays on Adam Smith*, 340–1, 573–4.

47 In England at least salary according to student numbers has never been introduced, on the grounds advanced by Mill that the university is an example of what he called 'market failure', that is because 'the uncultivated cannot be competent judges of cultivation' (*Principles of Political Economy*, 2, 519). A different form of assessment, through research, is now the norm, which has the effect, logically at least, of making teaching the least important part of an academic's job, and according to Smith's principles at least, the one that he or she is therefore most likely if not to neglect, at least to put as a last priority. In this sense, those arguments put forward in the 1850s by those at Oxford and Cambridge against the idea of universities as research institutions have to some extent been justified.

48 Blaug, 'The Economics of Education in English Classical Political Economy: A Re-Examination', in Skinner and Wilson, *Essays on Adam Smith*, 568–99, 591. See also Hollander, 'The Role of the State in Vocational Training: The Classical Economists' View', and Vaizey, *The Economics of Education*.

49 Marx, *Capital*, vol. 1, 484.

50 Godwin, *Enquiry Concerning Political Justice*, 616–17. State education was endorsed by Malthus in his *Essay on the Principle of Population*, who saw the advantage of this system of control – in this case, of the population.

51 On this aspect, see Heilbroner, 'The Paradox of Progress: Decline and Decay in *The Wealth of Nations*', in Skinner and Wilson, *Essays on Adam Smith*, 524–39.

52 West, 'Adam Smith and Alienation: Wealth Increases, Men Decay?', in Skinner and Wilson, *Essays on Adam Smith*, 522. On the classical economists and education see also West's useful essays, 'The Role of Education in Nineteenth-Century Doctrines of Political Economy'; and 'Private versus Public Education, A Classical Economic Dispute', in *The Classical Economists and Economic Policy*, ed. Coats, 123–43.

53 In the early part of *The Wealth of Nations* Smith by contrast does not excuse philosophers from the general process of the division of labour:

'Philosophers, or men of speculation, whose trade is not to do anything, but to observe everything . . . upon that account, are often capable of combining together the powers of the most distant and dissimilar objects. In the progress of society, philosophy or speculation becomes, like every other employment, the principal or sole trade and occupation of a particular class of citizens. Like every other employment too, it is subdivided into a great number of different branches, each of which affords occupation to a peculiar tribe or class of philosophers; and this subdivision of employment in philosophy, as well as in every other business, improves dexterity, and saves time. Each individual becomes more expert in his own peculiar branch, more work is done upon the whole, and the quantity of science is considerably increased by it' (I.i.9). For further discussion see Barrell, *English Literature in History*, Chapter 1.

54 For Kant's account of the essence of the university as the sublime, see Derrida, 'The Principle of Reason', 6. An extended analysis of the role of the philosopher in the *Wealth of Nations* would obviously have to relate it to that of the impartial spectator in the *Theory of Moral Sentiments* (1759). For an analysis of this figure and its relation to that of the 'Ideal Observer', see Campbell, *Adam Smith's Science of Morals*, and Raphael, 'The Impartial Spectator', in Skinner and Wilson, *Essays on Adam Smith*, 83–99.

55 See Skinner and Wilson, *Essays on Adam Smith*, 575.

56 Derrida, 'The Principle of Reason', 14.

bibliography

Bibliography................................

Abraham, Nicolas, The Shell and the Kernel, *Diacritics* 9:1 (1979), 16–28.

Adamson, John William, *English Education 1789–1902*, Cambridge, Cambridge University Press, 1930.

Adorno, Theodor W., *Aesthetic Theory*, trans. C. Leenhardt, London, Routledge & Kegan Paul, 1984.

—— *The Culture Industry: Selected Essays on Mass Culture*, ed. J. M. Bernstein, London, Routledge, 1991.

—— *Minima Moralia: Reflections from Damaged Life*, trans. E. F. N. Jephcott, London, New Left Books, 1974.

—— *Negative Dialectics*, trans. E. B. Ashton, London, Routledge & Kegan Paul, 1973.

—— *Prisms*, trans. Samuel & Shierry Weber, Cambridge, Mass., MIT Press, 1981.

Althusser, Louis, *Essays in Self-Criticism*, trans. Grahame Lock, London, New Left Books, 1976.

—— *Lenin and Philosophy and Other Essays*, trans. Ben Brewster, London, New Left Books, 1971.

Anchor, Robert, Bakhtin's Truths of Laughter, *Clio* 14:3 (1985), 237–57.

Anderson, Benedict, *Imagined Communities: Reflections on the Origin and Spread of Nationalism*, London, Verso, 1983.

Anderson, Perry, *In the Tracks of Historical Materialism*, London, Verso, 1983.

Anderson, R. D., *Education and Opportunity in Victorian Scotland: Schools and Universities*, Oxford, Clarendon Press, 1983.

Apter, E. & Pietz, W., eds, *Fetishism as Cultural Discourse*, Ithaca, Cornell University Press, 1993.

Arato, Andrew, ed., *The Essential Frankfurt School Reader*, Oxford, Blackwell, 1978.

Arnold, Matthew, *Culture and Anarchy*, ed. J. Dover Wilson, Cambridge, Cambridge University Press, 1932.

—— *Schools and Universities on the Continent*, ed. R. H. Super, Ann Arbor, University of Michigan Press, 1964.

Attridge, Derek, Bennington, Geoff, & Young, Robert, eds, *Post-Structuralism and the Question of History*, Cambridge, Cambridge University Press, 1987.

Bakhtin, M. M., *The Dialogic Imagination: Four Essays*, trans. Caryl Emerson & Michael Holquist, Austin, University of Texas Press, 1981.

—— *La Poétique de Dostoievski*, présentation de Julia Kristeva, Paris, Seuil, 1970.

—— *Problems of Dostoevsky's Poetics*, trans. Caryl Emerson, Minneapolis, University of Minnesota Press, 1984.

—— Rabelais and Gogol, *Mississippi Review* 11:3 (1983), 34–50.

—— *Rabelais and His World*, trans. Hélène Iwolsky, Cambridge, Mass., MIT Press, 1968.

—— *Speech Genres & Other Late Essays*, trans. Vern W. McGee, ed. Caryl Emerson & Michael Holquist, Austin, University of Texas Press, 1986.

Baldick, Chris, *The Social Mission of English Criticism, 1848–1932*, Oxford, Clarendon Press, 1983.

Balibar, Etienne, & Wallerstein, Immanuel, *Race, Nation, Class: Ambiguous Identities*, London, Verso, 1991.

Baran, Henryk, ed., *Structuralism and Semiotics*, New York, International Arts & Sciences Press, 1976.

Barrell, John, *English Literature in History 1730–80: An Equal, Wide Survey*, London, Hutchinson, 1983.

Barrett, Michèle, *Women's Oppression Today: Problems in Marxist Feminist Analysis*, London, Verso, 1980.

Barthes, Roland, The Structuralist Activity, in *The Structuralists from Marx to Lévi-Strauss*, eds Richard & Fernande DeGeorge, New York, Anchor Books, 1972, 148–54.

Bate, W. J., The Crisis in English Studies, *Harvard Magazine* Sept./Oct. 1982, 46–53.

Baudrillard, Jean, *Seduction*, trans. Brian Singer, Basingstoke, Macmillan, 1990.

Bauer, Dale, *Feminist Dialogics: A Theory of Failed Community*, Albany, SUNY Press, 1988.

Bauman, Zygmunt, *Intimations of Postmodernity*, London, Routledge, 1992.

—— *Modernity and Ambivalence*, Cambridge, Polity, 1991.

Becker, Gary, *Human Capital: A Theoretical and Empirical Analysis, with Special Reference to Education*, New York, National Bureau of Economic Research, 1964.

Bell, Daniel, *The Cultural Contradictions of Capitalism*, New York, Basic Books, 1978.

Bellot, H. Hale, *University College London, 1826–1926*, London, University College, 1929.

Benhabib, Seyla, *Critique, Norm, and Utopia: A Study of the Foundations of Critical Theory*, New York, Columbia University Press, 1986.

Benjamin, Walter, *Illuminations*, trans. H. Zohn, London, Fontana, 1973.

Bennett, Tony, *Formalism and Marxism*, London, Methuen, 1979.

Bennington, Geoffrey, *Dudding: Des noms de Rousseau*, Paris, Galilée, 1991.

—— *Legislations: The Politics of Deconstruction*, London, Verso, 1994.

Benoist, Jean-Marie, The End of Structuralism, *Twentieth Century Studies* 3 (1970), 31–54.

Bentham, Jeremy, *Chrestomathia*, eds W. H. Burston & M. J. Smith, *The Collected Works of Jeremy Bentham*, vol. 8, Oxford, Clarendon Press, 1983.

Benton, Ted, *The Rise and Fall of Structural Marxism: Althusser and His Influence*, London, Macmillan, 1984.

Bhabha, Homi K., *The Location of Culture*, London, Routledge, 1994.

—— ed., *Nation and Narration*, London, Routledge, 1990.

—— A Question of Survival: Nations and Psychic States, in *Psychoanalysis and Cultural Theory: Thresholds*, ed. James Donald, Basingstoke, Macmillan, 1991, 89–103.

Bloch, Ernst, *et al.*, *Aesthetics and Politics: Debates Between Bloch, Lukács, Brecht, Benjamin and Adorno*, London, Verso, 1977.

Booth, Wayne, Freedom of Interpretation: Bakhtin and the Challenge of Feminist Criticism, *Critical Inquiry* 9:1 (1982), 45–76.

Bourdieu, Pierre, *Distinction: A Social Critique of the Judgement of Taste*, trans. Richard Nice, London, Routledge, 1986.

—— & Passeron, Jean-Claude, *Reproduction in Education, Society and Culture*, trans. Richard Nice, 2nd ed., London, Sage Publications, 1990.

Brooks, Peter, The Idea of a Psychoanalytic Criticism, *Critical Inquiry* 13:2 (1987), 334–48.

Buck-Morss, Susan, *The Origin of Negative Dialectics: Theodor W. Adorno, Walter Benjamin, and the Frankfurt Institute*, New York, Free Press, 1977.

Bürger, Peter, *Theory of the Avant-Garde*, trans. Michael Shaw, Manchester, Manchester University Press, 1984.

Burleigh, Michael, & Wippermann, Wolfgang, *The Racial State: Germany 1933–1945*, Cambridge, Cambridge University Press, 1991.

Burstyn, Joan N., *Victorian Education and the Ideal of Womanhood*, London, Croom Helm, 1980.

Cain, William, *The Crisis in Criticism, Theory, Literature, and Reform in English Study*, Baltimore, Johns Hopkins University Press, 1984.

Cairns, David, & Richards, Shaun, *Writing Ireland: Colonialism, Nationalism and Culture*, Manchester, Manchester University Press, 1988.

Campbell, R. H., & Skinner, A. S., *Adam Smith*, London, Croom Helm, 1982.

Campbell, T. D., *Adam Smith's Science of Morals*, London, George Allen & Unwin, 1971.

Carroll, David, The Alterity of Discourse: Form, History, and the Question of the Political in M. M. Bakhtin, *Diacritics* 13:2 (1983), 65–83.

Caudwell, Christopher, *Illusion and Reality: A Study of the Sources of Poetry*, London, Macmillan, 1937.

—— *Studies in a Dying Culture*, London, The Bodley Head, 1938.

Clark, Katerina, & Holquist, Michael, *Mikhail Bakhtin*, Cambridge, Mass., Harvard University Press, 1985.

Clifford, James, *The Predicament of Culture: Twentieth-Century Ethnography, Literature, and Art*, Cambridge, Mass., Harvard University Press, 1988.

Coats, A. W., ed., *The Classical Economists and Economic Policy*, London, Methuen, 1971.

Coleridge, Samuel Taylor, *On the Constitution of Church and State According to the Idea of Each*, ed. John Colmer, London, Routledge & Kegan Paul, 1976.

Colmer, John, *Coleridge, Critic of Society*, Oxford, Clarendon Press, 1959.

Connell, W. F., *The Educational Thought and Influence of Matthew Arnold*, London, Routledge & Kegan Paul, 1950.

Copleston, Edward, *A Reply to the Calumnies of the Edinburgh Review against Oxford, Containing an Account of Studies Pursued at the University*, Oxford, 1810.

—— *A Second Reply to the Edinburgh Review, by the author of a Reply to the Calumnies of that Review against Oxford*, Oxford, 1810.

—— *A Third Reply to the Edinburgh Review, by the author of a Reply to the Calumnies of that Review against Oxford*, Oxford, 1811.

Copleston, William James, *Memoir of Edward Copleston, D.D., Bishop of Llandaff, with Selections from his Diary and Correspondence etc.*, London, 1851.

Court, Franklin E., *Institutionalizing English Literature: The Culture and Politics of Literary Study, 1750–1900*, Stanford, Stanford University Press, 1992.

Coward, Rosalind, & Ellis, John, *Language and Materialism: Developments in Semiology and the Theory of the Subject*, London, Routledge & Kegan Paul, 1977.

Cox, C. B., & Dyson, A. E., eds, *Fight for Education: A Black Paper*, London, Critical Quarterly Society, 1969.

—— *Black Paper, 2: The Crisis in Education*, London, Critical Quarterly Society, 1970.

Critical Inquiry, Forum on Bakhtin, 10:2 (1983).

Culler, A. Dwight, *The Imperial Intellect: A Study of Newman's Educational Ideal*, New Haven, Yale University Press, 1955.

Culler, Jonathan, *On Deconstruction*, London, Routledge & Kegan Paul, 1983.

—— *Structuralist Poetics: Structuralism, Linguistics, and the Study of Literature*, London, Routledge & Kegan Paul, 1975.

Cutler, Antony, Hindess, Barry, Hirst, Paul Q., & Hussain, Athar, *Marx's 'Capital' and Capitalism Today*, 2 vols, London, Routledge & Kegan Paul, 1977–78.

Dalal, Farhad, The Racism of Jung, *Race and Class* 29:3 (1988), 1–22.

D'Amico, Robert, *Historicism and Knowledge*, London, Routledge, 1989.

DeJean, Joan, Bakhtin and/in History, in *Language and Literary Theory*, Benjamin A. Stolz *et al.*, eds, Ann Arbor, University of Michigan Papers in Slavic Philology 5, 1984, 225–40.

Delamont, Sara, & Duffin, Lorna, eds, *The Nineteenth-Century Woman: Her Cultural and Physical World*, London, Croom Helm, 1978.

Deleuze, Gilles, *The Logic of Sense*, trans. Mark Lester, London, Athlone Press, 1990.

—— & Guattari, Félix, *Anti-Oedipus: Capitalism and Schizophrenia*, vol. 1, trans. Robert Hurley, Mark Seem, & Helen Lane, New York, Viking, 1977.

—— *A Thousand Plateaus: Capitalism and Schizophrenia*, vol. 2, trans. Brian Massumi, London, Athlone, 1988.

de Man, Paul, Dialogue and Dialogism, *Poetics Today* 4:1 (1983), 99–107, reprinted in *The Resistance to Theory*, Manchester, Manchester University Press, 1986, 106–14.

—— The Resistance to Theory, *Yale French Studies* 63 (1982), 3–20; reprinted in *The Resistance to Theory*, Manchester, Manchester University Press, 1986, 3–20.

Derrida, Jacques, Fors, trans. Barbara Johnson, *The Georgia Review* 31 (1977), 64–116.

—— Mochlos ou le conflit des facultés, *Philosophie* 2 (1984), 21–53.

—— Politics and Friendship: An Interview with Jacques Derrida, in *The Althusserian Legacy*, eds E. Ann Kaplan & Michael Sprinker, London, Verso, 1993, 183–231.

—— *Positions*, trans. Alan Bass, London, Athlone, 1981.

—— The Principle of Reason, The University in the Eyes of Its Pupils, *Diacritics* 13:3 (1983), 3–20.

—— *Specters of Marx: The State of the Debt, the Work of Mourning, and the New International*, trans. Peggy Kamuf, New York, Routledge, 1994.

Descombes, Vincent, *Modern French Philosophy*, trans. L. Scott-Fox & J. M. Harding, Cambridge, Cambridge University Press, 1980.

Dews, Peter, *Logics of Disintegration: Post-Structuralist Thought and the Claims of Critical Theory*, London, Verso, 1987.

Difference: On Representation and Sexuality, New York, The New Museum of Contemporary Art, 1985.

Dirlik, Arif, Culturalism as Hegemonic Ideology and Liberating Practice, *Cultural Critique* 6 (1987), 13–50.

Dollimore, Jonathan, Politics Teaching Literature, in *Literature, Teaching, Politics*, 2 (1983), 108–119.

Donato, Eugenio, Structuralism: The Aftermath, *Sub-Stance* 7 (1973), 9–26.

Eagleton, Terry, *Criticism and Ideology: A Study in Marxist Literary Theory*, London, New Left Books, 1976.

—— *Exiles and Emigrés: Studies in Modern Literature*, London, Chatto & Windus, 1970.

—— *Ideology: An Introduction*, London, Verso, 1991.

—— *The Ideology of the Aesthetic*, Oxford, Blackwell, 1990.

—— *Literary Theory: An Introduction*, Oxford, Blackwell, 1983.

—— Marxism, Structuralism, and Poststructuralism, *Diacritics* 15:4 (1985), 2–12.

—— *Walter Benjamin, or Towards a Revolutionary Criticism*, London, New Left Books, 1981.

—— Wittgenstein's Friends, *New Left Review* 135 (1982), 64–90.

Easthope, Antony, *British Post-Structuralism Since 1968*, London, Routledge, 1988.

Engels, Friedrich, *The Condition of the Working Class in England*, ed. Victor Kiernan, Harmondsworth, Penguin, 1987.

Etudes françaises, Bakhtine mode d'emploi, 20:1 (1984).

Fanon, Frantz, *Black Skin, White Masks*, trans. Charles Lam Markmann, London, Pluto, 1986.

Felman, Shoshana, ed., *Literature and Psychoanalysis: The Question of Reading: Otherwise*, Yale French Studies 55/56 (1977).

Ferry, L., Pesron, J.-P., Renault, A., eds, *Philosophies de l'université: L'Idéalisme allemand et la question de l'Université; textes de Schelling, Fichte, Schleiermacher, Humboldt, Hegel*, Paris, Payot, 1979.

Fineman, Joel, *The Subjectivity Effect in Western Literary Tradition: Essays Towards the Release of Shakespeare's Will*, Cambridge Mass., MIT Press, 1991.

Forgacs, David, Marxist Literary Theories, in *Modern Literary Theory*, eds Ann Jefferson & David Robey, London, Batsford, 1982, 134–69.

Foster, Hal, ed., *Postmodern Culture*, London, Pluto, 1985.

Foster, R. F., *Paddy and Mr Punch: Connections in Irish and English History*, London, Allen Lane, 1993.

Foucault, Michel, *The History of Sexuality*, vol. 1, trans. Robert Hurley, London, Allen Lane, 1979.

—— *Language, Counter-Memory, Practice: Selected Essays and Interviews*, trans. Donald F. Bouchard & Sherry Simon, Ithaca, Cornell University Press, 1977.

—— *The Order of Things: An Archaeology of the Human Sciences*, trans. anonymous, London, Tavistock, 1970.

Foulkes, A., *Literature as Propaganda*, London, Methuen, 1983.

Fox, R. G., ed., *Recapturing Anthropology: Working in the Present*, Santa Fé, School of American Research Press, 1991.

Freud, Sigmund, *Civilization and its Discontents*, trans. James Strachey, Pelican Freud Library, 12, Harmondsworth, Penguin, 1985.

—— *The Interpretation of Dreams*, trans. James Strachey, Pelican Freud Library, 6, Harmondsworth, Penguin, 1976.

—— *Moses and Monotheism: Three Essays*, trans. James Strackey, Pelican Freud Library, 13, Harmondsworth, Penguin, 1985.

—— *Totem and Taboo*, trans. James Strachey, Pelican Freud Library, 13, Harmondsworth, Penguin, 1985.

Frow, John, *Marxism and Literary History*, Oxford, Blackwell, 1986.

Fryer, Peter, *Staying Power: The History of Black People in Britain*, London, Pluto Press, 1984.

Gallop, Jane, *Reading Lacan*, Ithaca, Cornell University Press, 1985.

—— Reading the Mother Tongue: Psychoanalytic Feminist Criticism, *Critical Inquiry* 13:2 (1987), 314–29.

Garner, Shirley, Nelson, Kahane, Claire, and Sprengnether, Madelon, *The (M)other Tongue: Essays in Feminist Psychoanalytic Interpretation*, Ithaca, Cornell University Press, 1985.

Gasché, Rodolphe, Deconstruction as Criticism, *Glyph* 6 (1979), 177–215.

—— *The Tain of the Mirror: Derrida and the Philosophy of Reflection*, Cambridge, Mass., Harvard University Press, 1986.

Gellner, Ernest, *Nations and Nationalism*, Oxford, Blackwell, 1983.

Gibbon, Edward, *Memoirs of My Life*, ed. Betty Radice, Harmondsworth, Penguin, 1984.

Giddens, Anthony, *The Consequences of Modernity*, Cambridge, Polity Press, 1990.

—— *Modernity and Self-Identity: Self and Society in the Late Modern Age*, Cambridge, Polity, 1991.

Gilman, Sander L., *Difference and Pathology: Stereotypes of Sexuality, Race and Madness*, Ithaca, Cornell University Press, 1985.

Gilroy, Paul, *'There Ain't No Black in the Union Jack': The Cultural Politics of Race and Nation*, London, Hutchinson, 1987.

Glazer, Nathan, & Moynihan, Daniel P., eds, *Ethnicity: Theory and Experience*, Cambridge, Harvard University Press, 1975.

Godwin, William, *Enquiry Concerning Political Justice*, ed. Isaac Kramnick, Harmondsworth, Penguin, 1976.

Graff, Gerald, *Poetic Statement and Critical Dogma*, Chicago, University of Chicago Press, 1970.

—— *Professing Literature: An Institutional History*, Chicago, University of Chicago Press, 1987.

Green, V. H., *British Institutions: The Universities*, Harmondsworth, Penguin, 1969.

Greenblatt, Stephen J., ed., *Allegory and Representation: Selected Papers from the English Institute 1979–80*, Baltimore, Johns Hopkins University Press, 1981.

Grossberg, Lawrence, Nelson, Cary, Treichler, Paula, eds, *Cultural Studies*, London, Routledge, 1992.

Grumley, John E., *History and Totality: Radical Historicism from Hegel to Foucault*, London, Routledge, 1989.

Habermas, Jürgen, *Legitimation Crisis*, trans. Thomas McCarthy, London, Heinemann, 1976.

—— Modernity: An Incomplete Project, in *Postmodern Culture*, ed. Hal Foster, London, Pluto, 1985, 3–15.

—— *The Philosophical Discourse of Modernity: Twelve Lectures*, trans. Frederick Lawrence, Cambridge, Polity Press, 1987.

Halévy, Elie, *The Growth of Philosophical Radicalism*, 2nd ed., trans. Mary Morris, London, Faber & Faber, 1934.

Hall, Stuart, The Local and the Global: Globalization and Ethnicity, and, Old and New Identities, Old and New Ethnicities, in *Culture, Globalization, and the World-System*, ed. Anthony D. King, Basingstoke, Macmillan, 1991, 19–39, 41–68.

—— Minimal Selves, in *The Real Me: Post-Modernism and the Question of Identity*, ICA Documents 6, London, 1987, 44–6.

Harari, Josué V., Changing the Object of Criticism: 1965–1978, *Modern Language Notes* 94 (1979), 784–96.

—— ed., *Textual Strategies: Perspectives in Post-Structuralist Criticism*, London, Methuen, 1979.

Harris, Marvin, *Cultural Materialism: The Struggle for a Science of Culture*, New York, Random House, 1979.

Harte, Negley, *The University of London 1836–1986: An Illustrated History*, London, Athlone, 1986.

Hartman, Geoffrey H., *Criticism in the Wilderness: The Study of Literature Today*, New Haven, Yale University Press, 1983.

Hill, Christopher, ed., *Change and Continuity in Seventeenth-Century England*, rev. ed., New Haven, Yale University Press, 1991.

—— *The Intellectual Origins of the English Revolution*, Oxford, Clarendon Press, 1965.

Hindess, Barry, & Hirst, Paul Q., *Mode of Production and Social Formation: An Auto-Critique of 'Pre-Capitalist Modes of Production'*, London, Macmillan, 1977.

Hirschkop, Ken, & Shepherd, David, eds, *Bakhtin and Cultural Theory*, Manchester, Manchester University Press, 1989.

Hirst, Paul Q., The Necessity of Theory, *Economy and Society* 8:4 (1979), 417–45.

—— *On Law and Ideology*, London, Macmillan, 1979.

—— & Woolley, Penny, *Social Attributes and Human Relations*, London, Tavistock, 1982.

Hobsbawm, E. J., *Nations and Nationalism Since 1870: Programme, Myth, Reality*, Cambridge, Cambridge University Press, 1990.

Hollander, Samuel, The Role of the State in Vocational Training: The Classical Economists' View, *Southern Economic Journal*, 34 (1968), 294–309.

Houdebine, Jean-Louis, *Langage et Marxisme*, Paris, Klincksieck, 1977.

Howes, Craig, Rhetoric of Attack: Bakhtin and the Aesthetics of Satire, *Genre* 19:3 (1986), 25–43.

Jacoby, Russell, *Social Amnesia: A Critique of Conformist Psychology from Adler to Laing*, Hassocks, Harvester Press, 1977.

Jameson, Fredric, *Late Marxism: Adorno, or, the Persistence of the Dialectic*, London, Verso, 1990.

—— *The Political Unconscious: Narrative as a Socially Symbolic Act*, London, Methuen, 1981.

—— The Politics of Theory: Ideological Positions in the Postmodernism Debate, *New German Critique* 33 (1984), 53–65; reprinted in *The Ideologies of Theory: Essays 1971–1986*, 2 vols, London, Routledge, 1988, 2, 103–113.

—— *Postmodernism, or the Cultural Logic of Late Capitalism*, London, Verso, 1991.

—— *The Prison-House of Language: A Critical Account of Structuralism and Russian Formalism*, Princeton, Princeton University Press, 1972.

—— Wyndham Lewis as Futurist, *Hudson Review* 26:2 (1973), 295–329.

Jarausch, Konrad H., ed., *The Transformation of Higher Learning, 1860–1930: Expansion, Diversification, Social Opening, and Professionalization in England, Germany, Russia and the United States*, Chicago, University of Chicago Press, 1983.

Jay, Martin, *Adorno*, London, Fontana, 1984.

—— *Marxism and Totality*, Berkeley, University of California Press, 1984.

Jenkins, Geraint H., *The University of Wales: An Illustrated History*, Cardiff, University of Wales Press, 1993.

Kant, Immanuel, *The Conflict of the Faculties/Der Streit der Fakultäten*, trans. Mary J. Gregor, New York, Abaris Books, 1979.

Kaplan, Cora, *Sea Changes: Essays on Culture and Feminism*, London, Verso, 1986.

Kearney, H. F., *Gentlemen and Scholars: Universities and Society in Pre-Industrial Britain, 1500–1700*, London, Faber & Faber, 1970.

Killham, John, *Tennyson and The Princess: Reflections of an Age*, London, Athlone Press, 1958.

Kovel, Joel, *White Racism: A Psychohistory*, London, Free Association Books, 1988.

Kristeva, Julia, *Desire in Language: A Semiotic Approach to Literature and Art*, trans. Thomas Gora, Alice Jardine, & Leon S. Roudiez, New York, Columbia University Press, 1980.

—— *Nations Without Nationalism*, trans. Leon S. Roudiez, New York, Columbia University Press, 1993.

—— *Powers of Horror*, trans. Leon S. Roudiez, New York, Columbia University Press, 1982.

—— The Ruin of a Poetics, trans. Vivienne Mylne, in *Russian Formalism*, eds Stephen Bann & John E. Bowlt, Edinburgh, Scottish Academic Press, 1973, 102–119.

—— *Strangers to Ourselves*, trans. Leon S. Roudiez, London, Harvester Wheatsheaf, 1991.

Lacan, Jacques, and the école freudienne, *Feminine Sexuality: Jacques Lacan and the école freudienne*, eds Juliet Mitchell & Jacqueline Rose, London, Macmillan, 1982.

LaCapra, Dominick, Bakhtin, Marxism and the Carnivalesque, in LaCapra, *Rethinking Intellectual History: Texts, Contexts, Language*, Ithaca, Cornell University Press, 1983, 291–324.

Laclau, Ernesto, Psychoanalysis and Marxism, *Critical Inquiry* 13:2 (1987), 330–3.

—— & Mouffe, Chantal, *Hegemony and Socialist Strategy: Towards a Democratic Politics*, trans. Winston Moore & Paul Cammack, London, Verso, 1985.

Lacoue-Labarthe, P., & Nancy, J.-L., eds, *Les Fins de l'homme: A partir du travail de Jacques Derrida*, Paris, Galilée, 1981.

Leavis, Frank Raymond, *Education and the University: A Sketch for an 'English School'*, London, Chatto & Windus, 1943.

—— *English Literature in Our Time and the University*, London, Chatto & Windus, 1969.

Lévi-Strauss, Claude, *Introduction to the Work of Marcel Mauss*, trans. Felicity Baker, London, Routledge, 1987.

—— *Structural Anthropology*, vol. 2, trans. Monique Layton, London, Allen Lane, 1977.

—— *Tristes Tropiques*, trans. John & Doreen Weightman, London, Cape, 1973.

Lewis, Philip, The Post-Structuralist Condition, *Diacritics* 12:1 (1982), 2–24.

Linnekin, J., Cultural Invention and the Dilemma of Authenticity, *American Anthropologist* 93 (1991), 446–8.

Lodge, David, *After Bakhtin: Essays on Fiction and Criticism*, London, Routledge, 1990.

—— Double Discourses; Joyce and Bakhtin, *James Joyce Broadsheet* (June 1983), 1.

Loomba, Ania, Overworlding the Third World, *Oxford Literary Review* 13 (1991), 164–91.

Lukács, Georg, *The Meaning of Contemporary Realism*, trans. John & Necke Mander, London, Merlin Press, 1963.

Lyotard, Jean-François, *The Differend: Phrases in Dispute*, trans. Georges Van Den Abbeele, Manchester, Manchester University Press, 1988.

—— *The Lyotard Reader*, ed. Andrew Benjamin, Oxford, Blackwell, 1989.

—— *The Postmodern Condition: A Report on Knowledge*, trans. Geoff Bennington & Brian Massumi, Manchester, Manchester University Press, 1985.

Macherey, Pierre, *A Theory of Literary Production*, trans. Geoffrey Wall, London, Routledge & Kegan Paul, 1978.

Macksey, Richard, and Donato, Eugenio, *The Languages of Criticism and the Sciences of Man*, Baltimore, Johns Hopkins University Press, 1970. Reprinted as *The Structuralist Controversy*, 1972.

Malthus, T. R., *An Essay on the Principle of Population*, 2nd ed., London, 1803.

Marcuse, Herbert, *Negations: Essays in Critical Theory*, London, Free Association Books, 1988.

Martin, B., *A Sociology of Contemporary Cultural Change*, Oxford, Blackwell, 1981.

Marx, Karl, *Capital*, vol. 1, trans. Ben Fowkes, Harmondsworth, Penguin, 1976.

—— *The Eighteenth Brumaire of Louis Bonaparte*, in *Surveys from Exile, Political Writings*, vol. 2, ed. David Fernbach, trans. Ben Fowkes, Harmondsworth, Penguin, 1973.

—— *Selected Writings*, ed. David McLellan, Oxford, Oxford University Press, 1977.

—— & Engels, Friedrich, *Manifesto of the Communist Party*, Moscow, Progress Publishers, 1952.

McCannell, Juliet Flower, The Temporality of Textuality: Bakhtin and Derrida, *Modern Language Notes* 100:5 (1985), 968–88.

Medvedev, P. N., *The Formal Method in Literary Scholarship: A Critical Introduction to Sociological Poetics*, trans. Albert J. Wehrle, Baltimore, Johns Hopkins University Press, 1978.

Mill, John Stuart, *Dissertations and Discussions, Political, Philosophical, and Historical, reprinted chiefly from the Edinburgh and Westminster Reviews*, 4 vols, London, 1859–75.

—— *Mill on Bentham and Coleridge*, ed. F. R. Leavis, Cambridge, Cambridge University Press, 1950.

—— *Principles of Political Economy, with some of their Applications to Social Philosophy*, 2 vols, London, 1848.

Mitchell, Juliet, *Psychoanalysis and Feminism*, London, Allen Lane, 1974.

Mitchell, W. J. T., ed., *Against Theory: Literary Studies and the New Pragmatism*, Chicago, University of Chicago Press, 1985.

Mohanty, S. P., ed., Marx After Derrida, *Diacritics* 15:4 (1985).

Moi, Toril, *Sexual/Textual Politics: Feminist Literary Theory*, London, Methuen, 1985.

Montrelay, Michèle, *L'Ombre et le nom: Sur la féminité*, Paris, Minuit, 1977.

Morrow, John, *Coleridge's Political Thought: Property, Morality and the Limits of Traditional Discourse*, Basingstoke, Macmillan, 1990.

Morson, Gary Saul, ed., *Bakhtin: Essays and Dialogues on his Work*, Chicago, University of Chicago Press, 1986.

—— ed., *Literature and History: Theoretical Problems and Russian Case Studies*, Palo Alto, Stanford University Press, 1986.

Mueller, D. K., Ringer, F., & Simon, B., *The Rise of the Modern Educational System: Structural Change and Social Reproduction 1870–1920*, Cambridge, Cambridge University Press, 1989.

Musgrave, P. W., *Society and Education in England Since 1800*, London, Methuen, 1968.

Nairn, Tom, *The Break-Up of Britain: Crisis and Neo-Nationalism*, London, New Left Books, 1977.

Newbolt, Sir Henry, *The Teaching of English in England*, London, HMSO, 1921.

Newman, John Henry, *The Idea of a University, Defined and Illustrated*, ed. I. T. Ker, Oxford, Clarendon Press, 1976.

—— *Select Discourses from the Idea of a University*, ed. May Yardley, Cambridge, Cambridge University Press, 1931.

Nield, Keith & Seed, John, Theoretical Poverty or the Poverty of Theory: British Marxist Historiography and the Althusserians, *Economy and Society* 8:4 (1979), 383–416.

Norbrook, David, Life and Death of Renaissance Man, *Raritan* 8:4 (1989), 89–110.

Osborne, Peter, Adorno and the Metaphysics of Modernism: The Problem of a 'Postmodern' Art, in *The Problems of Modernity: Adorno and Benjamin*, ed. Andrew Benjamin, London, Routledge, 1989, 23–48.

Owusu, Kwesi, & Ross, Jacob, *Behind the Masquerade: The Story of Notting Hill Carnival*, Edgware, Media Arts Group, 1988.

Palmer, D. J., *The Rise of English Studies*, Oxford, Clarendon Press, 1965.

Parker, Andrew, *et al.*, eds, *Nationalisms and Sexualities*, London, Routledge, 1992.

Pechey, Graham, Bakhtin, Marxism, and Post-Structuralism, in *The Politics of Theory*, eds Francis Barker *et al.*, Colchester, University of Essex Press, 1983, 234–47.

—— On the Borders of Bakhtin: Dialogisation, Decolonization, *Oxford Literary Review* 9 (1987), 59–84.

Poster, Mark, *Existential Marxism in Postwar France: From Sartre to Althusser*, Princeton, Princeton University Press, 1975.

Prescod, Colin, Review of Paul Gilroy, '*There Ain't No Black in the Union Jack*': *The Cultural Politics of Race and Nation*, *Race and Class* (1988) 29:4.

Press, John, ed., *The Teaching of English Overseas*, London, Methuen, 1963.

Prospectus of the London University, London, 1825.

Rancière, Jacques, *La Leçon d'Althusser*, Paris, Gallimard, 1974.

Rasdall, Hastings, *The Universities of Europe in the Middle Ages*, 2nd ed., ed. F. M. Powicke & A. B. Emden, 3 vols, Oxford, Clarendon Press, 1936.

Rawson, Claude, The Crisis, and How Not to Solve It, *TLS* 10 Dec. 1982, 1371–2.

Reich, Wilhelm, *The Mass Psychology of Fascism*, trans. Vincent R. Carfagno, Harmondsworth, Penguin, 1975.

Roazen, Paul, *Freud and His Followers*, London, Allen Lane, 1976.

Robinson, Cedric J., *Black Marxism: The Making of the Black Radical Tradition*, London, Zed Press, 1983.

Robinson, Lilian S., *Sex, Class and Culture*, Bloomington, Indiana University Press, 1978.

Rogers, Pat, ed., *The Eighteenth Century*, London, Methuen, 1978.

Rose, Jacqueline, *Sexuality in the Field of Vision*, London, Verso, 1986.

Roszak, Theodor, ed., *The Dissenting Academy*, London, Chatto & Windus, 1969.

—— *The Making of a Counter Culture: Reflections on the Technocratic Society and Its Youthful Opposition*, London, Faber & Faber, 1970.

Roustang, François, *Dire Mastery: Discipleship from Freud to Lacan*, trans. Ned Lukacher, Baltimore, Johns Hopkins University Press, 1982.

Ryan, Michael, *Marxism and Deconstruction: A Critical Articulation*, Baltimore, Johns Hopkins University Press, 1982.

Sanderson, Michael, ed., *The Universities in the Nineteenth Century*, London, Routledge & Kegan Paul, 1975.

Schultz, Theodore W., Investment in Human Capital, *American Economic Review*, 51 (1961), 1–17.

Searle, John, *The Campus War: A Sympathetic Look at the University in Agony*, Harmondsworth, Penguin Books, 1972.

Segal, Ronald, *The Race War: The World-Wide Conflict of Races*, rev. ed., Harmondsworth, Penguin, 1967.

Sharratt, Bernard, *Reading Relations: Structures of Literary Production: A Dialectical Text/Book*, Brighton, Harvester, 1983.

Shelley, Percy Bysshe, *Essays, Letters from Abroad, Translations and Fragments*, ed. Mary Shelley, London, 1840.

Shiach, Morag, *Discourse on Popular Culture: Class Gender and History in Cultural Analysis, 1730 to the Present*, Cambridge, Polity, 1989.

Simon, Brian, *Education and the Labour Movement, 1870–1920*, London, Lawrence & Wishart, 1965.

—— *Studies in the History of Education, 1780–1870*, London, Lawrence & Wishart, 1960.

—— ed., *The Radical Tradition in Education in Britain: A Compilation of Writings by William Godwin [& others]*, London, Lawrence & Wishart, 1972.

Simpson, Renate, *How the Ph.D. came to Britain: A Century of Struggle for Postgraduate Education*, Guildford, Society for Research into Higher Education, 1983.

Skinner, Andrew S., & Wilson, Thomas, eds, *Essays on Adam Smith*, Oxford, Clarendon Press, 1975.

Slaughter, Cliff, *Marxism, Ideology and Literature*, London, Macmillan, 1980.

Smith, Adam, *The Correspondence of Adam Smith*, ed. Ernest Campbell Mossner & Ian Simpson Ross, Oxford, Clarendon Press, 1987.

—— *An Enquiry into the Nature and Causes of The Wealth of Nations*, ed. R. H. Campbell, A. S. Skinner, & W. B. Todd, 2 vols, Oxford, Clarendon Press, 1976.

—— *The Theory of Moral Sentiments*, eds D. D. Raphael and A. L. Macfie, Oxford, Clarendon Press, 1976.

Smith, Sydney, review of R. L. Edgeworth's *Professional Education* (1809), *Edinburgh Review* 15 (1809), 40–53.

Smith, Thomas Southwood, Literary Education, *Westminster Review* 1 (1824), 43–79.

Spivak, Gayatri Chakravorty, *In Other Worlds: Essays in Cultural Politics*, New York, Methuen, 1987.

—— *Outside in the Teaching Machine*, New York, Routledge, 1993.

Sprinker, Michael, Boundless Context: Problems in Bakhtin's Linguistics, *Poetics Today* 7:1 (1986), 117–28.

Stallybrass, Peter, & White, Allon, *The Politics and Poetics of Transgression*, London, Methuen, 1986.

Stephens, Michael D., & Roderick, Gordon W., *Post-School Education*, London, Croom Helm, 1984.

Stone, Lawrence, ed., *The University in Society*, Princeton, Princeton University Press, 1975.

Studies in Twentieth Century Literature 9:1 (1984), Bakhtin Special Issue.

Thompson, E. P., *The Poverty of Theory & Other Essays*, London, Merlin, 1978.

—— ed., *Warwick University Ltd: Industry, Management and the Universities*, Harmondsworth, Penguin, 1970.

Timpanaro, Sebastiano, *The Freudian Slip*, London, New Left Books, 1976.

Todorov, Tzvetan, *Mikhail Bakhtine: Le Principe dialogique, suivi d' Ecrits du Cercle de Bakhtine*, Paris, Seuil, 1981.

—— *Mikhail Bakhtin: The Dialogical Principle*, trans. Wlad Godzich, Minnesota, University of Minnesota Press, 1984.

—— *Nous et les autres: La Réflexion française sur la diversité humaine*, Paris, Seuil, 1989.

Turkle, Sherry, *Psychoanalytic Politics: Jacques Lacan and Freud's French Revolution*, London, Burnett Books, 1979.

University of Ottawa Quarterly 53:1 (1983), Bakhtin Special Issue.

Vaizey, John, *The Economics of Education*, London, Faber & Faber, 1962.

Vaughan, Michalina, & Archer, Margaret S., *Social Conflict and Educational Change in England and France 1789–1848*, Cambridge, Cambridge University Press, 1971.

Veeser, H. Aram, ed., *The New Historicism*, London, Routledge, 1989.

Viswanathan, Gauri, *Masks of Conquest: Literary Study and British Rule in India*, London, Faber, 1990.

Vogel, Lise, *Marxism and the Oppression of Women: Toward a Unitary Theory*, New Brunswick, Rutgers University Press, 1983.

Voloshinov, V. N., *Freudianism: A Marxist Critique*, trans. I. R. Titunik, New York, Academic Press, 1976.

—— *Marxism and the Philosophy of Language*, trans. Ladislav Matejka & I. R. Titunik, New York, Seminar Press, 1973.

Walcott, Fred G., *The Origins of Culture and Anarchy: Matthew Arnold and Popular Education in England*, London, Heinemann, 1970.

Ward, W. R., *Georgian Oxford: University Politics in the Eighteenth Century*, Oxford, Clarendon Press, 1958.

Weber, Samuel, *Institution and Interpretation*, Minneapolis, University of Minnesota Press, 1987.

—— The Intersection: Marxism and the Philosophy of Language, *Diacritics* 15:4 (1985), 94–112.

—— *The Legend of Freud*, Minneapolis, Minnesota University Press, 1982.

Webster, Charles, *The Great Instauration: Science, Medicine and Reform 1626–1660*, London, Duckworth, 1975.

Weeks, Jeffrey, *Sex, Politics and Society: The Regulation of Sexuality since 1800*, London, Longman, 1981.

Weir, Angela, & Wilson, Elizabeth, The British Women's Movement, *New Left Review* 148 (1984), 74–103.

West, E. G., The Role of Education in Nineteenth-Century Doctrines of Political Economy, *British Journal of Educational Studies*, 12:2 (1964), 161–72.

White, Allon, Bakhtin, Sociolinguistics and Deconstruction, in *The Theory of Reading*, ed. Frank Gloversmith, Brighton, Harvester, 1984, 123–46.

—— The Struggle Over Bakhtin: A Fraternal Reply to Robert Young, *Cultural Critique* 8 (1987–88), 217–41.

White, Hayden, The Authoritative Lie, *Partisan Review* 50:2 (1983), 307–12.

Widdowson, Peter, ed., *Re-Reading English*, London, Methuen, 1982.

Williams, Raymond, *Marxism and Literature*, Oxford, Oxford University Press, 1977.

Wolfenstein, Eugene Victor, *Psychoanalytic-Marxism: Groundwork*, London, Free Association Press, 1993.

Wollstonecraft, Mary, *A Vindication of the Rights of Woman*, ed. Miriam Kramnick, Harmondsworth, Penguin, 1975.

Wordsworth, William, *The Prelude, or the Growth of a Poet's Mind: An Autobio-graphical Poem*, London, 1850.

Young, Robert J. C., *Colonial Desire: Hybridity in Theory, Culture and Race*, London, Routledge, 1995.

—— Post-Structuralism: The End of Theory, *Oxford Literary Review* 5 (1982), 3–15.

—— Psychoanalytic Criticism: Has It Got Beyond a Joke?, *Paragraph* 4 (1984), 87–114.

—— Re. Reading *Re-Reading English*, *Oxford Literary Review* 6:2 (1984), 87–93.

—— ed., *Sexual Difference, Oxford Literary Review* 8:1–2 (1986).

—— Une tradition en crise, *Etudes françaises* 23/1–2 (1987–88), 47–74.

—— ed., *Untying the Text: A Post-Structuralist Reader*, London: Routledge & Kegan Paul, 1981.

—— *White Mythologies: Writing History and the West*, London, Routledge, 1990.

Zabel, Morton D., *Literary Opinions in America*, rev. ed., New York, Harper, 1951.

Zizek, Slavoj, *The Sublime Object of Ideology*, London, Verso, 1989.

Zuidervaart, Lambert, *Adorno's Aesthetic Theory: The Redemption of Illusion*, Cambridge, Mass., MIT, 1991.

Index......................................